ESSAYS IN
FISCAL AND
MONETARY POLICY

ESSAYS IN
FISCAL AND
MONETARY POLICY

Edited by
M. J. ARTIS
M. H. MILLER
for The Institute for Fiscal Studies

OXFORD UNIVERSITY PRESS
1981

Oxford University Press, Walton Street, Oxford OX2 6DP
London Glasgow New York Toronto
Delhi Bombay Calcutta Madras Karachi
Kuala Lumpur Singapore Hong Kong Tokyo
Nairobi Dar es Salaam Cape Town
Melbourne Auckland
and associated companies in
Beirut Berlin Ibadan Mexico City

Published in the United States by
Oxford University Press, New York

British Library Cataloguing in Publication Data
Essays in fiscal and monetary policy.
1. Macroeconomics
I. Artis, M.J.   II. Miller, M.H.
339   HB171
ISBN 0-19-829001-2

Set by Hope Services, Abingdon
and printed in Great Britain by
Richard Clay & Co Ltd., Bungay

PREFACE

The papers published in this volume have their origin in a seminar series on the interrelationship of fiscal and monetary policy, which was sponsored by the Institute for Fiscal Studies. The meetings were held during the academic year 1977-8, under the chairmanship of Sir Alec Cairncross. Organization was ably provided by Mrs Thelma Leisner, and finance by the Social Science Research Council. We are grateful to these individuals and institutions for their assistance as we are to David Wright, who prepared the index. The delay in the publication of the volume is not their responsibility but ours.

University of Manchester   M. J. ARTIS

University of Warwick   M. H. MILLER

CONTENTS

THE CONTRIBUTORS

A. P. Budd   London Business School

T. Burns   H.M. Treasury*

D. A. Currie   Queen Mary College, London

M. Fetherston   Department of Applied Economics, Cambridge

J. S. Flemming   Bank of England*

W. Godley   Department of Applied Economics, Cambridge

C. A. E. Goodhart   Bank of England

J. W. Grice   H.M. Treasury

P. E. Middleton   H.M. Treasury

National Institute of
Economic and Social Research

R. R. Neild   Cambridge University

The Editors

M. J. Artis   University of Manchester

M. H. Miller   University of Warwick*

*Present affiliations are shown. At the time the papers were first prepared Professor Miller was at the University of Manchester and John Flemming at Nuffield College, Oxford. Terry Burns, now Chief Economic Adviser to the Government, was then at the London Business School.

I

FISCAL AND MONETARY POLICY – AN INTRODUCTION TO THE ISSUES

M. J. Artis

The purpose of this introductory chapter is to provide some perspective on the principal issues discussed in the ensuing chapters of the volume. The seminar series from which these chapters originate was conceived of as focusing upon the kinds of consideration underlying the way in which fiscal policy is approached and assessed in contemporary macroeconomics, and in particular as illuminating the nexus between fiscal and monetary policy. The need for such discussions sprang directly from the observation that, at a time when many of the old certitudes of macroeconomic policy-making had been jettisoned, a stock-taking exercise would be useful. The chapter contributors were approached on the basis that they would have something useful to say in such a context.

There is no doubt that macroeconomics, and thus the theory that purports to guide the formation of monetary and fiscal policy at present, conveys the impression of being something of a shambles. There is certainly much less of a consensus within macroeconomics now than there was in the first half of the 1960s. At the policy level, the combination of inflation and recession has taught policy-makers some hard lessons; and the distress of policy-makers has been accompanied by a series of re-evaluations within analytical macroeconomics, without much sign as yet that anything approaching a new consensus has been reached. Even the statement that 'we are all monetarists now', which seemed to have a brief purchase on truth, is in doubt again, since the advent of the 'second wave' of monetarism—rational expectations monetarism.

Perhaps one useful way of characterizing the disintegration of consensus and the present dissension within macroeconomics would be to say that experience has cast doubt on the appropriate kinds of abstraction to make in a useful macroeconomics. Economic theory makes a great deal of use of distinctions between the short term and the long term, an analytical ordering that is informed, though not literally translated to calendar time dimensions, by empirical judgements about the relative speeds of adjustment of economic variables. At this level, it is clear that conventional *IS/LM* macroeconomics makes abstractions that clearly classify it as short-term theory. Indeed, the problem is that these abstractions, in the light of experience, seem to classify it as 'very' short-term theory. Much of the empirical and analytical advances in recent years seem to consist, on the one hand, of working out the significance and time form of responses of economic variables 'held constant' by the traditional analysis, and on the other of extending the analysis to embrace these responses and feedbacks in order to find out what new properties the model has when it is enhanced in this way. These enterprises have not always gone closely hand in hand, which in itself has contributed a certain disorientation and imparted a kind of restlessness to some of the analytical results, the calendar-time translation of whose steady state properties has often been desperately unclear. It seems that it must be possible to proceed in a more constructive way, for the price of not doing so is not only to prolong professional uncertainty but also, operationally, to confuse policy and deprive it of well-judged guidance. However, that no easy resolution is in sight is perhaps most dramatically demonstrated by the present confrontation of two new 'extreme' paradigms of macroeconomics: the macro-disequilibrium school and the rational expectations school. The latter relies on market-clearing and fast adjustment of prices; the former denies market-clearing and deprives prices of a helpful role in short-run adjustment.

Two reasons why it is not easy to resolve matters suggest themselves. First, it seems clear that the empirical data do not easily yield to the kinds of technique available in such a way as to readily confirm specific hypotheses. Second, it would in any case be naive to suggest that somehow we can, with the aid of empirical economics, arrive at a re-ordering of adjustment processes, allowing for an agreed reassessment of the most suitable abstractions to make for useful macroeconomics, and then proceed to a new consensus. Policy-makers are, or should be, interested in the longer-run consequences of their present actions even if these are not significant within the conventional period of policy relevance. This suggests—to borrow from John Flemming's comments later in this volume—that macroeconomic policy analysis ought to be cast in optimal control terms within which the 'longer-run' consequences of policy can be implicitly impounded in terminal conditions for the period over which policy is explicitly optimized. This has the virtue of avoiding the difficulty of locking macroeconomic analysis mistakenly into either a 'very short-term' or long-term mould, and is a constructive response to the present danger that the Keynesian baby will be thrown out with the bathwater while policy is conducted along monetarist lines, which may be entirely suitable for points on the full employment equilibrium path of the economy yet distinctly unsuited to dealing with the problems of getting back on to such a path.

This of course still leaves open the need to inquire into the nature of the responses suppressed by the conventional *IS/LM* account of macroeconomics, and to find out something about their time form and long-run consequences. This is an agenda involving both empirical and analytical work. In various ways, the chapter contributions to the present volume can be seen as contributing towards this.

One of the key abstractions of conventional *IS/LM* analysis is that it takes as given the stock of assets, both physical and financial, and focuses on flow equilibria. In these equilibria, stocks would be changing, but the abstraction allows the effect of this to be ignored—presumably on the assumption that the time period of reference of the model is, while long enough to be relevant, short enough that these feedbacks can be reasonably ignored. Some questioning of this presumption is perhaps implicit in the large volume of analytical literature devoted to examining the consequences of explicitly analysing the effects of asset accumulation; and is more explicit in the wealth-related consumption and expenditure functions employed in contemporary UK macroeconometric models. In the present volume David Currie analyses the role of wealth effects in his survey of the 'crowding-out' issue; however, while the formal results of traditional analysis of this issue are affected by the incorporation of the financing identities and wealth effects, Currie makes the point—no less important for being obvious once stated—that 'crowding-out', in conditions short of full employment, where it is predetermined *ex hypothesi* by physical supply constraints, is attributable to the result of the financing policy accompanying the fiscal stimulus. In the chapter contribution by Fetherston and Godley, the crucial role of wealth effects in the CEPG model (of which Fetherston and Godley's model is a version) in underpinning the characteristic 'New Cambridge' proposition concerning the spill-over from fiscal to balance of payments deficits is set out with extreme clarity. In their model (see simulation 1 for the clearest case), there is a desired wealth–income ratio for the private sector, and demand-determined output conditions. As a result, a fiscal stimulus that increases the wealth of the private sector invokes an adjustment of income to restore the desired wealth–income ratio, with a final equilibrium in which the injections of financial wealth from the budget deficit are offset by an equivalent drain from a deterioration in the current balance. While an adjustment of output and an offsetting drain of wealth to the overseas sector are one possible form of evolution of the system, another possible mechanism of adjustment comes via the 'inflation tax'. If inflation occurs, there is a drain of wealth via the implied inflation tax. A mechanism of this kind seems to play an important role in the LBS and NIESR models, as exemplified in the simulations of these models reported in this volume (there is further comment on this below). The analytical work in this area has proceeded without benefit of a well-documented empirical literature, and much of what empirical work there is has implied wealth effects by indirection, rather than directly. One reason for this has been the absence of reliable wealth data. Joe Grice's chapter in this volume, however, besides surveying the existing literature, also adds new evidence based on the use of explicit wealth data. The conclusions of this work are favourable to the existence of significant wealth effects on expenditure, though much remains to be done: not least, of course, to establish the significance or otherwise of wealth effects in asset demand functions.

Another respect in which the *IS/LM* analysis abstracted severely was in its treatment of inflation. This abstraction was of course, long since modified by the attachment of the Phillips Curve to the basic model. But the experience of the accelerating inflation of the 1960s, and the stagflation of the 1970s, led many economists to suggest that a short run in which inflation was so much of an afterthought was an unrealistic time-frame for adequate analysis. The popularity of the augmented Phillips Curve is an analytical consequence. The chapter contributions in this volume do not seek to deal with the issue directly, but endogenous wage–price responses and the nexus between the exchange rate, wages and prices are clearly significant in the model simulation evidence. And, of course, if wealth effects are important, then so too are inflation-induced wealth effects. Finally, if inflation is treated as endogenous, rather than as orthogonal to the system, the issue of policy measurement and policy-setting must take this into account. This theme recurs in Charles Goodhart's chapter on monetary policy and in the chapters by Budd and Burns and by Neild, where fiscal policy measurement is discussed. Budd and Burns argue that fiscal policy deficit measures should be adjusted for inflation, implicitly because of the tax-like effect of inflation. Neild recognizes, but prefers not to incorporate, this effect in his own preferred measure of fiscal policy. There is no doubt, whatever treatment is accorded to this phenomenon, that plausible orders of magnitude for it are in contemporary conditions very large in relation (for example) to the unadjusted budget deficit.

Traditional analysis also abstracts from, or, rather, makes special assumptions about, the role of expectations. John Flemming's note on the subject elaborates on this issue, which the rational expectations 'revolution' has brought forcefully to our attention. In particular, rational expectations has discomforting implications for many customary procedures in this area. First, the assumption of rational expectations makes something of a nonsense of some traditional distinctions between the short run and the long run: it can be caricatured as, in fact, making the long run the short-run solution. Second, it suggests that systematic demand management policies will be offset by private sector behaviour. Third, it inhibits recourse to simulation evidence to explore the consequence of different policies and makes more doubtful what can be learnt from past data. These results however do not follow without some amendment when careful consideration is given to a plausible set of behavioural assumptions even in combination with that of rational expectations. Flemming gives some reasons for being sceptical, but they are delivered in a constructive vein; a concession to rational expectations is implicit in his suggestion that monetary targets should be made conditional.

Policy issues are particularly addressed by Neild, Goodhart, Middleton and Budd and Burns. The former presents a measure of fiscal policy, based on the well-known high employment budget deficit measure. However, Neild is after slightly different game from that pursued by most users of this measure. He has in mind a measure that is designed to indicate whether long-run fiscal policy is appropriately set. This, in conjunction with some empirics, leads him to reject the notion of differential weighting of budget components and the use of the measure for short-run policy description. One argument in the latter context is that the availability of appropriate model simulations cuts out the need for such a policy indicator. Goodhart introduces other arguments against this kind of policy indicator, too, pointing out *inter alia* that in principle the effect of a change in the setting of any one policy instrument depends on the joint setting of all other instruments. Since not everybody has equal access to appropriate simulations (which should in principle be capable of dealing with Goodhart's objections), it may be that a valid need still exists for short-term indicators of policy stance. Budd and Burns suggest that an appropriate one is the fiscal deficit adjusted (upward) for inflation and for declines of output below capacity (trend). They suggest that such an adjusted fiscal measure is in fact the correlate of a monetary measure (the growth of real money supply), indicating that the two amount to the same thing; so that, although the policy *instruments* are different, measures of policy stance are really much the same. As their model indicates that the PSBR drives the money supply (*ceteris paribus*), and that output changes are essentially transitory, the adjustment in the long run working through to prices via the exchange rate, this is not surprising.

The National Institute paper sets out to describe the Institute's monetary sector and an important part of its fiscal sector, and provides simulation evidence of the response of the model as a whole (discussed below).

The paper by Middleton describes the way in which monetary and fiscal policy interact within the framework that is employed by the Treasury to examine these issues. The description embraces an account of the Treasury's monetary model, as well as an account of the way in which fiscal and monetary policy are seen as interacting. It is clear from this account that the financing identity of the government budget constraint, together with the role of the external sector, are seen as binding monetary and fiscal policy closely together.

This is also reflected in the simulations from the London Business School and National Institute presented in this volume. It seems worthwhile briefly to compare and comment upon these, and the most closely comparable simulation from the Fetherston–Godley chapter (although, as explained below, this simulation does differ in some important aspects from the other two).

COMPARATIVE SIMULATIONS

The three papers from the modellers provide evidence based on simulations of the way in which fiscal policy works. This evidence is worth careful inspection in so far as it indicates what factors it is that those concerned with the forecasting and analysis of the British economy have found important to take into account, and in so far as it demonstrates the net result of the interaction of a relatively complex set of forces. While analytical methods can illuminate outcomes for comparatively small systems, simulation methods seem indispensable for understanding the behaviour of more complex systems. They do, of course, have limitations. To begin with, it would be wrong to suppose that such methods somehow reveal the truth about the way the economy behaves; rather, they reveal the properties of systems built by modellers. Some of these properties will have been consciously built in by the modellers on the grounds that economic theory should be used to condition the empirical estimates, so that both the specification of relationships to be estimated and the estimation procedure already reflect to a degree the intuition of the modeller, who is perhaps most likely to 'let the data speak freely' when it comes to the estimation of lags in relationships. Second, simulation runs are counterfactual experiments or hypothetical examinations of the system, conducted under the assumption that everything about the system as specified remains unchanged in the event of the 'experiment' being run. But it is clear that this assumption is sometimes a very strong one; agents learn from, and come to anticipate, the results of policy actions and may modify their behaviour accordingly. A valid set of descriptive equations for the 1967 devaluation would not describe adequately the result of an equivalent devaluation today. Finally (though this is not an exhaustive list of qualifications), there is every reason to believe that initial conditions in the economy will affect the outturn of an experiment, but in the simulations reported here no attempt was made to pin them down to an identical time period, although all are for the post-floating period.

The once conventional wisdom concerning the effect of fiscal policy on the level of output in a small open economy with a floating (freely flexible) exchange rate maintained that it would be zero. This result depended on the assumption that, with perfect (flow) capital mobility, a bond-financed fiscal expansion must result in an appreciation of the exchange rate to preserve zero overall balance at an unchanged interest rate, reducing net exports by an amount sufficient to 'crowd out' entirely the fiscal expansion. The current and expected spot rate were assumed identical in this analysis, interest parity being thus preserved on the uncovered interest differential. Even with imperfect capital mobility, the assumptions of this analysis prohibited any positive output effect of bond-financed fiscal policy.[1] Money financing and monetary policy, generally, were by contrast assumed capable of affecting output by way of exerting a depreciating influence on the exchange rate and an expansionary effect on net exports.

Within this framework, some power could be restored to fiscal policy by amending the rather implausible assumption that exchange rates are not *expected* to change; since interest parity refers to the comparison of *covered* differentials, an alternative equilibrium could be envisaged providing for domestic interest rates to stand above (or below) world rates to an extent exactly offset by the expected depreciation (or appreciation) of the domestic currency. Thus, a fiscal expansion that led to an over-appreciation of the currency relative to its expected exchange rate could in principle provide for a *positive* output effect (always assuming that the demand for money is not completely interest-inelastic), at an increased interest rate.

A feature of the fiscal policy simulations reported below (Table 1.1) is that the output multipliers are rather low. However, as indicated in the bottom half of the table, this result has little to do with a deteriorating net export balance and nothing at all to do with an appreciation of the exchange rate. In a number of key respects, the view taken by UK econometric modellers achieves a consensus on the appropriate departure to make from the once-conventional wisdom sketched above.

First, as against the assumption made there that domestic wages and prices (the GDP deflator) are invariant to the exchange rate, UK modellers tend towards the assumption that an exchange rate change is not very 'effective' (or not effective at all) in the long run. The speed with which, and the way in which, exchange rate changes dissipate themselves in offsetting (or nearly offsetting) domestic wage and price changes varies considerably from model to model, however. The Cambridge Economic Policy Group (CEPG) assume a real-wage resistance form of wage equation (see Fetherston and Godley, Chapter 10 below, p. 170) and normal cost-based domestic prices; import prices in sterling terms reflect domestic prices to a small degree, and export prices in sterling terms reflect world prices (given the exchange rate) to a greater degree. The NIESR employs an augmented Phillips Curve (where, however, the coefficient on inflation is 0.8 rather than unity) and pricing assumptions qualitatively similar to those of CEPG. The London Business School (LBS) provides for a higher gearing of domestic prices directly to world prices, and for a 'Scandinavian' view of wage determination. All three models provide an interval in which a devaluation is effective, but CEPG and LBS allow no long-run effectiveness and the NIESR only a small degree of effectiveness in the long term. On the volume side, all three models recognize lagged responses which produce a J-curve of deteriorating current balance performance to begin with, followed by improvement and then by renewed deterioration as the reduction in exchange rate effectiveness catches up with the lagged volume responses. Space does not allow more expanded treatment of the models' wage–price–balance of payments–sector here,[2] but we have established the main outlines. In the long run, wages and prices are homogeneous of degree 1 in the exchange rate (or nearly so, in the case of NIESR); but lags in the pass-through of exchange rate changes to wages and prices, and in volume responses to relative prices and profitability, ensure that a regime of continuous depreciation would, in these models, improve the balance of payments.[3]

A second important departure from the once-conventional wisdom occurs in the modelling of capital flows. Where the traditional theory assumed a flow form of capital mobility, the bulk of empirical work in the field assumes that the correct specification is of a capital stock adjustment type. The Treasury is most explicit in the modelling of this feature, of which a striking characteristic is the oddly low degree of mobility implied by freely estimated coefficients, an oddity of which the authors are well aware.[4] Apart from the continuing flow associated with growth in world wealth, the implication of this approach to capital flow modelling is that a continuing capital flow can only be associated with a maintained *change* in interest differentials, a condition ruled out in consideration of long-run equilibria. For this reason the interest rate is likely to fall out of account in the examination of equilibria pertaining to a perturbation of a flow condition, especially as similar stock-adjustment considerations apply to the consideration of the financing of budget deficits.[5]

A third respect in which contemporary modelling departs from the once-conventional wisdom is in its handling of exchange rate expectations. As already indicated, the maintained assumption of the original statements of the conventional wisdom was that exchange rate changes were not expected to take place. Removing this assumption requires, to take its place, an account of how the exchange rate *is* determined. Here again, the Treasury has given the most detailed account among the model-builders. In this account, the spot exchange rate is required to move, in relation to its expected value, in such a way as, in combination with the highly imperfect capital stock adjustment response of capital flows, to provide for an expected appreciation/depreciation sufficient to clear the overall balance of payments. The expected value of the exchange rate is depicted as a weighted average of the current and a 'long-run equilibrium' rate, given by a relative money supplies formulation or a more direct version of purchasing power parity (PPP). Very roughly speaking, the view seems to be that the long-run exchange rate has to be one that will clear the current account, as follows naturally from the notion that capital flows are essentially capital stock adjustment in form. The LBS seems to adhere to a similar view, although their account is somewhat shorter on the dynamics of short-run adjustment in the exchange rate, which is made to depend rather more directly on a relative money supplies hypothesis. In the NIESR model, the exchange rate reflects PPP considerations directly, together with the uncovered interest rate differential and 'speculative' terms, while in the CEPG model, the exchange rate is considered to be a direct decision variable.[6]

A final highly significant departure from the conventional wisdom is provided by the incorporation in all the models of an 'inflation tax' arising from the hypothesis that in the face of inflation, which erodes the value of financial assets, agents will save in order to restore the real value of their wealth. In each of the products of the model-builders reported on here, the consumption function (private expenditure function in the case of the CEPG) is so specified as to provide for a rise in the savings ratio (as conventionally measured) in the face of inflation. The same is also true of the Treasury model.

The simulation results reported in Table 1.1, now hopefully fall into place. The table reports three simulations from this volume and one drawn from elsewhere (Ball, Burns and Warburton, 1978). The reason for including the latter is that the model from which it is derived is identical in all respects to that from which the Budd–Burns simulation (reported in this volume) is derived, and has the advantage that it corresponds exactly, in the shock that it simulates (a government spending increase), to that given by the NIESR and by Fetherston-Godley in this volume. The latter has, however, a slightly different status from

TABLE 1.1

Simulations of fiscal policy

A. Dynamic multipliers for fiscal policy: ratio of GDP increase (ΔY) to government spending stimulus (ΔG) or real tax cut ($-\Delta T$)†

	NIESR (ΔG)	Budd & Burns ($-\Delta T$)	Ball, Burns & Warburton (1978) (ΔG)		Fetherston & Godley (ΔG)
Quarter 1	0.68	0.07	1.01		
4	0.81	0.17	0.85	Year 1:	1.15
8	0.68	0.14	0.74		
12	0.43	0.02	0.54		
16	0.24	0.03	0.62	Year 5:	3.27

B. Crowding-in (+) and crowding-out (−):† ratio of expenditure changes to ΔG: quarters 4, (16)‡

	$/\Delta G$	NIESR		Ball, Burns & Warburton (1978)		Fetherston & Godley	
Government spending	ΔG	1.00	(1.00)	1.00	(1.00)	1.00	(1.00)
Consumer spending	ΔC	0.14	(−0.46)	−0.14	(−1.31)	0.15	(2.02)
Investment & stock-building	$(I+\Delta S)$	−	(−0.13)	0.38	(0.91)		
Net exports	$\Delta(X-M)$	−0.33	(−0.17)	−0.12	(0.02)	neg.	(0.25)
GDP	ΔY	0.81	(0.24)	0.85	(0.62)	1.15	3.27

† The simulation results quoted assume − except in the case of Fetherston–Godley (F–G), endogenous earnings, interest rate and exchange rate. In F–G, the exchange rate is chosen to clear the current account.

‡ For F–G, years 1, (5).

Sources: NIESR − Chap. 8, simulation 4, pp. 133–5; Budd & Burns − Chap. 9, Table 1, pp. 00–00; Ball, Burns and Warburton (1978) − simulation 2; Fetherston and Godley − Chap. 10, Table 3, pp. 00.

the others, inasmuch as it combines a government spending and devaluation shock sufficient to realize specified output and balance of payments targets with unchanged interest rates, while the NIESR and the two LBS simulations endogenize all of the money supply, exchange rate and interest rate. None of the simulations is a bonds-only financed fiscal shock, the money supply increasing in each.

Taking each in turn, it can be readily seen that in none of the first three simulations reported is the potency of fiscal policy especially marked. The lower half of the table attempts to give some indication of the source of the 'crowding out' simply by recording the change in expenditures as a proportion of the initiating increase in government expenditure.[7] This arithmetic indicates clearly enough that the relatively low values of the sixteen-quarter dynamic multiplier can be attributed to a crowding out of consumption expenditure. The same is true of the second LBS simulation, since the difference between this and the one appearing in the lower half of the table is apparently due (see Ball, Burns and Warburton, 1978) solely to the difference in import content between government and private consumption. It seems clear enough, moreover, that the crowding-out of consumption is to be attributed to an 'inflation tax', arising principally from the inflation induced by the depreciation in the exchange rate; this depreciation is not sufficient to cancel the income-induced rise in imports in the NIESR model, but is certainly helpful in that respect, as comparison of the NIESR's fixed and floating exchange rate simulations (Chapter 8 below, pp. 133-5) indicates. This is, in outline, what is to be expected. On the capital stock adjustment view of capital flows, increasing interest rates are required to stabilize the exchange rate in the face of current account deterioration, and these produce declines in wealth and consumption as well as reducing interest-sensitive expenditures (house-building especially). In the flexible rate framework, exchange depreciation avoids the need for such large interest rate movements and boosts net exports, at the expense of inflicting greater inflation, an inflation tax and cuts in consumption on the economy. While the fiscal multiplier is small, in accord with traditional theory, the crowding out falls primarily on consumption rather than on net exports, the exchange rate depreciating rather than appreciating. Although the timing and magnitudes are rather different, a similar summary describes the LBS simulations. Interest rates, again, affect both capital flows (implicitly) and debt holdings in stock adjustment fashion. The exchange rate depreciates with fiscal expansion, and crowding-out is due to the effect of inflation on consumption.

The Fetherston–Godley simulation is in rather different shape, though analytically the underlying model shares many of the same basic features: thus, the expenditure function allows inflation to reduce consumption; the wage–price system ensures that devaluation is 'effective' in the short run but ineffective in the long run; while interest rate changes adjust desired capital stock allocations. However, the exercise carried out in the Fetherston–Godley simulation differs from that in the other simulations, as already explained. The devaluation is aimed to clear the current balance in year 5, and (presumably) the positive contribution of net exports is close to its maximum along the adjustment path at that point; by contrast, the LBS and NIESR simulations both embody a continuously flexible exchange rate and exhibit positive current deficits by quarter 16. Since, in the Fetherston–Godley run, the exchange rate is managed so as to clear the current account, no part of the adjustment is borne by the capital account or interest rate adjustment. The constant interest rate–no devaluation multiplier is augmented by the engineered increase in competitiveness. Given the parameter values assigned in the model, the combined increase in the size of the initial shock to government expenditure together with the change in real net exports associated with the engineered devaluation must be approximately twice the size of the fiscal shock alone, so the substantial long-run GDP multiplier is not particularly surprising.[8]

CONCLUSIONS

The papers reprinted in this volume deal with various aspects of fiscal and monetary policy and their interrelationship, with particular reference to conditions in the United Kingdom. A central theme of this introductory chapter has been the disintegration of the consensus model of macroeconomic policy, identified with conventional *IS/LM* analysis and, in its policy aspect, the Tinbergen instruments –objectives framework. It has been suggested that analytical developments in the field can be viewed as explorations of the consequences of relaxing the simplifying assumptions of the conventional wisdom, relaxations that in a general way may be related to empirical judgements that traditional analysis suppressed economic responses that are in fact relevant over policy-relevant horizons. It has also been suggested that the reconstruction of a greater degree of consensus about policy impacts will require better informed empirical judgements and a more subtle analytical handling of the time dimensions of policy impact.

The chapters that follow do not indicate that any such reconstruction is yet at hand, but there is a wide measure of agreement among them about points of departure from conventional analysis. This is most notably true in respect of the significance given to the asset accumulation effects of fiscal policy. The question of the mode of financing of fiscal deficits–the management of the composition of the portfolios to which fiscal deficits add–is somewhat less systematically explored. One significant problem here is undoubtedly the difficulty of accounting for foreign exchange market behaviour and the formation of expectations in this market. The tension between the discipline imposed by foreign exchange market expectations and the exercise of discretion by the domestic policy-makers is an issue of the greatest practical importance to an open economy like that of the United Kingdom. Some of the papers in this volume, corresponding to the experience of the mid-1970s, reflect a particular form of resolution of this tension –the announcement and pursuit of monetary targets by the authorities. The difficulties with this resolution are many; but in particular, it seems to be a rather one-sided resolution in which substantial surrender of domestic policy-makers' discretion is involved; fiscal policy then also becomes heavily dependent upon monetary policy (a striking reversal, some would say, of the policy pattern of the 1960s). It seems likely that there is greater scope for discretionary demand management policy than this, and that in retrospect this period will be seen as a policy episode enjoined by highly specific historical circumstances: the more so as there is every reason for thinking that the pursuit of monetary targets in the Western world has failed to provide an answer to the problems to which it was addressed, while aggravating others.

The issues raised by the contributions to this volume are thus far from settled.

2

MONETARY AND FISCAL POLICY AND THE CROWDING-OUT ISSUE

D. A. Currie

This paper attempts to provide a survey of the theoretical literature concerned with the relative effectiveness of monetary and fiscal policy, and the related question of the crowding-out of private sector expenditures (or, more specifically in certain contexts, of private sector investment) by government expenditures. The debate over crowding-out has, of course, a long history, but it has assumed particular prominence over the past decade in the context of the monetarist/Keynesian debate. A number of empirical studies have attempted to determine the importance of crowding-out, both for the short and long term, but the problems of modelling all the possible channels through which crowding-out may work (or may be offset) mean that much further work is required. This paper concentrates on those arguments for and against crowding-out which rest on the interaction between monetary and fiscal variables, and attempts to assess the types of empirical evidence that are required to settle some of the theoretical issues involved. This emphasis means that arguments for crowding-out based on non-monetary channels of influence are largely neglected, though certain questions concerning the impact of fiscal parameters on the supply side of the economy are touched upon.

Much of the literature concerned with the longer-run effects of bond-financed fiscal changes has already been surveyed by the author (Currie, 1978), particularly for the closed economy and the open economy under fixed exchange rates. This paper analyses the short-run effects of monetary and fiscal policy; examines the longer-run effects of balanced budget fiscal policy (to contrast with those of bond-financed fiscal changes); and provides a more comprehensive analysis of the effects of monetary and fiscal policy under floating exchange rates. The object is to provide a concise survey of the existing, though rapidly expanding, literature in this area, and to consider the implications for the crowding-out debate. At the outset, it is helpful to summarize the four main themes around which our discussion is organized. These are as follows.

1. The fundamental reason for the occurrence of crowding-out is the familiar one of the existence of real constraints, either because of lack of capacity or because of labour shortages, on the expansion of real output in the economy. Thus those economists, such as monetarists, who espouse an expectations-augmented/excess-demand mechanism of inflation, whereby the economy naturally tends towards full utilization of resources (subject to uncertainty and

* I am indebted to Charles Goodhart and Joe Grice for helpful comments on an early draft of the material presented in this paper.

informational constraints), naturally believe in crowding-out in the longer run.[1] On this view, short-run expansionary effects of fiscal policy are achieved only at the expense of a permanently higher rate of inflation. A contrasting view is provided by those economists who reject this neoclassical view of the operations of the macroeconomy in favour of one based on a bargaining view of wage determination, relatively untempered by the state of demand, and on increasing returns to scale in production and embodied technical progress. On this view, fiscal policy may have short-run expansionary effects without higher inflation by raising the level of capacity and labour utilization; while in the longer run the effects may be sustained by boosting profitability and investment, lifting the economy on to a higher growth path.[2] It is not our concern in what follows to discuss the relative merits of these positions, but merely to draw out their implications for the crowding-out debate.

2. In addition to the existence of real constraints on the expansion of output discussed in (1), crowding-out may occur because of the operation of a variety of wealth effects resulting from fiscal changes. (These arise from the financing of any resulting fiscal deficit and from any induced price changes.) However, unless crowding-out must necessarily occur because of the constraints discussed under (1), such crowding-out really results from an inappropriate choice of monetary policy. If fiscal and monetary policy work suitably in tandem, this form of crowding-out need not occur. Attention has focused on it in the existing literature largely because of a tendency to examine the effects of fiscal policy unaccompanied by any accommodating monetary changes. While this may be of significance for the theoretical demarcation dispute between monetarists and Keynesians, it has no great interest from the policy perspective except to help to establish the appropriate mix between monetary and fiscal instruments.

3. Although much of the standard literature does not distinguish between the medium and longer-run effects of bond-financed fiscal deficits and balanced budget fiscal changes, the effects are quite distinct. This applies equally to a closed and an open economy. For this reason, it is necessary to distinguish policies that are usually lumped together under the general label of fiscal policy.

4. The longer-run effects of fiscal policy are quite sensitive to small changes in the theoretical specification of the model, particularly with respect to private sector behavioural equations. This makes it difficult to reach firm theoretical conclusions concerning even the qualitative effects of fiscal policy without evidence on these empirical issues, some of which remain unresolved. Thus the following analysis is intended, at least in part, to point to areas where further empirical evidence is required.

In view of point (3) above, it is necessary to sharpen somewhat the usual definitions of monetary and fiscal policy. With regard to the definition of monetary policy, we face an embarrassment of choice. In the following, we assume that constant monetary policy means the maintenance of given levels (or rates of change) of an appropriately chosen monetary aggregate. This leaves the choice of monetary aggregate open, and possible candidates include: the stock of high-powered money; a narrow definition of money, such as M1, including only cash in circulation and bank demand deposits; and a wide definition of money, such as M3, including all bank deposits. For what follows, the choice of high-powered money offers analytical convenience, since it permits a straightforward identification of monetary policy with government financing operations in those liabilities making up high-powered money.[3] However, monetary policy is usually defined in terms of a wider definition, and so we also consider this case in what follows. With a wider definition, fiscal changes, which modify interest rates and hence the non-bank private sector's cash holdings, require offsetting open-market operations if monetary policy is to be held constant.

With regard to fiscal policy, it is common in the literature to define this as changes in government expenditure or tax parameters which do not result in changes in the money supply (or deviations from the changes that would otherwise have occurred). However, this categorization is not adequate for our purposes, since it places bond-financed fiscal policy in the same category as balanced budget fiscal policy. Since it is a theme of the following analysis that the longer-run effects of these two types of policy are quite different, it is necessary to distinguish clearly between the two. Consequently, pure fiscal policy will refer throughout the following to balanced budget policy alone, while money or bond-financed fiscal changes will be referred to explicitly as such.[4] To make this separation between monetary and fiscal policy entirely clear-cut, it is necessary to assume that changes in the costs of servicing government debt, whether arising from changes in interest rates or from changes in outstanding debt, are offset by changes in other government transfers to the private sector. Otherwise changes in monetary policy will alter interest rates and outstanding government interest-bearing liabilities, and, therefore, will modify the stance of fiscal policy by altering net transfers to the private sector. We adopt this assumption throughout the following, except where we explicitly state to the contrary.

The usefulness of analysing the effects of balanced budget fiscal policy may depend on the type of problem under analysis. It is, of course, not very helpful to assume a budget balanced at each point of time, since it requires a capacity on the part of government to adjust either government expenditures or tax rates continuously so as to maintain balance between public revenues and outgoings. Clearly, the institutional mechanisms to effect such policy do not exist in practice. However, in the medium to longer run, much greater flexibility in fiscal policy exists (though political obstacles may intrude), and therefore the analysis of balanced budget fiscal policy assumes a practical significance. It is also of interest because it permits a comparison between the effects of balanced budget policy and those of bond-financed fiscal changes.

Throughout the following, except where explicitly stated otherwise, we assume that fiscal parameters are fixed in real terms. This is, of course, a simplification which may be questioned, since with a progressive tax system effective tax rates vary automatically with the price level (and, because of lags, with the rate of inflation). Again, however, there is ample scope for adjustment of policy to allow for these effects in the medium to longer run, and since this assumption seems most in the spirit of the existing literature, we adhere to it throughout.

Before analysing the effects of monetary and fiscal policy, it is necessary to clarify certain issues concerning wealth effects which assume considerable importance for longer-run analysis. Accordingly, the next section examines the theoretical arguments and empirical evidence for wealth effects in the money and goods markets. Section 2 deals with the relative efficacy of monetary and fiscal policy in a closed economy both in the short and the long run. Section 3 then extends the analysis to the case of an open economy under alternative exchange rate regimes and under alternative assumptions concerning capital mobility. The concluding section summarizes the main conclusions of the preceding sections, and tries to suggest lines of empirical research that would help to resolve some of the issues in question.

1. WEALTH EFFECTS IN MACRO-MODELS

Wealth effects may, in principle, enter the behavioural relationships specifying private sector behaviour in every market distinguished in a macro-model. In what follows, we shall consider those wealth effects that operate in goods and asset markets and neglect any such effects in labour markets. We are, therefore, concerned with the appropriate specification of private sector expenditure and asset demand functions.

The consistent specification of stock/flow macro-models has been discussed extensively by Brainard and Tobin (1968) and May (1970). In continuous-time models, wealth effects across net asset demand functions must necessarily sum to unity, expressing the tautology that the private sector must hold its net wealth in existing assets. Equilibrium at a point in time is determined by the joint equilibrium of asset and goods markets, for given values of exogenous and predetermined variables (which include existing asset stocks). This equilibrium also determines the private sector net surplus, and hence the rate of acquisition of net financial assets at a point in time. The flow supplies of these net assets determine the types of assets that are acquired, and hence the way in which asset stocks change over time; and the endogenous variables, including asset prices and income, change over time in such a way as to make the private sector willing to absorb wealth increases in this predetermined composition. In this process wealth effects operate in asset markets but also in goods markets: while the private sector must hold its current wealth in existing assets, it can plan to modify its wealth holdings over time by changing its savings plans and hence its flow of expenditures. (Whether this will, in fact, change its level of wealth, or instead change the flow equilibrium in such a way as to make the private sector content to hold its existing wealth, depends on the specification of other sectors, in particular of the government budget constraint and the balance-of-payments.)

The standard *IS/LM* model considers a goods market, a money market and an (omitted) bond market, and includes no wealth effect in the money demand and expenditure functions. The implicit bond demand function, therefore, has a wealth elasticity of unity, implying that the private sector wishes to absorb any net acquisition of assets in the form of bonds. So long as the government finances its deficit by bond issues, no disturbance to the flow equilibrium occurs.

An unrealistic feature of this specification is that the private sector's net wealth–income ratio can vary without limit, without any change in private sector expenditures. (Thus *IS/LM* analysis suggests that a flow equilibrium, with a government budget deficit and corresponding acquisition of bonds by the private sector, can be sustained, despite the ever-rising level of private sector bond holdings.) To avoid this, it suffices to include a wealth effect in either, or both, the money demand function and the expenditure function. A wealth effect in the money demand function means that a continuous acquisition of bonds (with no accompanying change in the money supply) can occur only with a steadily changing money market (and hence goods market) equilibrium. However, without the inclusion of a wealth effect in the goods market, it is still possible for the private sector's net wealth–income ratio to vary without limit: if the government finances with a money–bond ratio corresponding to the ratio of the wealth effects in the money and bond demand functions, no disturbance to the flow equilibrium need occur.[5] The inclusion of a wealth effect in the expenditure function avoids this: an increase in the level of wealth induces the private sector to increase its expenditures, so that an unchanging flow equilibrium is possible only with an unchanging level of wealth.

This discussion suggests that the standard *IS/LM* analysis should be modified by the inclusion of the level of real private sector net wealth in the money demand and expenditure functions.[6] This raises immediately the issue of what assets comprise private sector net wealth. Little dispute surrounds the inclusion of high-powered money (in so far as it is non-interest-bearing) and the capital stock. Much dispute surrounds the inclusion of government interest-bearing assets in net wealth. Thus it is often argued that such assets should not enter net wealth, since the coupon payments on government bonds have a net present value equal to the discounted associated future tax liability, which must, it is argued, bear on the private sector. This ultra-rational argument is of particular importance for what follows, since much of the analysis falls if bonds have a weight of precisely zero in private sector net wealth, but has continuing validity if the weight is non-zero, no matter how small.[7] The arguments as to why government bonds should count, at least in part, in net wealth are rehearsed in Grice (1977), Tobin (1978) and are touched on in Currie (1978). In view of these theoretical arguments, and in the light of the evidence concerning wealth effects on expenditures discussed below, we assume in what follows that government bonds count, if only in part, in net wealth, thereby discounting the ultra-rational arguments.

A further argument, deriving variously from Pesek and Saving (1967) and Patinkin (1967, 1969), suggests that bank demand deposits should enter net wealth. (Pesek and Saving argue this from the non-interest-bearing character of demand deposits, whereas Patinkin derives it from the capitalized value of a monopolized banking sector.) Fortunately, for our purposes, this question is not particularly critical, and we can, therefore, remain agnostic. To the extent that the Pesek–Saving–Patinkin position is valid, the wealth effects resulting from a monetary expansion will be increased.

From our earlier discussion, it is clear that any change in real private sector net wealth will generate wealth effects in asset or goods markets. However, it is convenient analytically to distinguish between different causes of changes in wealth. Thus we may distinguish between: the direct wealth effect, resulting from changes in the quantity (or, as discussed below, the composition) of assets outstanding; the interest-induced wealth effect, resulting from changes in valuation of existing longer-maturity asset stocks brought about by changes in interest rates; and the price-induced wealth effect, resulting from changes in the real value of wealth because of changes in the aggregate price level. Many econometric models include one or more of these wealth effects, but before surveying the empirical evidence, it is helpful to analyse the theoretical arguments.

Direct wealth effects may result from the financing of fiscal deficits or surpluses,[8] or from open-market operations. The analysis of these effects depends on the precise definition of wealth adopted. Thus if bonds are excluded from net wealth, government deficits or surpluses only have direct wealth effects to the extent that they are financed by high-powered money creation, while an open-market monetary expansion raises net wealth, so that the effects of monetary policy are enhanced by a direct wealth effect. To the extent that bonds count in net wealth, the direct wealth effects of monetary policy are reduced, while bond-financed fiscal deficits also have direct wealth effects. Indeed, if the Pesek–Saving–Patinkin argument is discounted, monetary policy has no direct wealth effects when bonds count fully in net wealth. However, if bank demand deposits are included in net wealth, monetary policy will continue to have direct wealth effects, since a monetary expansion can be expected to generate a multiple expansion of demand deposits that outweighs the withdrawal of bonds. Similarly, the wealth effects associated with fiscal deficits or surpluses will be greater the larger the recourse to high-powered money financing.

In addition to the direct wealth effect, we may also consider indirect wealth effects, resulting from induced revaluations of existing asset stocks. One such indirect effect, the interest-induced wealth effect, derives from the revaluation of longer-maturity fixed-interest securities and equities resulting from changes in the general level of interest rates. A further indirect effect may result from changes in the level of demand. If the increased level of demand raises realized and expected profitability, because of the higher level of capacity utilization, the value of equities will rise, thereby raising the general level of wealth. Finally, the price-induced wealth effect changes real private sector net wealth via changes in the aggregate price level, which alters the real value of nominally denominated government liabilities.

Turning now to the empirical evidence, there seems to be substantial evidence for the existence of wealth effects on private sector expenditures. The inclusion in a consumption function of a wealth variable broadly defined to include longer-maturity assets, valued at current market prices and deflated by an aggregate price index, suffices to capture all the wealth effects discussed above. A variable of this type is included in the MIT–PEN–SSRC (MPS) model for the US economy, and for the UK, Grice (1977) reports significant effects for such a definition. Other studies for the UK use a narrower definition of wealth confined to liquid assets, which excludes the operation of the interest-induced wealth effect while allowing for the direct and price-induced wealth effect. Thus the Treasury model formerly incorporated a liquid asset effect in the consumption function, while the most recent version may be interpreted as including an explanatory variable defined to be the cumulative sum of past savings, appropriately deflated. (This specification ignores the effect of changing asset valuations on wealth.) The London Business School model specifies non-durable consumption to depend, *inter alia*, on the liquid asset–disposable income ratio (see Laury, Lewis and Ormerod, 1978). Similarly, Townend (1976) reports a significant effect of liquid assets on personal sector expenditure, explaining the high savings ratio of recent years.

However, the available evidence does not resolve the theoretical debate over the appropriate definition of private sector net wealth. The use of a liquid assets definition, including interest-bearing assets, is sufficiently wide to violate the ultra-rational argument that interest-bearing government liabilities should not count in net wealth, but does not include longer-maturity debt which, on the contrary view, should properly be included. However, Grice (1977), using more recent wealth data than the other studies, provides evidence that less liquid private sector assets are also of importance in the determination of consumption. Such studies, therefore, provide little support for the ultra-rational position, though the tentative nature of this evidence should be stressed. Whether bank demand deposits are counted as net wealth (as suggested by Pesek and Saving and Patinkin) depends on the precise definition of liquid assets or wealth adopted: if bank advances are deducted to arrive at the definition of net wealth (as, for example, in Grice), it is implicitly assumed that bank deposits do not contribute at all to net wealth. However, given the multi-collinearity between alternative definitions that include or exclude bank demand deposits, it seems unlikely that empirical testing will be able to discriminate between them. As we have noted above, this question can be left open in what follows, and it suffices to take a position against the ultra-rational view that government bonds should not enter, even in part, in net wealth.

Turning now to the evidence for wealth effects in the money demand function, the evidence is much more ambiguous. It is fairly usual to argue that wealth will be an important determinant of money demand (see, for example, Friedman, 1956, and Tobin, 1958). However, in the MPS model and some other large models of the US economy, money demand is specified to depend only on a measure of the level of transactions and short-term interest rates (see Ando and Modigliani, 1975; Modigliani and Ando, 1976). This is justified by Ando and Shell (in an appendix to Ando and Modigliani, 1975) on the grounds that interest-bearing assets dominate money as a portfolio investment.[9] They also point to the exhaustive study of the US money demand function by Goldfeld (1973), who concluded that such a specification was superior on predictive grounds. However, Goldfeld admits a limited role for wealth changes, and his main conclusion is challenged by the findings of Khan (1974), who finds that a long rate of interest is superior in the money demand function. This issue is of particular importance in our following analysis, but is clearly unresolved for the US.

For the UK, the lack of reliable wealth data has hindered investigation of this question. Because of this, most empirical studies of the relative explanatory power of wealth and income in the money demand function have used a permanent income proxy for wealth rather than an explicit wealth measure. The problem with this is that it removes any link between actual asset holdings and money demand, except via the level of interest payments on assets if permanent income is defined appropriately to include these.[10] This specification treats reductions in tax liability and increases in interest income as equivalent, pound for pound, and fails to capture any differences resulting from considerations of risk and private sector portfolio balance. Such a specification is appropriate only in the ultra-rational world where government bonds do not count as net wealth.

The existence of a wealth effect on money demand may well depend on the definition of money adopted. Thus wealth effects may be minimal with a narrow definition of money, such as M1, which includes only cash and bank demand deposits held primarily for transactions purposes. With a wider definition of money such as M3, which also includes time deposits, considerations of portfolio balance may become more important so that a wealth effect may be present. This point has considerable significance for what follows (and we shall, therefore, return to it), for it implies that the effects of fiscal policy (unaccompanied by changes in monetary policy) may depend critically on how constant monetary policy is defined.

It is generally assumed in the literature that the wealth effect in the money demand function is positive. This implicitly assumes that government bonds are closer substitutes for capital than for money. However, as Tobin (1971) and Tobin and Buiter (1976) point out, the opposite may be the case, so that bonds act as substitutes for money in private sector portfolios. This is more likely the wider the definition of money adopted and the shorter the maturity of the government bonds in question. If this is so, contraction of the money supply brought about by open-market operations in short-maturity government bonds may have only limited effects on interest rates, the level of private sector wealth and hence on aggregate demand, because the reduced supply of money is matched by a fall in the demand for money as a result of increased holdings of short-maturity bonds. In the absence of any strong evidence in support of this argument, we shall largely neglect it in what follows, leaving it to the reader to note the necessary modifications to the analysis and results that follow if it is adopted.

2. MONETARY AND FISCAL POLICY IN A CLOSED ECONOMY

Following our review of wealth effects in the previous section, we can now consider the relative effectiveness of monetary and fiscal policy in a closed economy. We start by considering the question for the short run in the familiar context of the *IS/LM* model, and then proceed to add additional features of analysis. Initially, we assume that fiscal changes are of the balanced budget variety, while monetary changes arise solely from open-market operations, so that we may abstract from the interconnections between monetary and fiscal policy arising from the financing of fiscal deficits. Later we drop this restriction to point to the different long-run effects of balanced budget fiscal changes and bond-financed fiscal changes.

The standard textbook exposition of the relative efficacy of monetary and fiscal policy is conducted in the context of *IS/LM* analysis. In the absence of wealth effects of any kind, the relative effectiveness of the two policies depends only on the relative size of the interest elasticities of the private sector expenditure and money demand functions. An increased expenditure elasticity lowers the absolute effectiveness of fiscal policy since it increases the extent to which the fiscal stimulus is offset by the induced rise in interest rates, reducing private sector expenditures; while it raises that of monetary policy by increasing the effect of a given change in interest rates on aggregate demand. A reduced interest elasticity of money demand increases the rise in interest rates that accompanies a given fiscal stimulus, and therefore lowers the effectiveness of fiscal policy; while it raises that of monetary policy by increasing the change in interest rates resulting from a given change in the money supply. Thus the larger the ratio of the expenditure elasticity to the money demand elasticity, the greater the relative efficacy of monetary to fiscal policy.

This analysis provides the simplest possible argument for crowding out for monetary reasons. Expansionary fiscal policy unaccompanied by monetary expansion induces a rise in interest rates and a fall in interest-sensitive private sector expenditures, thereby limiting the expansionary effects of the fiscal stimulus. Such an offset will be only partial, however, except in either of the extreme cases of a completely interest-inelastic money demand function or an infinitely interest-elastic expenditure function, neither of which receive any empirical support. Two points should be made about this form of crowding-out.

First, government expenditures assume no privileged role in the argument: an increase in consumer demand can crowd out private sector investment; or in an open economy with less than perfect capital mobility an increase in exports can have the same effect. Second, as Buiter (1977) suggests, it seems more appropriate, particularly for policy purposes, to note that this form of crowding-out can be ascribed more to restrictive monetary policy than to expansionary fiscal policy. Accommodating monetary policy, offsetting the induced rise in interest rates by a degree of monetary expansion, permits the full expansionary effects of fiscal policy to come through. In the absence of real constraints on output, no crowding-out need occur.

A further qualification concerns the appropriate definition of income in the money demand function. If a narrow definition of money is adopted, it is appropriate to assume that the demand for money is based on transactions considerations, so that a pre-tax measure of income should be used. With wider definitions, however, wealth considerations become more important, so that the broader demand for money may become more influenced by post-tax income. In this case, expansionary balanced budget fiscal policy will tend to dampen (or even, for extreme parameter values, reverse) the rise in interest rates, because the increased tax rates will tend to reduce money demand. This factor will tend to diminish the extent of crowding-out with constant monetary policy.

The inclusion of wealth effects in the private sector money demand and expenditure functions modifies this analysis somewhat.[11] No direct wealth effects occur provided that we adhere to our definition of net wealth as comprising outstanding government liabilities of all types. However, to the extent that bonds count only in part in net wealth, or to the extent that bank demand deposits are counted, monetary policy will be accompanied by a direct wealth effect, which increases both the absolute and relative short-run effectiveness of monetary policy.[12]

Of greater significance is the interest-induced wealth effect, operating both on private expenditures and on money demand. This is most easily thought of as adding to the interest elasticities of the respective functions, and may, therefore, be incorporated into the standard *IS/LM* analysis by simply modifying the slopes of the two curves. A large wealth effect on private sector expenditures therefore lowers the short-run effectiveness of fiscal policy, since the expansionary effects are partly offset by the induced rise in interest rates and consequent decline in expenditures in response to lower asset prices and reduced private sector wealth. By contrast, with a large wealth effect on money demand, a fiscal stimulus induces a fall in private sector wealth via declining asset prices, and this in turn tends to lower the demand for money, offsetting in part the increase in the demand for money resulting from the expansionary effects of the fiscal stimulus in the goods market. Consequently, interest rates rise less, so that the offsetting effects of the decline in interest-elastic expenditures is reduced, and so fiscal policy has larger expansionary effects. The converse arguments apply to monetary policy. It follows that a large wealth effect on private sector expenditures lowers both the relative and absolute short-run effectiveness of fiscal policy, and raises that of monetary policy, while a large wealth effect on money demand has the opposite effects.[13]

A further indirect wealth effect may result from changes in the level of demand. If the increased level of demand raises profit expectations because of the higher level of capacity utilization, the value of equities will rise. This will add to the expansionary effects of both monetary and fiscal policy if the expansionary impact of the wealth effect in the goods market outweighs the contractionary impact of the wealth effect in the money market; otherwise it will offset in part the expansionary effects. For fiscal policy, this indirect effect, therefore, works in the opposite direction to that of the interest-induced wealth effect, while for monetary policy the two wealth effects work in the same direction.

Monetary and fiscal policy may also exert wealth effects via induced price changes and consequent changes in the level of real wealth. In the absence of any wealth effects, an increase in the price level tightens money market conditions via a reduced real money supply, and, therefore, leads to a rise in interest rates and a fall in aggregate demand. A wealth effect in the goods market reinforces this contractionary effect, because the rise in the price level and the associated fall in asset prices lowers the real value of nominally denominated debt in the hands of the private sector, and will, therefore, curtail expenditures. A wealth effect in the money market reduces this contractionary effect, since the fall in real wealth lowers the real demand for money, and hence reduces the necessary rise in interest rates to restore money market equilibrium. As before, the net effect of the two wealth effects depends on their relative effects on demand: the contractionary effect of a price rise via the wealth effect in the goods market may be greater or smaller than the expansionary effect of the wealth effect in the money market. However, even if the net effect of the wealth effects is expansionary, the reduction in the real supply of money necessarily ensures that the net effect of a price increase is contractionary. Thus to the extent that expansionary fiscal or monetary policy raises the aggregate price level in the short run, the absolute effectiveness of both policies is reduced, but there is no strong reason why their relative effectiveness should be altered.[14]

In practice, many econometric models incorporate the opposite effect, whereby the stimulus to demand lowers prices (or, more realistically, lowers the rate of increase of prices) by reducing unit costs. In this case the price change helps to enhance the expansionary effect, rather than curtail it. Empirical work on the pricing behaviour of firms for the UK by Neild (1963) and Nordhaus and Godley (1972) suggests that prices are determined on the basis of long-run unit costs, so that any short-term price effects will be absent. (For a recent discussion, see Godley, 1977; and for a contrary view see the comments on this paper by Parkin.)

Before turning from the impact effects of monetary and fiscal policy to the longer-run effects, it is worth discussing one further effect which is not usually discussed in the context of *IS/LM* analysis. If we abandon the assumption of a fixed price (or money wage) level, some explicit consideration of the impact of policy changes on inflationary expectations becomes necessary even for an analysis of impact effects. If increases in government expenditures or the money supply raise inflationary expectations directly on impact, then several effects are likely to occur. First, the rise in inflationary expectations acts to offset the increase in nominal interest rates resulting from expansionary fiscal policy, so that the increase in real interest rates is reduced.[15] Indeed, if price expectations are sufficiently sensitive to policy changes the real interest rate may even fall on impact. Similarly, expansionary monetary policy will result in a larger fall in real interest rates than would occur in the absence of these induced inflationary expectations. Since private sector investment (and other interest-sensitive expenditures) will depend on the real, rather than the nominal, rate of interest, this will increase the expansionary effects of both fiscal and monetary policy.[16] Against this must be set the effect of lower anticipated real rates of return on monetary and non-monetary nominally denominated assets. If private sector holdings of such assets are relatively insensitive (in real terms) to the rate of return, so that the private sector decides to maintain the real value of such assets, then the resulting rise in the savings ratio will tend to offset, and might in extreme cases even reverse, the usual expansionary effects of monetary and fiscal policy. However, to the extent that the desired real stock of nominally denominated assets falls as a result of the lower real return, the rise in the savings ratio will be mitigated by the attempt of the private sector to run down these asset holdings.[17] Given these divergent forces, it is hard to reach any firm *a priori* conclusions concerning the influence of price expectations on the short-run effectiveness of monetary and fiscal policy.

So far in our analysis, we have abstracted from lags in the effects of policy instruments. Lags in the response of expenditures, particularly investment where decision and order book delays are generally lengthy, mean that the effects analysed so far may take some time to work through (though as Tucker, 1968, points out, lags in the response of money demand to interest rates may speed up the process by inducing an overshooting of interest rates in the adjustment path). This means that our discussion of short-run effects should more appropriately be thought of as relating to the medium term. But then the working out of these effects may not be strictly separable from the operation of the price and asset changes over time, to the analysis of which we turn in a moment. If these latter effects become significant only over a longer time horizon, then the separation may be approximately maintained with great gain in analytical convenience (as in the work of Brunner and Meltzer, 1972, 1976), but the validity of this procedure can only be established empirically. Otherwise the analytical solution of medium-term multipliers becomes intractable, and it is necessary to have recourse to dynamic simulations of estimated models incorporating the necessary channels of influence.

Turning now from the analysis of short-run effects to consider the longer-run effects of monetary and fiscal policy (where we continue to confine attention for the moment to balanced budget fiscal changes), we must allow for the effects of changing prices and a varying capital stock. The effect of price changes is captured to some degree in almost all econometric models. Thus the large Keynesian models have typically incorporated some form of Phillips Curve relationship, which ensures that the higher levels of demand induced by either monetary or fiscal policy result in a somewhat higher rate of inflation, at least after the once-for-all effect on prices of the fall in unit costs has worked through. The implication of this is that the expansionary output effects of a once-for-all increase in government expenditure or the money supply must necessarily be eroded in the long run: the rise in the price level progressively tightens monetary conditions until the initial expansionary effects are eventually entirely offset, the economy eventually returning to its initial level of demand.[18] Thus increases in government expenditure necessarily crowd out private sector expenditures on a one-for-one basis. However, the relevance of this for policy purposes is limited; for the time horizon over which such crowding-out occurs is extremely long, so that expansionary fiscal or monetary policy stimulate the level of output and employment over a five- or ten-year time span. Furthermore, as for the simple fixed-price *IS/LM* case, the crowding-out that occurs in such models arises essentially from restrictive monetary policy. If the authorities are willing to accept a higher rate of inflation in return for a higher level of demand, underwritten by a faster rate of monetary expansion, such models predict that higher levels of output and employment are permanently sustainable. Thus in the absence of binding constraints on the expansion of real output, crowding-out occurs only because of an inappropriate combination of monetary and fiscal policy.

The argument of the previous paragraph neglects the effects of higher rates of inflation on price expectations and hence, in turn, on wage and price determination. If this effect is only partial, as in the NIESR model (see Laury, Lewis and Ormerod, 1978), so that the long-run trade-off between unemployment and inflation is steeper than the short-run, but not vertical, then the argument still stands. A different picture emerges from those models that include a long-run vertical Phillips Curve, so that price expectations feed through to wage and price determination on a one-for-one basis. (The Treasury and London Business School models incorporate such a mechanism—(see Laury, Lewis and Ormerod (1978). However, the empirical basis for this specification, as for alternative ones, is recognized to be weak.) In such models, permanent gains in output are unsustainable (neglecting capital-deepening effects, which we consider in a moment). Temporary gains in output are obtained only at the expense of a permanently higher rate of inflation, and once-for-all changes in either fiscal or monetary policy generate no long-run cumulative gains in output. This limits considerably the scope for any form of demand management policy, which on this view should be confined to maintaining the appropriate stance of long-run policy, together, perhaps, with some judicious short-term changes to hasten adjustment towards the long-run equilibrium. In this case, crowding-out necessarily occurs because of real constraints on output in the economy. This contrasts with our previous cases, where crowding-out resulted only because of an inappropriate combination of monetary and fiscal policy.

Induced changes in the capital intensity of production modify somewhat this analysis of the longer-run effectiveness of monetary and fiscal policy. A fiscal stimulus unaccompanied by monetary expansion necessarily raises the real rate of interest in the long run as the upward pressure on prices tightens money market conditions. If a well-behaved neoclassical production function is assumed, the rise in real interest rates will in the longer run induce capital shallowing, thereby lowering output levels. This argument suggests that fiscal policy lowers both the cumulative and the long-run level of national income. Thus we obtain a form of super-crowding-out, whereby government expenditures displace private sector expenditures on a more than one-to-one basis. (As we note later, this result is specific to balanced budget fiscal policy. The longer-run effects of bond-financed fiscal deficits are quite distinct.) By contrast, monetary policy lowers the long-run real rate of interest by raising the ratio of monetary to non-monetary financial assets, and hence induces capital deepening. Thus in such a world, a one-shot increase in the money supply raises both the cumulative and the long-run level of output.[19]

However, several qualifications to this argument need to be considered. First, as noted above, with a wider definition of money, money demand may depend on post-tax income. In this case, the crowding-out resulting from an increase in government expenditure matched by taxes is reduced because of the dampening effects of higher tax rates on money demand. Second, changes in tax rates may influence labour supply and wage determination. In theory, of course, tax rates may affect labour supply in either direction, depending on the slope of the individual's supply curve of labour. However, higher marginal tax rates may tend systematically to reduce the labour supply of marginal members of the workforce, such as married women, therefore adding to the crowding-out resulting from balanced budget fiscal policy. Finally, it may again be argued that this form of super-crowding-out, resulting from changes in capital intensity, results from an inappropriate combination of policy: accommodating monetary policy, which maintains the level of real interest rates, avoids any change in capital intensity as a result of fiscal policy, and, therefore, reduces the possibility of super-crowding-out.

A more serious objection is that this view of the long-run effects of monetary and fiscal policy relies heavily on the view of labour market behaviour underlying the neoclassical version of the long-run vertical Phillips Curve. (For a different derivation with distinct implications, see Rowthorn, 1977.) A rather different view emerges from analyses based on a bargaining view of the labour market, where wage bargains are determined by target real post-tax wages largely untempered by the state of labour market demand, and prices are determined as a mark-up on unit costs. (See, for example, the writings of the Cambridge Economic Policy Group; for recent empirical evidence, see Henry, Sawyer and Smith, 1976.) Such an analysis suggests that an expansion of output lowers pressures on profits and prices by increasing take-home pay and thereby meeting wage aspirations. If investment responds to higher profitability, the result can, therefore, be a sustained increase in output. However, balanced budget fiscal policy may not be a very effective means of achieving this expansion: although it will boost the level of demand, the accompanying increase in tax rates will tend to offset the associated beneficial effects. For a higher tax burden on wages will increase pressures for higher pre-tax wages in compensation, while higher taxes on profits will stem the rise in investment.[20] On this view, fiscal policy with unchanged tax rates (and, therefore, requiring deficit financing) is likely to be more effective.

Finally in this section, we turn to consider the effects of a bond-financed fiscal stimulus. Since this is analysed in Currie (1978), the discussion here is merely summary. The impact effect of such a stimulus is, of course, qualitatively (though not quantitatively) identical to that of a balanced budget change (unless the private sector successfully predicts future government financing policy and its consequences, a possibility that we neglect here). However, for medium-term and longer-run analysis, it is necessary to consider the implications of the financing of the ensuing government budget deficit. Here the longer-run analysis depends critically on whether the issue of government bonds has an expansionary or a contractionary effect on the level of aggregate demand; that is, whether the contractionary effect of new bond issues in the money market is outweighed by the expansionary effect via the wealth effect in the goods market. If the net effect is contractionary, then the issue of bonds to finance the budget deficit resulting from an increase in government expenditure will generate a fall in output, a decline in tax revenues, a widening budget deficit and the necessity of a still larger issue of government bonds.[21] In this case, if the initial fiscal stimulus is maintained, cumulative instability results, and an ever-increasing degree of crowding-out of private sector expenditures results. In practice, the fiscal stimulus will be either reversed or accompanied by monetary expansion. Thus the initial fiscal stimulus cannot be sustained without an accompanying monetary expansion. Similarly, a once-for-all monetary expansion by means of open-market operations is unsustainable without accommodating fiscal changes if cumulative instability is to be avoided. This is because the expansionary effects of such a policy raise tax revenues and create a budget surplus, which must then be financed by bond purchases. Under the same conditions, such purchases will result in a further rise in demand, a further rise in tax revenues, a growing budget surplus, and a still larger volume of bond purchases. Thus, if indefinitely large expansions or contractions of aggregate demand are not to result, monetary and fiscal policy must necessarily work in concert in the long run, and the question of the relative efficacy of the two policies becomes otiose. However, if bond financing is expansionary in its effects, then independent stances for monetary and fiscal policy become possible. In this case, the long-run effects of fiscal policy are expansionary, while those of monetary policy are offset. For the long-run level of real output and income will be determined by the government budget constraint and the necessity of budget balance in the long run. Thus the long-run level of income is determined entirely by the fiscal parameters of the government budget constraint, and monetary policy has no role to play in its determination.[22] The long-run fiscal multiplier is given by the inverse of the marginal tax rate, so that the long-run multiplier effects of fiscal policy are larger than in the short run. In contrast to balanced budget fiscal policy, bond-financed deficits, if stable, generate no crowding-out even in the long run.[23]

The prospect for stability of bond-financed deficits (and of open-market changes in the money supply) is much more problematic when a long-run vertical Phillips Curve is incorporated, with the associated assumption that unemployment tends towards its 'natural' long-run level (for a fuller discussion, see Currie, 1978), for the attainment of long-run equilibrium requires a balanced government budget in the long run. For this to occur, an increase in government expenditure financed by bonds must induce a corresponding rise in taxes via an increase in real income in the long run. Since unemployment is assumed to tend towards its natural level in the long run, this can occur only via capital-deepening. But the upward pressure on real interest rates provided by the increase in government expenditure and bond issues makes it more probable that capital shallowing and long-run instability will be the outcome. However, it may once more be noted that this form of instability arises from an inappropriate choice of financing method: it may be shown that mixed money and bond financing (such as a policy aimed to stabilize real interest rates) need present no stability problems (see Currie, 1977). Thus the inclusion of this form of inflationary mechanism reinforces the main lesson for policy formulation, that monetary policy must accommodate to the stance of fiscal policy (or vice versa) if long-run instability is to be avoided.

3. MONETARY AND FISCAL POLICY IN AN OPEN ECONOMY

The previous section focused on the effects of monetary and fiscal policy in a closed economy, which may be thought of most usefully as the world economy. In this section, we consider the case of an open economy, and the extent to which the effects of monetary and fiscal policy are felt domestically or are instead exported via the balance of payments. We assume throughout that the economy in question is small in relation to the rest of the world, and therefore we neglect any second-round feed-back effects whereby domestic changes influence economic conditions in the rest of the world which then react back on the domestic economy. We first analyse the case of fixed exchange rates under alternative assumptions concerning capital mobility, and then examine the case of floating exchange rates. We are concerned in this section to draw out the implications of alternative assumptions concerning the balance of payments for the effectiveness of policy. To avoid a proliferation of alternative cases, we therefore neglect in what follows some of the issues discussed for the closed economy in the previous section. This is not to suggest that these questions are unimportant (for, as the previous section showed, the qualitative effects of policy may depend on them), but is intended merely to keep the analysis within manageable proportions.

We consider first the effects of once-for-all changes in monetary and fiscal policy under a fixed exchange rate with zero capital mobility. The analysis is similar to that for a closed economy, except that it is necessary to allow for the wealth changes that occur via the balance of payments and for changes in the competitiveness of domestically produced goods relative to overseas production. We first neglect changes in competitiveness and focus on the effects of induced wealth changes. Expansionary monetary policy will, on impact, lead to a rise in the level of demand via a fall in interest rates and a rise in the level of imports. Thus the impact effects will be similar to those for the closed-economy case, though of smaller magnitude, since part of the expansionary effect will spill over into higher imports, and hence raise the demand for overseas, rather than domestic, goods. However, the resulting trade deficit will lead to a subsequent drain on private sector wealth, which will modify over time this initial impact. In the absence of sterilization of the balance of payments effects on the domestic money stock, this drain of wealth will take the form of a gradual decline in the money stock. The consequent tightening of monetary conditions domestically will lead to a fall in private sector expenditures, thereby reducing the trade deficit. Eventually the trade balance will return to zero, so that the level of imports, and hence income, must be at their initial levels.

Thus the effects of monetary policy with fixed exchange rates are offset in the longer run by subsequent monetary adjustments, and the stimulus to demand is entirely exported in the long run to the rest of the world via wealth changes. Because of the fall in wealth, interest rates must in the long run fall relative to their initial level in order that aggregate demand is unchanged. Thus interest-elastic expenditures, such as investment, will be stimulated at the expense of wealth-sensitive expenditures, such as consumption. The level of the money stock in final equilibrium relative to its initial level (prior to the open-market purchases of bonds) depends on the by-now familiar condition of whether bond issues are expansionary or contractionary in themselves. If expansionary, then the reduction in the outstanding bond stock exerts a contractionary effect (relative to the initial equilibrium), which must be offset by a rise in the money stock. (This none the less represents a fall relative to its level after the initial open-market monetary expansion.) If contractionary, then the money stock in long-run equilibrium will be below its initial level.

Alternatively, the monetary authorities may sterilize the monetary effects of the trade deficit by offsetting bond purchases, so that the drain in wealth takes the form of a fall in private sector non-monetary financial wealth. If bond issues are expansionary in themselves, then the effects will be similar (though not identical) to those analysed above. The drain in wealth will lower aggregate demand, thereby reducing the trade deficit; and eventually income will return to its former level with a balanced trade account. Since the money supply is higher as a result of the initial open-market operations, interest rates will again be lower; but because the decline in wealth takes the form of non-monetary, rather than monetary, wealth, the induced fall in interest rates will be larger than before. Hence, if bonds issues are expansionary, sterilization will give a larger boost to interest-elastic private expenditures at the expense of wealth-sensitive expenditures.

However, if bond financing is contractionary in its effects, then cumulative instability ensues if sterilization policies are adhered to; for the drain of non-monetary wealth resulting from the initial trade deficit will raise the level of demand, inducing a further deterioration of the trade balance, a larger drain of wealth; and so the process continues. Thus, the type of instability, noted for the closed economy, that may result from bond financing of government deficits applies similarly to the financing of the balance of payments in an open economy.[24] Instability is more likely the larger the wealth effect on money demand, which therefore suggests a greater possibility of instability if constant monetary policy is defined with respect to a broad definition of money, such as M3, rather than a narrow one, such as M1 (see section 1).

In contrast to monetary policy, the effects of balanced budget fiscal changes under a fixed exchange rate regime (and still ignoring relative competitiveness) depend critically on the specification of the import function. We suppose first that each component of final demand has the same import content, so that imports depend on national income. In this case, the longer-run effects of fiscal policy are similar to those of monetary policy. The impact effect of a balanced budget fiscal stimulus is to raise the level of domestic demand and generate a trade deficit. In the absence of sterilization, the consequent drain of money tightens monetary conditions progressively until the balance of payments returns to equilibrium. This requires that imports return to their initial level, and because of the assumed specification of the import function, the same is true of national income. In the long run, therefore, the expansionary effects are entirely exported, and private sector expenditures are crowded out on a one-for-one basis. The same argument applies when sterilization occurs, provided that bond financing is stable. If, however, it is not, cumulative instability, as for the case of monetary policy, will result.

If government expenditure is directed at domestically produced goods with low import content, then the effects may be rather different. For in this case, a balanced budget increase in government spending may generate a trade surplus in the short run, despite the expansion of domestic demand. (This occurs because of the resulting fall in the average import propensity as government spending with low-import content displaces other expenditures.) The trade surplus leads to an acquisition of wealth by the private sector. If this increase in wealth has an expansionary effect (either because it takes the form of increased money holdings or, if sterilization occurs, because bond financing is stable), then the level of demand rises, thereby tending to eliminate the surplus. In the long run, therefore, balanced budget fiscal policy has permanent expansionary effects on the domestic economy, while exerting a contractionary effect, via wealth changes, on the rest of the world. Partial crowding-out may still occur, since a non-zero import propensity of government expenditure means a rise in imports attributable to government spending, and hence an offsetting fall in private expenditures in the long run to maintain trade equilibrium. Only in the extreme, and implausible, case of a zero import content of government spending does no crowding-out occur.[25] As before, if sterilization occurs and bond financing is unstable, then cumulative instability results, in this case taking the form of a continuing contraction of domestic demand and an ever-widening trade surplus.

This analysis is, of course, complicated once induced price adjustments are allowed for. In this case, the initial rise in demand may generate price increases (though the qualifications noted in our discussion of the closed economy case should be reiterated), and hence a weaker initial trade position (because of loss of relative competitiveness) and a less expansionary effect on the domestic economy. In the longer run, any induced price increases will tend to depress demand, and this process of adjustment will interact with the wealth adjustments discussed above. Eventually, a constant level of relative competitiveness must be established, so that the rate of inflation is zero (or, more generally, equal to that prevailing in the rest of the world). If there is any form of monotonic relationship between the rate of inflation and the level of demand in the labour market, then this requires that labour market conditions must in the long run return to their initial position. In the absence of capital-deepening, the level of output will return in the long run to its initial level, wealth and relative competitiveness adjusting to ensure that this is consistent with equilibrium in goods and financial markets.[26] Thus fiscal policy necessarily crowds out private expenditures on a one-for-one basis. Capital-shallowing will result in super-crowding-out as a result of fiscal policy, while capital-deepening ensures that crowding-out, if it occurs, will be only partial.

With a well-behaved neoclassical production function, capital-deepening can result only from a fall in the rate of interest.[27] This is more likely to result from expansionary monetary policy, which lowers the ratio of non-monetary to monetary wealth, than from fiscal policy, which exerts an initial upward pressure on interest rates. It is also more likely with sterilization, since then the drain in wealth resulting from the initial balance of payments deficit will place a downward pressure on interest rates by again lowering the ratio of non-monetary to monetary wealth. By contrast, non-sterilization will tend to raise interest rates. Thus, with a fiscal stimulus and non-sterilization, for example, the most likely outcome is a long-run fall in the level of output combined with some loss of relative competitiveness.[28]

Turning now to consider the effects of capital mobility under fixed exchange rates, we must incorporate into the analysis the implications of wealth adjustments via the capital account of the balance of payments. The impact effects of such adjustments are generally recognized to modify the analysis of the impact effects of monetary and fiscal policy. The greater the degree of capital mobility, the greater the extent to which the interest rate changes resulting from monetary and fiscal policy will be stemmed by induced flows of money capital. Thus expansionary fiscal policy will induce a capital inflow which offsets the upward pressure on interest rates, thereby increasing the expansionary impact effects. Monetary policy, by contrast, induces a capital outflow, reducing the fall in interest rates and hence the expansionary effects of the policy. The effects of these capital movements on the interest rate may be offset by sterilization, but the greater the degree of capital mobility the more difficult the implementation of such policies becomes. In the extreme case of perfect capital mobility, fiscal policy has its maximum impact effect, while monetary policy is entirely nullified in the short run.

In analysing the longer-run effects of policy with capital mobility, it is important to distinguish the different effects of the current and capital accounts on the wealth holdings of the private sector. The net wealth position of the private sector alters only via deficits or surpluses on the current account, and is unaffected by capital account transactions. However, the composition of private sector portfolios (in particular, the ratio between monetary and non-monetary wealth) is influenced by the overall balance of payments, together with the sterilization policies adopted by the authorities. In the extreme case of perfect capital mobility, where sterilization is impossible, adjustments via the capital account will ensure that the private sector is in portfolio equilibrium at prevailing world interest rates. In these circumstances, open-market sales of bonds will merely result in the additional bonds being taken up by overseas holders, thereby changing stocks of foreign exchange but with no effect on the domestic money stock. Monetary policy is, in this case, useful only for influencing the quantity of government bonds held overseas and the level of foreign exchange reserves, and, as noted above, is unable to influence the level of domestic output either in the short or the long run.

The longer-run effects of fiscal policy under conditions of perfect capital mobility with a fixed exchange rate are similar to those under zero capital mobility, with the difference that, with interest rates fixed at their world level, no capital-shallowing or deepening can occur. Thus, if we adopt a neoclassical view of the long run, output must necessarily return to its initial level, or, more generally, in the context of a growing economy (which we neglect here), to its initial growth path. Thus, relative competitiveness must remain unchanged to maintain external equilibrium if imports depend on national income, or must fall (so that domestic prices rise) if government spending has a lower import content than the average. Adjustments in the level and composition of wealth ensure that this position is consistent with equilibrium in goods and asset markets. For goods market equilibrium to result, the level of wealth must fall so that private sector expenditures are lowered sufficiently to offset the fiscal stimulus to demand (less any offset resulting from a loss of competitiveness). If no changes in competitiveness occur in the long run, changes in wealth can occur only via the current account, which must, therefore, be in cumulative deficit over the adjustment path, since the rate of change of private sector wealth is in this case equal to the current account surplus. For money market equilibrium to be maintained, the money stock must then fall to offset the reduction in money demand resulting from the decline in wealth. In the absence of any partial attempt at sterilization, the change in the money supply is equal to the overall balance of payments surplus (equal to the sum of the current and capital accounts), which must, therefore, show a cumulative deficit, so that foreign exchange reserves fall as a result of the process of adjustment.[29] But if government expenditure has a different from average import propensity, the consequent long-run change in domestic prices will influence the level of real wealth and money holdings over the above changes via the balance of payments. In this case, no simple results concerning the cumulative external deficit can be deduced.

Allowance for changes in interest payments in the current account modifies this conclusion somewhat. Since fiscal policy leads to an inflow of money capital from overseas, the interest burden in the current account is increased. This suggests that some improvement in the trade account is necessary in the long run to offset this. If labour market conditions and the absence of capital-deepening mean that output cannot change in the long run, this can be achieved only by a rise in competitiveness or a fall in prices. On this argument, fiscal policy (used in isolation from other policy changes such as a devaluation) will lead to a fall in prices, achieved by a cumulative contractionary effect on the level of output. Thus, although no super-crowding-out occurs in the long run, this will be observed in the adjustment process. But this argument, although valid for the static case, may not apply when account is taken of growth and inflation. For, in this case, capital flows will occur in long-run equilibrium to maintain and expand the real value of portfolios. The increase in the country's share of world liabilities resulting from a fiscal stimulus will increase this capital inflow in the long run and hence permit a worsening in the trade account. If this effect outweighs the interest payments effect, fiscal policy will lead to a rise in prices in the long run.

Before turning to the case of floating exchange rates, it is convenient to note the contrast between the long-run effects of balanced budget changes and other types of fiscal policy. In the above analysis, the private sector's balance on current account and overall external transactions necessarily tends to equilibrium because of changes in the level and composition of wealth. However, this arises because of the assumption that the government budget is maintained in balance throughout. More generally, the current account can be unbalanced to the same extent as the government budget, so that the additions to private sector wealth resulting from the budget deficit are just offset by the external deficit. Thus an increase in government expenditure unmatched by tax increases will, in the long run, lead to a position where the budget deficit is just equal to the current account deficit if no problems of instability intrude.[30] Such a position will not be sustainable, of course, because it requires an indefinite depletion of foreign exchange reserves (or continuous increase in official overseas borrowing); but policy changes will be necessary to alter it since no endogenous forces operating on the private sector will act to modify it.

This long run equilibrium, where the external current account deficit equals the government budget deficit, may be reached via different adjustment mechanisms. Thus, if price adjustments are neglected, an increase in government expenditure must induce a sufficient rise in domestic output if stability obtains, so that the external deficit arises from an increase in the level of demand induced by wealth adjustments. (Instability may, of course, result if the private sector acquisition of wealth is in the form of bonds, and the contractionary effects of this via the money market outweigh the expansionary effects in the goods market.) Alternatively, adjustment may take place via a rise in the domestic price level, generating a fall in external competitiveness, and a deterioration in the external account sufficient to match the government deficit. In general, one would expect adjustment via both routes. Because changes in income induce changes in the level of tax revenues, the greater the extent to which adjustment takes place via a rise in output, the smaller the equilibrium budget deficit and hence the smaller the deterioration in the external account. Conversely, the greater the extent to which adjustment takes place through a rise in prices and a loss of competitiveness, the larger the resulting external deficit and the greater the degree to which the expansionary effects of fiscal deficits (noted in Section 2) are exported to the rest of the world.

On a neoclassical view of the long run, the most likely result of bond-financed fiscal deficits is a rise in interest rates and capital-shallowing, leading to a fall in real output in the long run. In this case, the resulting deterioration in the external account, brought about by price rises, will exceed in magnitude the increase in government expenditure. However, as for the closed economy, this form of super-crowding-out may be avoided by a mixed financing policy aimed at stabilizing interest rates, so that capital-shallowing is avoided. Under conditions of high capital mobility, such a policy becomes increasingly unavoidable, so that it becomes impossible to discuss monetary and fiscal policy in isolation. Stability for these cases is rather less problematic than for the closed-economy case discussed in Section 2, since equilibration can occur via increases in the external deficit rather than by capital-deepening, as is necessary for the closed economy.

Now we turn to consider the effectiveness of monetary and fiscal policy under a floating exchange rate regime. Under zero or limited capital mobility, the analysis of the effects of monetary and fiscal policy on output is similar to that for the closed-economy case, the effect of demand changes on the external account being offset by changes in the terms of trade resulting from exchange rate changes and induced domestic price changes. It is, therefore, possible to concentrate on the more interesting case of a high degree of capital mobility. For analytical ease, we focus on the limiting case of perfect capital mobility, which we take to be the case where expected real rates of return on all financial assets are equalized by arbitrage irrespective of currency denomination.[31]

The standard textbook results for this case, deriving from the work of Flemming (1962) and Mundell (1968), are that the effects of monetary policy on aggregate demand are enhanced as capital mobility increases, while those of fiscal policy are reduced, in the limit having no power to influence the level of demand. This occurs because an increase in government expenditure tends to raise interest rates, inducing a potential capital inflow to stem this rise, causing an appreciation of the exchange rate. In the limiting case of perfect capital mobility, the interest rate cannot alter, and the appreciation proceeds to the point where the stimulus to demand is entirely offset by a reduction in net overseas demand induced by the fall in international competitiveness. The increase in government expenditure, therefore, entirely crowds out net exports. By contrast, monetary policy tends to push down interest rates and to induce a potential capital outflow, which generates a fall in the exchange rate, enhancing the expansionary demand effects of monetary policy. In the extreme case of perfect capital mobility, the depreciation of the exchange rate causes an increase in demand sufficient to stem the downward pressure on interest rates.

Recent work has cast considerable doubt on the usefulness of these results even for the fixed-price case.[32] Niehans (1975) suggests that trade flows are determined by long-run or 'permanent' exchange rate levels, so that the short-run effect of exchange rate changes will be limited. Thus the Flemming-Mundell argument loses much of its force in the short run, and the effects of monetary expansion on income may be perverse even if trade flows are sufficiently insensitive to short-run exchange rate changes that the Marshall–Lerner (or more generally the Bickerdike–Robinson) conditions are not satisfied. Furthermore, as Dornbusch (1976) also emphasizes, any change in exchange rates will be checked by speculative capital flows if exchange rate expectations are regressive, again limiting the force of the argument.[33] If the assumption of a fixed price level is abandoned, then it becomes necessary to allow for expectations concerning the rate of change of prices and the exchange rate. As was argued for the closed-economy case, a fiscal or monetary stimulus may be expected to raise inflationary expectations and lead to expectations of a depreciating exchange rate. In this case, it is possible that a fiscal stimulus will lead to a *fall* in the exchange rate, with the currency going to a forward discount. In order for exchange rate equilibrium to be maintained, domestic interest rates would have to rise to off-set the forward discount, and this would raise money velocity and permit an expansion of demand. In this case, the short-run expansionary effects of fiscal policy would be enhanced, not offset, by capital movements.

The short-run validity of the Flemming-Mundell results therefore seems in doubt. Recent studies that examine longer-run wealth adjustments question its applicability in the longer run (see Katz, 1977, and Kenen, 1977). They point to the fact that the short-run equilibrium noted by Flemming and Mundell cannot be a long-run one, since it requires a trade imbalance with corresponding changes to private sector wealth. Thus, a balanced budget fiscal stimulus gener-ates an initial trade deficit via an appreciation of the exchange rate (ignoring the objections of the previous paragraph), which then leads to a fall in private sector wealth. As wealth falls, the decline in the demand for money places a downward pressure on interest rates, inducing a potential capital outflow and a decline in the exchange rate, thereby stimulating output via an increase in net exports. In the long run, the level of private sector wealth will be lower and income will be higher than initially, in such proportions as to maintain money market equi-librium. Private sector expenditure falls, but since income rises in the long run this crowding-out is only partial. Since the trade account must balance in the long run (so that wealth is not changing) despite the rise in income, the exchange rate must be lower in the long run than its initial position.[34]

By contrast, an increase in the money supply which generates an initial trade surplus leads to an increase in private sector wealth. This places upward pressure on interest rates via the wealth effect in the money market, inducing a potential capital inflow and an appreciation of the exchange rate. This appreciation pro-ceeds to the point where the deterioration in competitiveness and the fall in net exports reduces income sufficiently to maintain money market equilibrium despite the rise in wealth. Long-run equilibrium eventually obtains when the trade account balances. The further appreciation of the exchange rate after the initial impact depreciation means that the longer run effects of monetary policy are more limited than in the short run.

The implication of this analysis, as Katz (1977) demonstrates, is that it is perfectly possible for fiscal policy to have enhanced impact under perfect capital mobility (compared with the case of zero mobility) with floating exchange rates, while monetary policy has reduced impact. As for preceding points of analysis, the issue hinges on the significance of the wealth effect on money demand which permits the change in money velocity. If this wealth effect is significant, it is perfectly possible for the effectiveness of fiscal policy to be enhanced by greater capital mobility under floating exchange rates, while that of monetary policy is reduced. Indeed, in the extreme case where there is no wealth effect on expendi-tures but a positive one on money demand, the effectiveness of monetary policy is entirely neutralized in the long run under perfect capital mobility. For there is then a unique exchange rate and level of income which gives goods market equilibrium with a balanced external account (for given levels of government expenditure and exports), the level of wealth adjusting to ensure money market equilibrium. Conversely, for this special case fiscal policy has enhanced effect. Thus the short-run Flemming–Mundell conclusions can be entirely overturned. Kenen presents some preliminary empirical results confirming the usefulness of this type of analysis for the US.[35]

We may once more draw the contrast between the effects of balanced budget fiscal policy and those of bond-financed fiscal deficits. An increase in government expenditure financed by bonds has the usual impact effects noted by Flemming and Mundell (ignoring the objections noted above). However, since the level of output remains unchanged, the resulting budget deficit is equal to the full increase in government spending. Since the trade account deteriorates by the same amount to offset the stimulus to demand, the impact equilibrium is characterized by a position where the trade deficit is entirely matched by the budget deficit. Hence no ensuing private sector wealth adjustments occur, nor does any form of crowding-out. In this case, the short-run equilibrium also holds for the long run, and may continue as long as no policy change (forced by loss of confidence perhaps) occurs. The government deficit is financed by the issue of bonds which are taken up by the overseas sector as the counterpart to the trade deficit. This provides no disturbance to private sector asset equilibrium. Thus the Flemming–Mundell results, although inapplicable to the longer-run analysis of balanced budget fiscal policy, are valid for the longer-run effects of bond-financed deficits.[36]

These results are based on the assumption of a fixed price level. With flexible prices, the scope for any long-run effects from once-for-all changes in monetary and fiscal policy is limited. With the rate of interest determined by the world level, any scope for capital-deepening is absent. With a neoclassical production function, no long-run output effects are possible. Turnovsky and Kingston (1977) argue that monetary policy, in the form of open-market operations, has long-run demand effects, but these arise from the change in interest payments on interest-bearing financial assets held by the private sector. Since we have assumed throughout that these effects on the level of interest payments are offset by compensating changes in other government transfers, we neglect them.

To summarize the conclusions of this analysis, we may first note that the analysis provides no strong reasons to suppose that the impact effects of either monetary or fiscal policy on aggregate demand will be negligible, irrespective of the exchange rate regime. Under a fixed or flexible exchange rate regime, the longer-run effects of monetary policy tend to be offset by induced wealth adjustments. The longer-run effects of fiscal policy under fixed exchange rates will also tend to be offset (unless government expenditure has a significantly lower import content), but under a floating exchange rate regime the longer-run effects may be augmented. Whether these demand effects will be translated into output changes depends on the specification of labour market and pricing behaviour adopted. On a neoclassical view, output will respond only in the short run, with the longer-run effects on demand being dissipated through price rises. (Some output effects may be obtained under conditions of less than perfect capital mobility by capital-deepening: some capital-deepening may result from expansionary monetary policy, but fiscal policy is more likely to generate the opposite.) The analysis of longer-run results under alternative non-neoclassical views of the labour market, which none the less allow for variable prices, would seem to be a fruitful area of further analysis.

The results presented here do, however, confirm the main arguments presented in the introduction to this chapter. If real constraints on the expansion of output exist, because of labour market constraints, then the long-run scope for expansionary fiscal or monetary policy is negligible, so that crowding-out in the longer run is then inevitable. If these constraints do not exist, then there is always an appropriate combination of monetary and fiscal policy (and exchange rate changes, if we are considering the adjustable peg exchange rate case) that permits a sustained expansion of output, even in the long run. Thus crowding-out arises either for familiar reasons, or because of an inappropriate choice of policy instruments. Our subsidiary themes—that balanced budget fiscal policy and bond-financed fiscal deficits have quite distinct longer-run effects, and that the effects of fiscal policy may depend on minor questions of model specification —have also been supported.

4. CONCLUSIONS

This paper has been concerned to examine the relative efficacy of monetary and fiscal policy, first for a closed economy (in the first section) and then for an open economy under differing assumptions concerning the exchange rate regime and the degree of capital mobility. Our main conclusions have been summarized in the opening section, and so in conclusion we simply provide some remarks on the implications of our analysis for empirical work.

Our analysis has illustrated how critically these effects depend, at least in the longer run, on the ensuing wealth and price adjustments. It would, therefore, seem that empirical investigation should be aimed at these areas, particularly to establish the significance (or otherwise) of the wealth effects examined theoretically here. In particular, the question of whether the issue of government bonds is expansionary or contractionary in terms of its net effect on aggregate demand would seem to be of particular importance. This question might initially be approached by examining for the UK the relevance of a wealth effect in the demand for money function, since, if a transactions approach proves superior, the whole issue may be side-stepped (as Modigliani and Ando, 1976, suggest for the US).

The major problem facing such a study is likely to be the lack of good-quality wealth data for the UK. A similar problem is likely to arise in using existing econometric models to resolve any of the issues raised in this paper, since many of the theoretical linkages discussed here are missing from these models. Whether this absence reflects the irrelevance of these channels of influence or the problems of modelling these effects with existing data is, of course, an empirical question which can be resolved only by careful investigation.

However, it would certainly be interesting to simulate existing econometric models to see to what extent their performance corresponds to theoretical predictions. The results discussed in this paper suggest that the precise specification of the type of fiscal policy assumed may be important. Thus the results of monetary changes with a balanced government budget maintained throughout by conscious changes in fiscal parameters may well vary in its effects from the same changes, with unchanged fiscal parameters and hence a varying budget deficit. Similarly, the longer-run effects of balanced budget fiscal changes may be quite different from those of bond-financed fiscal deficits with given fiscal parameters. Longer-run results will, however, be highly sensitive to the specified inflationary mechanism, and may, therefore, exhibit marked variation between models. Simulations to highlight any such results would be of particular interest.

WEALTH EFFECTS AND EXPENDITURE FUNCTIONS: A SURVEY OF THE EVIDENCE

J. W. Grice

The main purpose of this paper is to consider some of the more important recent evidence regarding the effect of wealth on personal expenditures. It is by no means a comprehensive survey of all of the empirical work that has gone on in this area, and to a large extent it focuses specifically on the role of wealth in the United Kingdom. Still less is it a comprehensive critique of the theoretical work that has been undertaken, where the issues involved permeate most areas of macroeconomics. Empirical work cannot proceed in a vacuum, however, and if we wish to use the information given by the available data efficiently, it is first necessary to be clear what questions it is to which we require answers. Part of the paper therefore examines the theoretical context of wealth effects in an attempt to delineate more clearly what these questions are.

There are five main sections of the paper. In the first, we consider why a study of wealth effects is relevant at all. Section 2 examines the mechanism by which wealth effects might operate, while Section 3 considers what assets and liabilities might count as wealth in this connection. The fourth section surveys some of the main studies of wealth effects in the United States and the United Kingdom to see what light they shed on the issues raised in the earlier sections. Finally, two recent studies are described which do seem to suggest that, in the United Kingdom at least, wealth effects may have an important role in determining personal consumption. A summary of the main conclusions ends the paper.

1. THE RELEVANCE OF WEALTH EFFECTS

A prior question to consideration of either theory or data is to ask why wealth effects should be relevant at all to macroeconomics. It seems fair to say that the earliest interest in wealth effects centred mainly on their theoretical implications rather than on whether they might be important in practice. Pigou (1943) is normally credited with having first formulated their existence (though Haberler (1941) has an alternative claim). Principally, he was concerned with refuting Hansen's 'Keynesian' assertion that an under-employment equilibrium could exist indefinitely if the economy became enmeshed in the inconsistency case or in the liquidity trap. To do so, he postulated that real money balances were an argument in the function determining private expenditures. As is well known, under certain conditions this of itself is sufficient to obviate the long-run possibility of involuntary unemployment. But he made no attempt to suggest how important an argument these real balances are, or, indeed, whether empirical evidence supported their presence at all.

Similarly, Patinkin's work (1965) pays scant attention to empirical issues. Wealth effects form the cornerstone of his integration of monetary and value theory so that a large part of the construction would fall if it could be shown that wealth effects on expenditure simply did not exist in the real world. But in fact the second edition, a volume of some 700 pages, devotes only a short note at the end to empirical justification, and the evidence presented there in favour of wealth effects having operated is by no means overwhelming.

Our first reason, then, for an empirical interest in wealth effects is to determine the status of theory in the Pigou-Patinkin tradition. We want to know whether these theories are just interesting abstract analyses or whether, further, they have real-world application. It should be noted that the resolution of this question becomes particularly important when considering what should be optimal fiscal and monetary policy. To see this point, consider the ways by which private sector wealth in an economy may be changed. First, there may be a direct change associated with saving or dissaving, even if all other variables remain constant. Second, there may be revaluations of existing wealth which take place in the absence of net saving. The predominant variables that may give rise to such revaluations are changes in nominal interest rates, which will alter the nominal capital value of any fixed-interest debt held, and changes in the price level, which will alter the real value of any assets held in money-fixed terms. Finally, changes in the level of demand may cause wealth to change by altering the capacity utilization of fixed physical capital assets, and hence their profitability. Now the four factors concerned here—the level of savings, interest rates, the price level and the pressure of demand—are all variables that one might expect to be sensitive to fiscal and monetary policy, at least in the short run. If wealth effects exist, therefore, and policy is not conducted to allow for this, then unexpected and possibly perverse results may occur. For example, a tax cut aimed at stimulating consumption may actually reduce consumption if in consequence the price level rises and reduces the real value of personal wealth. To determine whether this eventuality will in fact occur we need to know not only whether wealth does exert an effect on consumption but, further, precisely what the strength of that effect is.

But, in truth, it is probably not for these reasons that there has been a recent flurry of activity in the estimation of wealth effects. Most recent attention has, rather, been stimulated by the failure of 'conventional' consumption functions to track recent personal savings at all closely. In almost all OECD countries there has been a sharp upwards movement in the savings ratio, which typically would not have been predicted by the econometric models used in those countries. As Figure 3.1 shows, this sudden upward movement has been particularly marked in the United Kingdom. Throughout the 1960s the savings ratio remained fairly constant at an average of about 8-9 per cent. It rose somewhat in 1972 and 1973 but jumped sharply to a plateau in 1974 which has been pretty much sustained ever since. Conventional consumption functions of, say, the permanent

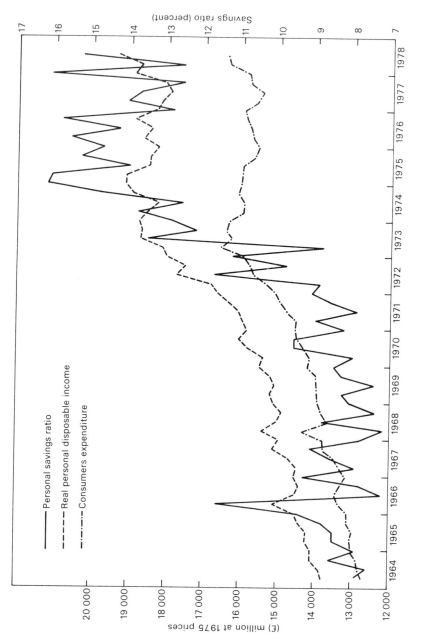

Fig. 3.1. Saving behaviour in the United Kingdom, 1964(I)–1978(II), at 1975 prices

income or habit persistence types, which relate expenditure simply to lagged personal disposable income terms, in fact had little difficulty in explaining the 1972 and 1973 data. Over this period, disposable income rose at an unprecedented rate, and either hypothesis would have forecast a high rate of savings. On the one hand, the permanent income hypothesis suggested that most of the increase was initially regarded as transitory and therefore not consumed: on the other, the habit persistence model postulated that consumers would take time to adjust to the higher income levels so that again savings would at first be high. In 1974, however, real personal income stagnated and showed little variation until the first half of 1977, when it fell sharply. During all this time the savings ratio remained very high by historical standards, quite contrary to what the conventional equations predicted. An old equation in the Treasury model, for example, which related consumers' expenditure only to lagged values of income components, predicted consumption in this period to be, on average, more than 5 per cent higher than it actually was.

Obviously, a wealth effect must be a prime candidate in the explanation of these events. The price level rose very quickly after 1973, presumably destroying the real value of a substantial proportion of personal assets fixed in money terms. The observed excess saving may therefore have been of a replacement nature. However, a number of other explanations have been put forward to account for the high savings, which we should consider as well.

First, perhaps the most common explanation is that we have simply been observing an upsurge of precautionary saving in the face of increased uncertainty. In the most general sense, while one may concede that an abnormal degree of uncertainty may have induced extra saving, it is extremely difficult to test this theory because of the problems of obtaining an appropriate measure of consumer certainty. To that extent the theory is unattractive, since we have no direct method of confirming or refuting it. There are however more specific versions of the uncertainty argument which are more readily testable. A crude unemployment theory of uncertainty would suggest that the level of unemployment should correlate with the degree of uncertainty since the probability of a given member of the workforce finding himself out of work depends upon the level of unemployment. In practice, however, this factor alone does not seem capable of explaining the recent behaviour of savings. Indeed, work by Bean (1978) suggests that the high unemployment of recent years may actually have decreased saving as the negative transitory income effect engendered by unemployment has outweighed any associated precautionary saving. A slightly more refined theory suggests that precautionary saving is associated with the expected duration of unemployment as well as its absolute probability, and that it should therefore be correlated with the rate of change of unemployment. In this respect, Bean's results do attribute a small negative influence on consumption to the rate of change of unemployment, but they are capable of explaining only a small proportion of the observed rise in saving. Moreover, they would not explain why saving remained high in 1976 and 1977 when the increase in unemployment was not rapid. These generally rather negative conclusions are corroborated by those reported by Townend (1976).

Another more specific uncertainty theory attributes the precautionary saving to the recent high rates of inflation. Certainly, the correlation between savings and inflation seems to have been much closer since 1962 than that between savings and unemployment. But this alone does not necessarily imply that uncertainty has generated the extra saving. If it had, one might have expected that consumers would have hedged against it by purchasing durable goods, assets less likely to be affected by financial instability. But, in fact, it is precisely purchases of these goods that have been most depressed, at least up to the end of 1977. Like the uncertainty-consequent-upon-unemployment theory, therefore, the uncertainty-consequent-upon-inflation theory is not without its difficulties.

Another theory, which used to be popular, postulated that the savings ratio rose after 1973 because of sharp rises in 'committed savings', that is, savings such as mortgage debt repayments or life assurance contributions which arise from longstanding decisions rather than from new discretionary decisions to save. The issue is discussed in the *Midland Bank Review* (1977), but it seems clear from the conclusions of that discussion as well as from the Bank of England's analysis of the data that most of the rise in the savings ratio came from changes in discretionary, not committed, savings. Professor Revell has recently constructed a more detailed classification of committed and discretionary saving for the Treasury. Preliminary analysis using these data has pointed to the same conclusions.

Finally, mention should be made of the 'rational money illusion' hypothesis put forward by Deaton (1978). Consumers are taken to have only imperfect knowledge of changes in the general price level so that they are not always able to distinguish changes in relative prices from changes in the absolute price level exactly. Suppose, now, that there is an inflation not entirely anticipated by consumers. Since they therefore under-predict the price level in general, they ascribe too much of the price rises in specific goods to relative increases and, acting microeconomically rationally, purchase less of each good. Thus savings rise: by the opposite process, when a fall in the inflation rate occurs that is not anticipated, savings fall. There is thus a direct mechanism linking savings and unanticipated inflation. This effect could well be important and deserves further attention, but a drawback is that we need to measure consumers' inflation expectations, not an easy process. Moreover, so far the results suggest that the best fit is obtained when one assumes that all inflation is unanticipated. It seems very difficult to believe that this really was the case over the last few years. We take up this point again in the next section.

In conclusion, therefore, while wealth effects are not the only possible cause of the high savings of recent years, most of the other major explanations do have drawbacks which make us want to consider their possibility fairly carefully.

2. MECHANISMS OF THE WEALTH EFFECT

A good taxonomy of wealth effects is provided by Tobin (1975) and the first part of this section draws freely from it. To make the classification, we postulate a private sector expenditure function as follows:

$$E = C + I$$
$$C = C(Y, r, \frac{W}{P} \ldots)$$
$$I = I(Y, r, \ldots)$$

where

E = total private expenditure
C = private consumption
I = private investment
Y = aggregate output
W = private sector wealth in nominal terms
P = the price level
r = the real interest rate.

For the moment we leave the question of what assets should be included in W, only assuming that it can move independently of changes in P. First, consider the effects of changes in the price level on expenditure. As prices fall, the real value of the quantity of money rises, assuming a constant nominal amount, and the interest rate may fall stimulating both consumption and investment. This is the Keynes effect. Keynes himself, however, does not appear to have thought that this effect would be very strong, and he maintained it would disappear entirely in a liquidity trap case. Note that, in any case, while this is a situation where the expenditure function is not homogeneous of degree zero in prices, it does not depend upon wealth and is therefore strictly outside the scope of this survey.

By way of contrast, the Pigou effect is a genuine wealth effect. As the price level falls, the value of any private sector assets fixed in nominal value rises, with the consequence that the propensity to consume out of the given income may rise. Thus, as with the Keynes effect, expenditure in real terms is no longer independent of the price level. This long-run result, however, is complicated by the existence of 'distributional' effects. The wealth term for the private sector consolidates out debits and credits that are entirely inside the private sector. While this may be correct in an accounting sense, it may also be economically misleading: not only could these inside debts be very large in relation to net private sector wealth, but we also know something about their directional effect on expenditure. On the whole, debtors became debtors because they have higher than average propensities to spend, while creditors are likely to remain creditors only if they continue with below-average spending propensities. Thus a rise in the price level, by reducing the value of debits and credits simultaneously, effectively transfers wealth from low-spending to high-spending individuals. In the short term, therefore, if it is caused by a change in the price level, the wealth effect may be perverse: a reduction in the general price level may reduce expenditure. Only in the longer term, when all of the debts inside the private sector have rescaled themselves to the changed price level, will these distribution effects cease and the wealth effects become unidirectional again. It is interesting to note in this connection that the very existence of the Pigou effect depends upon a kind of distribution effect. If outside debts were also to rescale themselves to changed price levels in the long run, then a change in the price level could have no effect at all on activity.

These effects, what we might call 'classical' or 'static' wealth effects, are well known, and a number of studies have attempted to test for their presence. Less well known, however, is the 'flow' Pigou effect mentioned by Tobin but derived in more detail by Sjaastad (1976). In what follows, we assume a closed economy. Notationally, real variables will be represented by lower case letters while upper case letters denote nominal magnitudes.

Conventionally, the private sector income relevant to expenditure is taken as disposable income y^d where

$$y^d = y - t$$

where

y = private sector output
t = total taxes net of transfers.

Bailey (1971) notes, however, that we also need to take into account the effect on the private sector of what the government does with its revenues. Principally, they are likely to be used to finance government expenditure, g, which may in part be perceived by the private sector as though it were income to itself. But the perceived income may not be the same as the actual expenditure. If the government uses its revenue to purchase goods and then dump them in the sea, there will presumably be no increase in perceived private sector income. On the other hand, by virtue of its peculiar legal position, there are some expenditures that the government may be able to make to more effect than could the private sector. It may be better for society as a whole, for example, for the government to build and maintain the road system than for it to refrain from doing so and hand the money thus saved back to the private sector. In such cases, the perceived increase in income will be greater than the government expenditure. In general, it seems reasonable to identify the change in perceived private income as $h(g)$ where h is some function such that

$$h(0) = 0$$

and

$$h' > 0.$$

Now, taxation is not the only means by which the government finances its expenditure. Given that we are allowing for the whole benefit of government expenditure via the $h(g)$ function, we must allow for the cost of that part of it financed by debt issue. Here we need to consider the ultra-rationality proposition. Most modern statements of this argument derive from Buchanan (1958). Basically the proposition is that it is a matter of indifference whether the government raises its revenues from bonds or from taxation. Unlike private sector debt, government debt is not necessarily secured on productive capital: it may, instead, be secured on the taxing power alone. Consequently, the issue of government debt now entails a stream of future tax liabilities to service and redeem this debt, since no productive capital is formed to yield output to provide this service. Discounting these future liabilities within a perfect capital market, their present value will be exactly equal to the value of the debt issue. Hence, the equivalence of taxation and government bond issue.

If we were to accept this argument, we should need to net off the per period increase in government debt, as well as taxation, in defining disposable income. But there are a number of reasons why to do so may be extreme.

1. Individuals may not have to face all future tax liabilities consequent upon debt issue. Some of these may accrue to descendants.[1]

2. Capital markets may not be perfect. In particular, taxation arrangements may drive a wedge between the market rate of interest at which the bonds are issued and the social rate of time preference at which the future tax liabilities are discounted.

3. Individuals may simply not be perfectly ultra-rational in this sense.

4. Even if they are ultra-rational, the equivalence of taxation and bond issue depends upon the government's not engaging in productive capital formation. If it does so with the proceeds of bond issues, then income from this capital will itself service the debt just as with private debt issues. In practice, government does indulge in investment as well as consumption, and in many cases the majority or all of the public debt is covered by publicly owned capital.[2]

A more general formulation would therefore allow the possibility of ultra-rationality but would also permit incomplete or zero effects of this kind. One way of doing so would be to characterize the perceived decrease in private income from the issue of public debt per period, b, by $\phi(b)$ where ϕ is a function such that

$$\phi(0) = 0$$

and

$$0 \leqslant \phi' \leqslant 1.$$

When $\phi' = 1$, therefore, we have the extreme ultra-rationality case where taxation and bond issue are identical: at the other extreme, $\phi' = 0$ and no taxation is perceived when bonds are sold. Partial ultra-rationality occurs when ϕ' takes intermediate values.

There exists a third way in which governments can finance their expenditures, namely by expanding the money supply. Closely allied to this is what Friedman has christened the 'inflation tax', which we should consider next. This takes the form of the reduction in the real value of money-fixed wealth of the whole private sector as the result of a price change per period. For a closed economy the principal assets affected will be the stock of outside money and, to the extent that they are regarded as net wealth at all, the stock of government bonds. Using the ϕ function defined above, we can then describe the inflation tax as I, in nominal terms, where

$$I = \pi M + \pi(1-\phi')D$$

and

π is the rate of inflation
M is the stock of outside money
D is the stock of outstanding government bonds
I is the inflation tax perceived to be levied on private sector income.

Putting these points together, we can derive an expression for 'perceived' private sector income, y^*, that is, private sector income allowing for the full effects of government expenditure and its financing. Thus

$$y^* = y - t + h(g) - \phi(b) - \pi m - \pi(1 - \phi')d$$

or, in nominal terms,

$$\frac{Y^*}{P} = \frac{Y}{P} - \frac{T}{P} + h\left(\frac{G}{P}\right) - \phi\left(\frac{B}{P}\right) - \pi\left[\left(\frac{M}{P}\right) - (1-\phi')\left(\frac{D}{P}\right)\right].$$

Now, the government's instantaneous budget financing identity is given by

$$\frac{G}{P} = \frac{T}{P} + \frac{(\dot{D})}{P} + \frac{(\dot{M})}{P}$$

Noting that $B/P = (\dot{D})/P$, we can substitute for T in the perceived income expression. Thus,

$$\frac{Y^*}{P} = \frac{Y}{P} - \frac{G}{P} + h\left(\frac{G}{P}\right) - \phi\left[\frac{(\dot{D})}{P}\right] + \frac{(\dot{D})}{P} + \frac{(\dot{M})}{P} - \pi\left[\frac{M}{P} + (1-\phi')\left(\frac{D}{P}\right)\right].$$

Assume that, in some sense, the public and private sectors are in equilibrium so that the marginal return to society of a little extra public expenditure is equal to that from a little extra private expenditure, given the prevailing opportunity sets. Then $h' = 1$ and

$$\frac{Y^*}{P} = \frac{Y}{P} + \frac{(\dot{D})}{P} - \phi\left[\frac{(\dot{D})}{P}\right] - \pi(1-\phi')\left(\frac{D}{P}\right) + \frac{(\dot{M})}{P} - \pi\left(\frac{M}{P}\right).$$

We can take as benchmarks the cases where:

1. $\phi' = 0$

Then

$$\frac{Y^*}{P} = \frac{Y}{P} + \frac{(\dot{D})}{P} - \frac{\pi D}{P} + \frac{(\dot{M})}{P} - \pi\left(\frac{M}{P}\right)$$

$$= \frac{Y}{P} + (\gamma - \pi)\left[\frac{D}{P} + (\lambda - \pi)\right]\left(\frac{M}{P}\right)$$

where

$\lambda = \dot{M}/M$ is the rate of creation of outside money

$\gamma = \dot{D}/D$ is the rate of creation of government bonds.

2. $\phi' = 1$

$$\frac{Y^*}{P} = \frac{Y}{P} + \frac{(\dot{M})}{P} - \pi\left(\frac{M}{P}\right)$$

$$= \frac{Y}{P} + (\lambda - \pi)\left(\frac{M}{P}\right).$$

Hence, in either case real perceived income is equal to real pre-tax output plus the rate of change of the real stock of outside money. In the case where public sector debt issue is not regarded as taxation at all, perceived income is augmented by the rate of growth of real government bonds outstanding. But in either case, income as viewed by the private sector is a negative function of the rate of inflation. If, further, we suppose that private sector expenditure is a positive function of this perceived income, then clearly expenditure will be negatively related to the rate of inflation. This is the dynamic Pigou effect. Note that, in contradistinction to the static Pigou effect, it is here the rate of change of the price level that is relevant, not the price level itself.

This distinction is important and can give rise to confusion. By definition, over time inflation implies a rising price level and may therefore involve a series of static wealth effects on expenditure. If this is the mechanism involved, then a halt to inflation may not have any immediate impact on expenditure. Initially, all that will happen is that the price level will stop rising. Observed savings will continue to be high and consequently expenditure to be depressed until real wealth is restored to its desired level. By sharp contrast, the dynamic effect operates instantaneously on expenditure even if the price level is fixed. (Instantaneously, of course, the rate of inflation may vary while the price level itself is constant.) If this is the mechanism at work, therefore, changes in the rate of inflation should have an immediate impact on expenditure since the effect is then directly from the inflation rate and not indirectly via the price level.

An alternative approach to the matter, which throws further light on the nature of this mechanism, is to consider the flow wealth effect as an issue in inflation accounting. Keynes (1936) effectively defines income as that level of expenditure that the consumer can make indefinitely without changing his real wealth. In a world where the price level was fixed so that inflation was always zero, income as conventionally measured in the national accounts would indeed correspond closely to this definition. But this is no longer true when inflation occurs. To the extent that wealth is held in assets that are not automatically re-valued in line with prices, part of 'income' each period will need to be earmarked to compensate for the erosion of the value of these assets. The amount of income that needs to be earmarked in this way will depend directly upon the change in price level per period, that is on the rate of inflation. If wealth is to be maintained, this earmarked income is clearly not available for consumption, and it is precisely this that the dynamic Pigou effect picks up.

Before leaving this section, one other role of the wealth effect should be noted. In principle, wealth may affect personal behaviour in any of the markets in which persons operate. One such market where, until recently, wealth has not received much attention is the labour market. In the theoretical analysis of labour supply and time allocation developed by Becker (1965), wealth may act as a proxy for unearned income. Barzel and Mcdonald (1973) also emphasize the importance of wealth in the context of the labour supply, and, working with United States data, the empirical study of Ashenfelter and Heckman (1974) found a strong and significant effect. In the United Kingdom, Greenhalgh (1977) has reported a connection between changes in wealth and married female labour force participation.

It is not straightforward to ascertain the strength of this effect, because Greenhalgh uses a proxy for wealth rather than a direct measure. One can say, however, on the basis of her aggregate equation, that a 1 per cent rise in her proxy would result in a reduction in the labour supply of some 14,000–18,000, given the present demographic structure of the population. It is not without interest in this connection that the sharp rise in savings observed in the UK after 1973 was accompanied by an equally sharp rise in the labour supply. It is tempting to ask whether the same wealth effect may not have been responsible for both phenomena. At least the question deserves further attention.

3. DEFINITION OF THE WEALTH TERM

Within the general problem of what assets should be included in the wealth term, a specific question has arisen in recent years as to what role, if any, in the consumption function liquid assets play. After reviewing the general problems, we therefore focus on this issue.

Pigou himself includes only the money stock within his wealth term. Because he is interested only in the steady-state effects of price level changes, he is driven to include only money-fixed assets, of which money itself is clearly the paradigm. Even within these limited terms, this does not appear to be correct: in a modern economy, most of the money stock is 'inside', an asset of one part of the economy but a liability of another. Thus, in the long run this component should presumably be excluded from consideration. Now consider public sector debt. Like money, the vast majority of such debt is also money-fixed, so *prima facie* this also should be included. Arguments against inclusion essentially turn on the ultra-rationality postulate. If the economy does behave in an ultra-rational fashion, then clearly the net wealth represented by public sector debt must always be exactly zero. In the review of ultra-rationality in the preceding section, however, there seemed good reasons why the economy need not behave in this way, particularly if the public sector engages in capital formation. In that case, the question of whether public debt should be excluded or not becomes an empirical matter and not one that can be decided by theoretical consideration alone.

Equity and overseas debt clearly do form part of the wealth of the private sector since they represent claims on income-yielding capital (though it would obviously be double-counting to include both the productive capital and the equity, separately valued). Pigou presumably excluded them because they are not money-fixed assets and therefore are not relevant to the long-run analysis of the effects of a change in the price level. From value theory, we should expect that the real value of these assets should depend upon the marginal product of the relevant capital; in the long run, this real value must be independent of the general price level. Yet in a general, not necessarily long-run, analysis of the effects of wealth on expenditure, these points do not apply. First, not being overwhelmingly concerned with the effect of price level changes as was Pigou, we are rather concerned with the effect of any perceived change in wealth whether it arises from the price level, money illusion or, indeed, changes in the marginal productivity of capital. Second, in the short term, possibly for institutional reasons but also because of imperfect short-term knowledge, nominal values of such assets do not adjust fully and immediately to changes in the price level. Whether the private sector takes any account of such short-run discrepancies is again an empirical matter and not one upon which one can pronounce from theory alone. These same points may be said to apply to wealth held as housing or as other durable goods.

To the general question, therefore, of what assets constitute private wealth, it does not appear possible to give definite answers. Like money, wealth is whatever the economy chooses to regard as wealth, so that we can only infer from the data the assets encompassed by this choice. But we can be more positive on the role of liquid assets in private expenditure functions. A number of studies (see Section 4 below) have included liquid assets in the consumption functions with some apparent success. It is open to us, therefore, to ask whether these results can have any bearing on the matters before us.

Perhaps the first question to raise is what function liquid assets fulfil in the consumption function. There would seem to be two possibilities: (1) that the degree of liquidity itself is a factor in private expenditure, independent of the wealth and income positions; (2) that, in some sense, private liquid assets are a satisfactory proxy for total wealth. The first of these, that liquid assets measure liquidity, is not easy to accept; for it is difficult to see why persons' desired liquidity should ever differ from their actual liquidity except for the trivial reason that their total wealth may differ from their desired wealth. In the United Kingdom there are four major categories of personal liquid assets: notes and coin, National Savings, bank deposits and building society deposits. Over most of the period from which expenditure functions are normally estimated, the supply of most of these assets was not controlled, primarily because the authorities were committed to controlling interest rates rather than the money supply. Hence, having the total wealth to do so and the supply of liquid assets not being restricted, persons must always have been able to be exactly as liquid as they wished. If liquidity should affect consumption at all, it can do so only when actual and desired quantities diverge. Since, for the most part, this possibility does not arise, liquid assets, as a measure of liquidity, must have a very limited role in the consumption function.

More plausible is the second suggestion, that liquid assets are a good proxy for total wealth. Certainly they have the advantage that they are easy to measure, whereas total wealth can be measured only with notorious inaccuracy. Moreover, it has been suggested that liquid assets may even be a more appropriate wealth measure in the consumption function than a wider measure, because they are in some sense 'strategic'. Many, if not most, households will hold all of their financial wealth in the form of liquid assets: ownership of illiquid assets such as public fixed interest debt or equities is not widespread. Unfortunately, these arguments alone will not allow us to utilize observed liquid assets as a wealth proxy. Suppose, first, that we divide the economy into the many consumers who hold all of their wealth in the form of liquid assets and the relatively few who have more extensive portfolios. One problem is that the extensive portfolio consumers are individually likely to be the heaviest consumers, since in general we should expect them to be the wealthiest members of the economy. In spite of their small numbers, therefore, these consumers may not be negligible within total expenditure. Moreover, they are likely to be furthest away from subsistence income levels and therefore will have most scope for making discretionary changes to consumption. If we are primarily interested in explaining marginal changes in income, therefore, this group cannot be ignored.

A second serious problem arises from the fact that we cannot distinguish from the overall liquid assets series that belong to the liquid assets-only consumers and those that belong to the extensive portfolio consumers. To illustrate the point, suppose there is a relative rise in the rate of interest relevant to liquid assets, all other relevant variables held constant. Liquid assets-only consumers will be encouraged to hold more financial assets, and since, by definition, they have no illiquid assets, their only means of doing so is to refrain from consumption. Hence, as expected, the effect is to reduce expenditure. Extensive portfolio consumers, however, will try to increase their liquid assets holdings, not only by decreasing consumption, but by rearranging their portfolios away from illiquid assets. Evidence from public sector debt demand equations and from the demand for money suggest that this movement may be relatively large. But if liquid assets itself is an argument in the expenditure function, the effect of these portfolio flows, which in reality arise purely from portfolio management reallocations, will be to increase forecast expenditure. Thus we would have the entirely counter-intuitive result that an increase in the rate of interest on liquid assets alone results in higher consumer expenditure.

A further point to note in this connection is that liquid assets-only consumers may not in fact be predominant; they may, indeed, be a minority. While direct holdings of illiquid financial assets are not numerically great, indirect holdings via the medium of life assurance or pension funds are widespread. Moreover, holdings of non-financial wealth are very common. Well over half the population live in owner-occupied housing, and virtually all consumers own some wealth in the form of stocks of durables. Whether or not these forms of wealth are relevant to expenditure is, of course, an empirical matter, but it is certainly not open to us to dismiss their possible relevance *a priori*.

At the end of this discussion, therefore, we still have no very satisfactory reason for including liquid assets, on their own, in the private sector expenditure functions. On the one hand, it is hard to see how liquidity itself can have been relevant when, for the most part, the supply of liquid assets has not been constrained. On the other hand, liquid assets need not necessarily represent a good or 'strategic' proxy for total wealth while attempts to use them as a surrogate in this way could lead to perverse results. All in all, formulations of the consumption function where liquid assets represent the only wealth term ought to leave us distinctly uneasy.

4. SOME EMPIRICAL RESULTS

A number of points have been raised by the discussion of the previous sections which, being empirical in nature, can be settled only by examination of the data. Perhaps the main questions to be asked are as follows.

1. Does wealth affect private sector expenditures and, if so, by what mechanism in practice?

2. What assets are regarded by the private sector as wealth within the context of any such wealth effect?

3. What evidence is there for ultra-rationality with respect to public sector debt?

4. More specifically, what evidence is there for a liquid assets representation of wealth as compared with a wider definition embracing illiquid and non-financial assets?

Bearing these questions in mind, what then do the empirical studies show? Perhaps not surprisingly, most empirical work relating to wealth effects and expenditure has been carried out for the United States and there is now a considerable number of these studies.

Doubtless owing to lack of good time-series data, the first attempts to evaluate the effects of wealth on expenditure were based on cross-sectional savings surveys. Klein (1954) reported a significant link between liquid assets and consumption using data from the 1949 US Survey of Consumer Finances, but Fisher (1956) failed to find any such striking relationship from the 1953 UK savings survey. Thore (1961) carried out a similar analysis of the Swedish savings survey of 1957 but again found no strong link. This early evidence from cross-sections is therefore inconclusive.

Over time, however, a growing number of time-series studies of the consumption function became available which also examined the empirical justification for relating consumption to holding of liquid assets. Patinkin (1965, note M) lists twelve such equations, all for the United States, based on seven published studies viz. Klein (1950); Christ (1951); Klein and Goldberger (1955); Fox (1956); Zellner (1957); Griliches *et al.* (1962); Morishima and Saito (1964). These equations differed mainly in the period over which they were estimated and in their definition of liquid assets. Various estimation periods between 1902 and 1960 were used, while some defined liquid assets by M1 and others by the wider M2 (US definitions in both cases). Two features stood out, however, from these rather disparate specifications. First, in almost all cases the coefficient on the liquid assets term was of the expected sign and strongly significant (in ten out of the twelve cases the relevant t ratio was greater than 2.5). But, second, the size of the estimated coefficients showed considerable variation; Fox's study, for example, gave an implied elasticity of consumption with respect to liquid assets of 0.05, while Zellner had estimated an elasticity more than seven times greater. Further evidence of the instability of these formulations was given in a striking fashion by the equations reported by Klein and Goldberger. Estimating their equation over the period 1929–50, they found only a small and insignificant coefficient on the liquid asset term: adding two extra years to the end of the estimation period resulted in a tripling of the coefficient associated with a t ratio barely less than three. In spite of the apparent significance of liquid assets, therefore, these results must be treated with caution. Patinkin himself, in fact, does not believe that any of these studies test the version of the real balance effect which he was advancing. First, he defines real balances as all the net financial assets of fixed money value, not just liquid assets. 'Secondly, and far more important, they give the impression that it is real balances *per se* which influence consumption, instead of real balances as a component of total wealth. As has been constantly emphasised above, it is this latter formulation which is implied by our analysis' (1965, p.658). In order to test the static wealth effect properly, clearly we need to include other assets in the wealth terms, and it is to studies of this nature that we turn next.

One of the major reasons why there had been an early concentration on liquid assets formulations was undoubtedly the difficulties involved in calculating data for other forms of wealth. Hamburger (1955) constructed his own total wealth series and fitted it with some success to a consumption function. The accuracy of this wealth series has been questioned, however, while Brumberg (1953) criticized, seemingly justifiably, the labour income term that had been used. A better estimate of wealth was provided by Goldsmith (1956). One of the series presented was the net worth of the household sector which covered a wide range of personal assets including all financial assets. This series thus seems more appropriate to test the static wealth effect properly.

Ando and Modigliani (1963) were the first to test for the relevance of this net worth series and they did so within the context of the life-cycle hypothesis. Over a long estimation period 1929–59 (excluding wartime years) they were able to establish a strong positive correlation between consumption and net worth. Despite poor data, roughly similar results were found for 1900–28. But these conclusions have been challenged by at least three other studies: Evans (1967) pointed out that the model fitted badly to post-war quarterly data and that when estimated over that period the wealth effect appeared to be totally absent. This conclusion was confirmed by Maddala (1966), who suggested that the difference between pre-war and post-war results might be due to the increased proportion of durables expenditures within total consumption. Since durables themselves are an important form of holding wealth, the effect of changes in total wealth on consumption may not be unambiguous. On a separate point, Branson and Klevorick (1969) reported the results of adding a price term to the Ando–Modigliani model and found a significant effect. Concomitant with this apparent money illusion was a reduction in the net worth coefficient, to such a low level that it probably measured no more than consumption out of non-labour income. However, it is difficult to accept that the Branson and Klevorick formulation is itself correct. While a finding of temporary money illusion would not be surprising, their model entails permanent long-run money illusion. Possibly this finding is spuriously induced by estimating the equation over a period when the price level showed little variation. It would be very surprising indeed if the same result were to obtain when sharper changes in the price level are observed. Nevertheless, these points must raise a question mark over the Ando–Modigliani results. Similar doubts apply to the results reported by Arena (1963), which are derived from essentially the same model. Mayer (1972) in any case notes that over the period 1948–58 even the best of Arena's equations fails to out-perform a naive no-change model of consumption.

Two other studies both attempt to test for the presence of a widely defined static wealth effect but, not having reliable direct estimates of wealth, solve out wealth from the formulation, effectively proxying it by a long lag on income. Working with US data of various sub-periods within 1929–60, Spiro (1962) obtains significance on his wealth-proxying terms which suggests the presence of a wealth effect. For post-war years, Mayer also found that the model outperforms the naive no-change model. Evans, however, criticized the formulation on technical grounds, in particular because the method of deflation to constant price terms implied a lack of long-run price homogeneity. Moreover, it is not clear how good a proxy for wealth has been employed. A long lag on income would not pick up, for example, autonomous past changes in the savings ratio which would have affected actual wealth. Nor would it have picked up changes in wealth brought about by fluctuations in stock prices or by changes in interest rates. As a specific test of the wealth effect, therefore, the Spiro results are somewhat unsatisfactory. The same is true of the results from UK data reported by Ball and Drake (1964). The wealth proxy is very similar to that used by Spiro and is subject to the same criticisms. While they too find their wealth proxy to fit the data well, it is not clear that a genuine wealth effect is indicated by these results.

Reverting to US studies, Munnell (1974) and Feldstein (1976) have recently found evidence of a somewhat unusual form of wealth effect within what they have called the 'Extended Life Cycle hypothesis'. Feldstein estimated a model similar to that of Ando and Modigliani, using a standard Goldsmith measure of household net worth, and comparing it with one where accumulated social security reserves were included in the formulation. He concluded from the statistical results that consumers do regard social security reserves as part of their wealth and that the propensity to consume out of this form is not significantly different from that out of direct holdings of assets. Munnell's conclusions were closely similar. These studies have not yet been subjected to detailed criticism, but whatever the ultimate conclusion as to their value, the impact of social security on private sector expenditures is clearly a subject that deserves further attention.

A final American study to be cited is that of Mishkin (1976). Mishkin's work relates only to consumer durables expenditures but, since this is one of the most volatile components of demand, is none the less of interest. He postulates that, not only is the total net financial worth of persons relevant to expenditure, but so also is its composition. In particular, he finds that negative wealth—debts— have a depressing impact on expenditures nearly five times greater than the expansionary effects of positive gross wealth. While, again, these results do not seem conclusive, they do suggest that compositional effects warrant further investigation. In a later paper (Mishkin, 1977), he has suggested that compositional movements of this kind can explain a major part of the 1973-5 recession on the United States. In particular, he identifies movements in common stocks valuations as being a crucial aspect of the balance sheet. In this respect, Mishkin provides empirical confirmation of the arguments advanced by Modigliani (1971).

Turning to the UK studies of wealth, we find no such rich panoply available. Five studies are mentioned here. An interesting, comparatively early, study was made by Stone (1964). He constructed a direct personal wealth measure by taking a point estimate for wealth in 1961 and using cumulated savings to re-present changes before and after that point. In a regression, the resulting series turned out to be a significant positive influence on consumer spending with a t statistic of 2.2. While suggestive, however, some doubt must attach to this result: (1) the estimation period was fairly short (1955–63); (2) it is not clear how good a representation of wealth movements is given by this procedure; (3) no proper account of dynamic structure was taken.

Chronologically, the next study to test for wealth effects was that of Hilton and Crossfield (1970). In this case, they constructed a direct measure of wealth and once again found a significant effect on consumption. They also found that the effect was concentrated on non-durables with little effect on durable expenditures, when they were estimated separately. Another important finding was that liquid assets entered separately had an insignificant and perverse effect. Dynamics were better treated in this study, which also had the benefit of a longer estimation period. It is therefore unfortunate that Townend (1976), over a longer estimation period, should have reached diametrically opposed conclusions. He found that, while liquid assets were closely related to consumption (albeit with a fairly small quantitative impact), wider measures of wealth were not relevant. In view of the discrepancy between this finding and that of the previous study, it would be interesting to identify what factors had caused the difference in results. Unfortunately, Townend does not give details of the derivation of his wider series, which would enable this to be done. Some support for the liquid assets hypothesis is provided by a simple model estimated by Forsythe (1975), but he appears not to have considered the possibility of wider wealth effects.

A fifth study of interest is that of Deaton (1972), which considered wealth in the framework of the life-cycle model. Direct data for personal net wealth were taken from the Revell and Roe studies (Revell, 1967) and its effect tested quarterly on personal consumption of non-durable goods, 1955–66. In spite of the difficulties of correct specification and estimation involved in this model, wealth is shown as having a significantly positive effect on non-durable consumption, and the main question is whether the size of these effects is sufficiently large for them to be important. Deaton illustrates the strength of his effect by noting that a 25 per cent reduction in ordinary share values at the beginning of 1969 would have caused a £4.58 billion capital loss to shareholders, measured in 1958 prices; but the maximum reduction in consumption that would ensue would be only £22.6 million. While the effect would continue, with lessening impact, for some time, Deaton nevertheless concludes: 'in normal circumstances ignoring wealth effects causes little error; in times when stock market values change very rapidly, especially in financial crises, there is significant impact.'

From this work, Laidler (1978) has recently concluded that wealth effects in the United Kingdom are not very important and therefore do not have a prominent role in the transmission mechanism. This would seem incorrect. Over the estimation period of the Deaton equation, there was very little non-trend variation in personal wealth holdings, with only minor cycling about a rising trend. Since 1966 the situation has changed markedly with fluctuations of a much greater amplitude occuring. The principal factor behind this effect has been the greater variability of the inflation rate, but also of importance has been the increased volatility of the stock market and the real capital gains and losses that have been made by house-owners. Together, these contributions to wealth have resulted in an irregular rise in its real value to persons of perhaps 30 per cent between 1966 and mid-1973 followed by a fairly steady fall of about the same magnitude to the end of 1977. Given this experience, and assuming that the parameters of the Deaton equation still held, the wealth movement would certainly not be negligible since they would have caused changes of several per cent to consumers' expenditure. Contrary to Laidler's conclusion, therefore, Deaton's results underline the importance of wealth effects in the United Kingdom.

All the above studies, for both the United States and the United Kingdom, represent attempts to test one or another aspect of the static wealth effect. Attempts to test the dynamic wealth effect can be quickly surveyed because, to the author's knowledge, there are no such studies. Some indirect evidence is given, however, from studies that have found the rate of inflation to be a negative factor on consumption. Working with US data, Juster and Wachtel (1972) found a consistent link of this nature, as did Defris (1977) from Australian data. Neither was able to suggest a satisfying economic rationale for this phenomenon but rather believe that inflation must have a negative impact on consumer confidence and hence on expenditure. While this could be the true explanation, this evidence would also be consistent with the operation of the dynamic Pigou effect. Similarly, the evidence adduced by Deaton in support of the 'rational money illusion' hypothesis could be consistent with a dynamic wealth effect. In particular, the somewhat strange finding that the best fit of the rational money illusion specification is obtained on the assumption that no inflation is anticipated might, at least in part, be explained by a dynamic Pigou effect, even if rational money illusion were operating in tandem.

5. TWO RECENT STUDIES OF WEALTH EFFECTS IN THE UNITED KINGDOM

It should be clear from the above, fairly selective, survey that there is no shortage of empirical studies of wealth effects, especially for the United States. But the overall effect is one of confusion; while several studies have found evidence of wealth affecting expenditure, most appeared to be subject to justifiable criticism. This confusion is reflected in the major econometric models. We find the Wharton model having only a tiny effect from liquid assets on private consumption while the MPS model has a strong direct effect between expenditure and total net worth.

With regard to the UK, the evidence seems somewhat clearer, if only because there have been fewer studies. All five studies cited show evidence of some form of wealth effect operating, and only Townend specifically quotes evidence against a wider wealth effect. None the less, the econometric models are by no means unanimous: it is possible to find the published version of the NIESR consumption function having no wealth effect, the last published Treasury equation having a real liquid assets term and the LBS equation having a somewhat stronger liquid assets term, intended to proxy, we are told, a much wider wealth effect (see Laury *et al.*, 1978). A recent important study by Davidson *et al.* (1978) has added further weight to the arguments in favour of a wealth effect. This study is interesting because it sets out not to test for wealth effects but rather as an exercise in econometric methodology to explain why published studies of consumers' expenditure in the United Kingdom have produced substantially different conclusions. To this end, they propose that, among other requirements, an entirely successful econometric model should be able to explain why other, different, published conclusions were reached and what mis-specification had led to these erroneous results. As an illustration of this methodology, they consider three earlier studies of UK consumption—Hendry (1974), Ball *et al.*, (1975) and Wall *et al.* (1975)—none of which explicitly allow wealth effects. The study proceeds by testing for the possibility of various statistical mis-specifications that could have occurred in these earlier models: autocorrelation of the errors, multicollinearity between the explanatory variables, the effects of measurement errors, etc. At each stage in the procedure, great emphasis is laid on testing the explicit and implicit restrictions imposed by the models to see whether in fact these restrictions could be consistent with the available data. Eventually the authors decide that the major mis-specification involved in these earlier models was 'a serious, but hard to detect, dynamic misspecification'. More specifically, this dynamic mis-specification is a failure to allow the possibility than the income–expenditure relationship could initially have been in disequilibrium. Correcting for this error, they obtain a model as follows:

$$\Delta_4 \log C_t = 0.49 \, \Delta_4 \log Y_t - 0.17 \Delta_1 \Delta_4 \log Y_t - 0.06 \log (C/Y)_{t-4}$$
$$ (0.04) (0.05) (0.01)$$

$$+ \, 0.01 \, \Delta_4 D_t$$
$$(0.003)$$

where

C_t = consumer's expenditure on non-durable goods at 1970 prices

Y_t = real personal disposable income

D_t = a dummy variable picking up forestalling effects prior to the 1965 budget.

The implications of this model are: (1) that the savings ratio this quarter is much the same as that four quarters ago; (2) that the savings ratio will be the higher, the faster has been the intervening growth in income; (3) that this short-run behaviour will be modified in the longer term if there is an initial divergence between consumption and income. It is noted that the other three formulations considered may be regarded as special cases of this one. It is the third term in the right-hand side that is of particular interest because, if we integrate both sides of the equation, we find the level of consumption depending negatively upon cumulated negative saving. However, no wealth effect is implied because the wealth implied by this cumulated saving is not deflated. But the study goes on to show that a substantial improvement in fit is obtained if price level and price change terms are added. The equation then becomes:

$$\Delta_4 \log C_t = 0.47 \, \Delta_4 \log Y_t - 0.21 \, \Delta_1 \Delta_4 \log Y_t - 0.10 \log (C/Y)_{t-4}$$
$$\quad\quad (0.04) \quad\quad\quad\quad (0.05) \quad\quad\quad\quad\quad (0.02)$$
$$+ 0.01 \Delta_4 \, D_t - 0.13 \Delta_4 \log P_t - 0.28 \Delta_1 \Delta_4 \log P_t$$
$$(0.003) \quad\quad (0.07) \quad\quad\quad\quad (0.15)$$

where

P_t = the consumer expenditure deflator.

In this case, integrating both sides and taking the third and fifth terms together from the right-hand side, we find that the level of consumption now depends upon the deflated stock of cumulated past savings or, at least, a close approximation thereto (see the appendix to this paper). We also find some evidence that the rate of inflation is negatively related to the level of consumption.

It should be emphasized that Davidson *et al*. themselves do not characterize their model as containing a wealth effect but rather justify their disequilibrium terms on statistical grounds. However, a natural economic interpretation of these results would be that a wealth effect is implicated. Similarly, the observed negative impact of inflation would be consistent with a flow wealth effect. Here the authors interpret their results as support for Deaton's rational money illusion hypothesis, but, for the reasons advanced above, a more plausible interpretation could be in terms of a dynamic Pigou effect.

While the terms relevant to wealth in the above formulations are moderately well determined, the most striking feature about them is their predictive success. When estimated only as far as 1973 (III) they predict up to the end of 1977 with prediction errors well within the estimated standard errors of the equation. In view of the fact that conventional models have had enormous difficulty in explaining precisely this period, this performance is quite staggering. Indeed, for these reasons, the current Treasury model now contains an equation of this form.

In an important respect, therefore, the Davidson study may be regarded as providing evidence of wealth effects in the Stone mode. Recent work within the Treasury (see Grice, 1977) has followed the alternative approach of estimating updated direct measures of wealth and testing for their relevance. This process was considerably aided by the intensive work on personal wealth holdings, undertaken by the Central Statistical Office (CSO) and others for the Royal Commission on the Distribution of Income and Wealth. A summary is given in CSO (1978). Using this information and other already available data, it was possible to derive a time-series for personal wealth, embracing most forms of assets, quarterly from 1963 to 1975. Static wealth effects were tested by means of the following form:

$$C = a + \sum_{i=0}^{M} b_i \, Y_{t-i} + \sum_{j=0}^{N} c_j \, (W/P)_{t-j}$$

where

C = consumers' expenditure at 1970 prices
Y = real personal disposable income
W = nominal personal wealth (on various definitions)
P = the consumer expenditure deflator
M, N are integers

Flow wealth effects were tested by the formulation

$$C = a + \sum_{i=0}^{M} b_i \, Y_{t-i} + \sum_{j=0}^{N} c_j \, \overline{(W/P)}_{t-j}$$

where

$$\overline{(W/P)} \;=\; \Delta \, (W/P)$$

$$\doteqdot \left(\frac{\Delta W}{W} - \frac{\Delta P}{P} \right) \left(\frac{W}{P} \right)$$

Interpretation of the static formulation is straightforward. The flow effect formulation allows expenditure to be related not to the stocks of wealth but rather to the rate of change of wealth. In turn, this effect can be decomposed into effects owing to the rate of increase of nominal wealth ($\Delta W/W$) and those owing to the rate of inflation ($\Delta P/P$). The main results from this work using various definitions of wealth are shown in Tables 3.1 and 3.2. It would seem that we can draw the following conclusions.

1. Static wealth effects perform better than dynamic ones. When both static and dynamic price terms were included, the effects became indeterminate, possibly owing to correlation between the price level and the rate of inflation

over this data period. Further data for 1976 and 1977, when this correlation was broken, may be helpful in this respect.

2. The apparent significance of liquid assets, when included alone in the formulation, disappears when wider wealth measures are also included.

3. The best fits appear to be obtained over this period when wealth is defined to include all financial assets but not physical ones.

4. On the artificial assumption that only a static wealth effect operated, then a 1 per cent rise in the price level at the end of 1975 would have reduced consumers' expenditure by about £10 million in 1970 prices permanently within two years. On the alternative assumption that only a flow wealth effect existed, a 1 per cent sustained inflation at the end of 1975 would have reduced consumers' expenditure by about £12 million in constant 1970 prices each quarter there onwards.

The advantage of this study as compared with that of Davidson *et al.* is that, by using direct measures of wealth, it provides a direct test of the wealth hypothesis and allows us to make some specific answers to the questions raised in the earlier section of this survey. Its disadvantage is that it may be econometrically unsatisfactory, in particular because there may be dynamic mis-specification. The logical next step would therefore seem to be to combine these approaches and examine the effects of substituting the direct wealth measures into the Davidson framework. At the present stage, however, the two studies together do seem to point strongly towards the importance of wealth effects in the United Kingdom.

6. SUMMARY AND CONCLUSION

The first section of this paper examined the behaviour of savings in the United Kingdom and noted the extreme difficulty that conventional models have had in explaining this behaviour since 1973. A wealth effect was identified as a potential source of this problem while other possible explanations appeared to have difficulties. Next, we considered by what mechanism the wealth effect operated and distinguished the classic or static wealth effect from the lesser-known flow or dynamic effect. Attention was drawn to the possible importance of wealth effects on the supply side of the economy as well as on demand. In Section 3 consideration was given to what assets should be included in the definition of wealth and this seemed to be largely an empirical question. Some doubts were cast, however, on the common practice of using liquid assets series to represent wealth in general.

What progress has been made in answering the list of empirical questions drawn up at the beginning of the fourth section? Sections 4 and 5 reviewed some of the relevant evidence. The answer must be that progress has been uneven. Specifically for the United Kingdom, the weight of evidence appears to favour the operation of a sizeable static wealth effect on expenditure. There is also

TABLE 3.1.
Static Wealth Effects

Equation	Constant	Y	RNLA	RILLI	Variables† RNW	RNHW	RNFW	$\bar{R}^2$	SE	DWS
1	514.8	0.443 (8.75)	0.129 (6.96)					0.984	80.83	1.82
2	388.2	0.744 (8.70)	0.0145 (0.37)	0.0196 (2.28)				0.988	71.99	2.27
3	1289.0	0.564 (5.60)			0.0132 (1.72)			0.978	95.55	1.31
4	−1671.8	0.925 (16.66)				0.0327 (3.86)		0.983	85.18	1.67
5	−809.8	0.827 (2.59)					0.0234 (4.35)	0.983	84.19	1.71

†*RNLA* = real net liquid assets of persons
RILLI = real net illiquid assets of persons
RNW = real net total wealth of persons
RNHW = as *RNW*, *less* holdings of life assurance and pension fund assets
RNFW = real net financial wealth of persons

TABLE 3.2
Dynamic Wealth Effects†

Equation	Constant	Y	$RNLA$	$RILLI$	RNW	$RNHW$	$RNFW$	$\bar{R}^2$	SE	DWS
					Variables					
6	1773.3 (3.32)	0.698 (11.03)	0.128 (0.36)					0.961	125.97	0.95
7	1014.6 (2.66)	0.807 (17.56)	−0.243 (1.01)	0.080 (6.14)				0.983	83.57	2.21
8	1298.8 (5.38)	0.763 (25.11)		0.067 (4.69)				0.977	96.24	1.33
9	1539.7 (6.84)	0.733 (29.93)			0.053 (3.60)			0.975	101.09	1.20
10	1545.5 (6.89)	0.732 (26.04)				0.100 (4.22)		0.975	100.17	1.26
11	1525.1 (6.69)	0.733 (25.02)					0.062 (3.82)	0.974	102.35	1.20

† All coefficients refer to long-run effects. *T*-ratios are in brackets.

evidence that would be consistent with a dynamic wealth effect but its existence has not been demonstrated overwhelmingly and it must almost certainly be less important quantitatively than the static effect, if it exists at all. With regard to the composition of wealth, the truthful answer must be that these issues have scarcely begun to be tackled. However, two tentative conclusions may be advanced.

1. Changes in physical wealth are less important, if at all, in determining expenditure than changes in financial wealth;

2. Wealth effects are wider in scope than liquid assets alone.

All in all, a considerable amount of work remains to be undertaken before we can be satisfied on any of these issues. But what is clear from the available evidence is that wealth effects are sufficiently important to make further investigation necessary. We can ignore their possibility at our peril.

APPENDIX

WEALTH AND THE DAVIDSON–HENDRY FORMULATION

The Davidson–Hendry equation may be written:

$$\Delta_4 \log CND = \alpha\Delta_4 \log Y + \beta \Delta\Delta_4 \log Y + \gamma \log (CND/Y)_{-4} + \delta\Delta_4 \log P$$

$$(3.A1)$$

where

CND = real non-durable consumption
Y = real personal income
P = the consumer price deflator
$\alpha, \beta, \gamma, \delta$ are parameters

In dynamic equilibrium, this yields a permanent income relationship

$$CND = KY \qquad (3.A2)$$

where

$$K = exp\,\{[(1-\alpha)\Delta_4 \log Y - \delta\Delta_4 \log P]\,\gamma\} \qquad (3.A2a)$$

Now, introducing wealth, let

W^* = nominal wealth
W = real wealth
S = real savings
θ = fraction of portfolio held in money-fixed assets
k = wealth–income ratio

We have

$$\Delta W \doteq S_{-1} - \theta W_{-1} \Delta \log P. \qquad (3.A3)$$

Thus

$$k\,(1 + \Delta \log Y) = (1 - \theta \log P)k_{-1} + (S/Y)_{-1}. \qquad (3.\text{A}4)$$

It holds approximately that

$$\log\,(CND/Y) \doteqdot S/Y. \qquad (3.\text{A}5)$$

From expressions (A2), (A2a) and (A5), it follows that, in equilibrium,

$$k = (\alpha - 1)\,\Delta_4 \log Y + \delta \Delta_4 \log P / \gamma\,(\Delta \log Y + \theta \Delta \log P). \qquad (3.\text{A}6)$$

Therefore (A3) may be re-expressed as

$$\Delta_4 \log W \doteqdot 4\,(S/Y)_{-4} - \theta \Delta_4 \log P$$
$$\doteqdot -4\,(CNDkY)_{-4}/k - \theta \Delta_4 \log P \qquad (3.\text{A}7)$$

Using (A7), the Davidson–Hendry equation may be re-expressed as

$$\Delta_4 \log CND \doteqdot \alpha\,\Delta_4 \log Y + \beta \Delta \Delta_4 \log Y + \eta \Delta_4 \log W$$

where

$$\eta = -\delta/\theta = -\gamma k/4.$$

I am indebted to C.R. Bean for this derivation.

THE MEASUREMENT OF FISCAL POLICY*

R. R. Neild

At the Seminar I described the main problems that Terry Ward and I had encountered in applying the concept of the constant employment budget (or 'full employment' budget) to Britain. Since then a book incorporating our results has been published by the IFS (Ward and Neild, 1978). Since much of what I said at the Seminar can be found in that book, what follows is a much amended paper. It concentrates on two questions that were raised at the Seminar, and on which there is something to add to what is said in the book: first, whether it is useful to have a single aggregate measure of fiscal policy; second, whether it is possible to construct such a measure.

USEFULNESS

It is possible to formulate and assess macroeconomic policy without an aggregate measure of fiscal policy. One can use a model in which the various components of the budget are represented separately in more or less detail. Different taxes and types of expenditure, represented in this way, can then be treated as separate instruments; and in order to assess alternative policies, those instruments can be manipulated so as to see, from simulation runs with the model, the effect that different combined settings of them is estimated to have on target variables, such as employment, prices, or the foreign balance. The balance in the budget will be treated neither as an instrument nor as a target, but may be calculated and linked to financial flows.

That, by and large, was the approach that ruled from the last war until a few years ago—though to start with the models were crude in the extreme. Now, however, the formulation of policy is focused on the balance in the budget, as it was before the war. The balance in the budget, defined in Britain as the public sector borrowing requirement,[1] is used by the government and by commentators as a summary measure of fiscal policy and as a target. Yet it has serious deficiencies in both uses. As a measure of fiscal policy it is deficient in that it is influenced by changes in income (which may be caused by exogenous events or by fiscal policy itself) as well as by discretionary changes in the instruments of fiscal policy, i.e. expenditure schedules, tax rates and other charges. Thus, even if all tax rates, charges and expenditure schedules stay constant, a variation in

---

*I have worked so closely on these problems with Terry Ward that it is hard to say where his ideas end and mine begin. I am most grateful to him and to Mr K.J. Coutts for comments on a draft of this paper, but I of course am responsible for any imperfections that remain.

income will change the yield of taxes and charges and the value of endogenous outlays; and that will cause the balance in the budget to change. As a target, it is dangerous because it will induce perverse action: if income falls as a result, say, of a rise in the propensity to save, the balance in the budget will deteriorate and the achievement of a given target will require discretionary action to tighten fiscal policy, which, in turn, will diminish income further. These are long-established defects, but they are ignored in much current discussion. For this reason alone, there are good grounds for seeking a better summary measure of fiscal policy than the actual, uncorrected balance in the budget.

Among economists, there has been an awakening of interest in the financial sector of the economy, and the balance in the budget has become a feature in most macroeconomic models. The plausibility of the relationship between the financial balances of different sectors tends to be used as a test of the plausibility of the model and of the forecasts it produces. And the balance in the budget is often used as a summary measure of fiscal policy changes that have occurred or would be required to generate different outcomes. But the same objections arise: diagnosis and prescription require the ability to measure discretionary actions, but these are mixed together with endogenous effects if the uncorrected balance in the budget is used. Moreover, understanding of differences between different models might be helped if one could start out from broad agreement about what fiscal action had been taken or was under consideration.

Finally, in a seminar on the relationship between fiscal policy and monetary policy, it is sensible to seek a measure of fiscal policy—and monetary policy—in the hopes of making discussion precise. Measurable concepts tend to be more useful than non-measurable ones.

On the other hand, the usefulness of an aggregate measure of discretionary fiscal action has been questioned on the grounds that it is not possible to obtain a pure measure because the effects on the economy of a given discretionary change will vary with the economic circumstances, including the setting of other instruments. A variant of this argument is that, on a monetarist approach, one is concerned with the change in the money supply, which again will vary with economic circumstances. These arguments really concern the feasibility, not the usefulness, of obtaining a pure measure of discretionary action. This we can consider in two stages: what the problems are in theory, and what they are like when you tackle them in practice.

THE PROBLEMS IN THEORY

The calculation of a summary measure of discretionary fiscal action can be regarded as a problem of combining the setting of all the constituent instruments in the budget (expenditure schedules, tax rates and charges).

No one disputes that, in the first instance, the different items in the budget should be combined according to the receipts and expenditure to which they give rise at an actual or hypothetical level of income. And the case for using a standardized hypothetical level of income, as one does in calculating the Constant Employment Balance, does not need to be repeated here. The main question at issue concerns whether the receipts and expenditure to which different instruments give rise should be weighted on the grounds that their effects on demand and income differ, and, if so, how.

In discussion of these issues a good deal of confusion has arisen because of failure to distinguish between the measurement of short- and long-run effects. There are two important differences.

1. In the short run, there are well-established differences in the effect on demand of changes in different budget items because of differences in the lags with which spending, i.e. consumption and investment, respond to them. As the lags work themselves out, these differences are likely to decline and may become negligible.

2. Weights based on short-run effects can be applied only to *changes* in fiscal policy:[2] there is no sense in applying them to the *absolute values* of all expenditures and receipts as if they were all being introduced afresh in each period.

A figure for the change in fiscal policy weighted according to short-run leaks into gross savings (and possibly imports) measures the short-run change in spending (or output, if the import leak is allowed for) induced by the budget change under consideration. But such a measurement does not permit one to judge at all directly whether the change is of the right amount. To do that one must (1) predict how the absolute values of one's target economic variables (such as output, employment, prices and the foreign balance) will move in the short run in the absence of a policy change; (2) decide what are the desired values for the same variables over the same period; and (3) judge from this comparison what is the desirable change in the weighted balance in the budget. It seems simpler, if one has a short-run model of the economy—and there are plenty around—to use it and not generate with it a synthetic measure of this kind, unless, say, one needs a rough ready-reckoner for quickly comparing alternative policy packages after one has first determined with the aid of the model the appropriate scale of action measured in terms of short-term effects. But short-run effects alone should not dictate the choice of policy.

The case for a measure based on the long-run effects of budgetary policy (meaning the effects after both investment and consumption have adjusted fully to the policy) is that, in so far as one knows the normal long-run relationship of the private sector's financial balance to the level (and rate of change) of income, one can use such a measure directly to judge whether the *absolute* size of the balance in the budget at any specified level (and rate of change) in income is appropriate. This stems from the flow of funds identity:

$$G - T = S - I + M - X$$

G = government expenditure

T = government receipts
S = private sector savings
I = private sector physical investment
M = current payments abroad
X = current receipts from abroad.

If we assume that the target foreign balance is zero, we can ignore $M - X$. What one then judges is whether $G - T$ will match the long-run or normal value of $S - I$, which will be generated if income is at the level and on the path that is under consideration.

If, for simplicity, we ignore the rate of change in income and consider a static world, the exercise is to judge whether the following equality is achieved:

$$G - t\,Y^* = \alpha\,Y^* \qquad\qquad (4.1)$$

where

t = the aggregate rate of tax in relation to GNP
α = the long-term private sector coefficient of *net* savings (i.e. the acquisition of financial assets) in relation to GNP
Y^* = target GNP.

Anyone who makes a direct judgement as to whether the balance in the budget is of the right size—be it the actual or the planned balance; be it adjusted to a constant employment basis or not—is implicitly or explicitly making a judgement about the private sector net savings coefficient.

The suggestion that the policy-maker should in this way use a long-term measure in order to judge whether fiscal policy is consistent with long-term equilibrium in the economy does not necessarily mean that he should or should not depart from the long-run equilibrium setting of the budget in order to offset short-run fluctuations. What is important is that his summary measure will permit him to see whether such action will take him far from the estimated equilibrium setting for the budget, and how far the action taken will be self-correcting (see Ward and Neild, 1978).

With this approach based on long-term effects, the question of whether and how to weight different items depends on whether and how the leak into long-run private sector *net* savings (i.e. the net acquisition of financial assets) differs from one budget item to another. We can consider a series of alternative cases, taking, for simplicity, a closed economy and assuming that marginal and average leaks are equal.

Case A

There is no significant difference in the long-term leaks into net savings associated with the different fiscal instruments included in the budget, and the uniform leak does not change from one period to another or with alternative policies in one period:

$$\alpha_1 = \alpha_2 = \ldots = \alpha_n = k.$$

Conclusion: do not weight. The unweighted constant employment balance measures fiscal policy. It can be compared with αY^*, the estimated private sector net savings at constant employment, in order to judge the appropriateness of the fiscal stance.[3]

Case B

As in Case A, but α varies from one period to another, or with alternative policies in one period, e.g. different monetary policies.

Conclusion: do not weight. The unweighted constant employment balance measures discretionary policy. As in Case A, it can be compared with estimated net savings by the private sector at constant employment in order to judge the appropriateness of fiscal stance, but the latter will now be given by $\alpha_t Y^*_t$, where α_t is the long-term savings propensity appropriate to the period.

Case C

The leaks differ from item to item but stay constant from one period to the next.

$$\alpha_1 \neq \alpha_2 \text{ etc.}$$

Conclusion: weighting is needed. But the relevant weights are the reciprocals of the long-term leaks into net savings, and if you apply these you arrive at income. This can be seen from the equation for the income of a closed economy:

$$Y = G_1 \frac{1}{\alpha_1} + G_2 \frac{1}{\alpha_2} + \ldots G_n \frac{1}{\alpha_n} - t_1 Y \frac{1}{\alpha_{n+1}} - t_2 Y \frac{1}{\alpha_{n+2}} \ldots$$

where a separate item is introduced for each budget instrument or group of instruments that is found to have a leak (α) into long-term private sector net savings different from other instruments. In other words, the weighted budget balance *is* income, if your weights are net savings. Moreover, if you weight the *constant employment* budget, introducing Y^* into the tax terms in the above equation in place of endogenous Y, you arrive at a curious semi-mythical figure for Y in which tax revenues tY are computed by reference to one level of income while the equation throws up another level of income. By comparing this figure with Y^* you get an indication of the direction and extent to which fiscal policy needs to be adjusted if Y^* is to be achieved, and you can, by a process of iteration, find values of the G's and t's that are consistent with the achievement of Y^*. An alternative procedure is to use endogenous Y in the tax terms in the equation and see how far, with different values of the G's and t's, the resulting non-mythical (in the sense above) figure for Y thrown up by an iterative solution of this equation differs from Y^*, the constant employment level of income.

In short, the constant employment balance must yield to rather more involved forms of analysis if it is established that there are significant differences in the leaks into net savings associated with different budget items. But this does *not* mean that discretionary fiscal policy can no longer be measured. Since in this case the α's in the equation above are *ex hypothesi* constant, Y is a measure of fiscal policy: it can change for no reason other than a change in policy.

Case D

The leaks differ from item to item and their relative magnitudes change from one period to another, owing to exogenous and/or endogenous factors, including the relative setting of different instruments, both fiscal and other.

Conclusion: the same as Case C, except that the measurement of fiscal policy requires the use of the classic prescriptions for dealing with shifting weights: in comparing two periods (or two alternative fiscal policies applied to one period), compare the results arrived at with base-year weights and end-year weights, and so on. In this context, this means calculating Y on the same basis as in Case C, except that two sets of values of α, each generated by the model, are applied to each measurement.

It can be seen that, as regards varying leaks, the problem of arriving at a measure of discretionary policy is the same as that we live with from day to day in making indices of prices, production and many other economic magnitudes— indices that we use contentedly enough. There seem no grounds for accepting the notion that, if the long-term economic effects of different fiscal instruments differ and/or change significantly, we must reject measurement of discretionary action.

So far we have considered only the implications of differences in the characteristics of the leaks into net savings; we have assumed that all the endogenous items in the budget, here described as tax rates (though there are endogenous expenditures, notably unemployment benefits), are related directly to total income, thus ignoring the fact that the bases by reference to which taxes are in fact levied are various constituents of income and expenditure which may bear a relationship to total income, that varies with the level of activity. This too can best be seen as a weighting problem and approached in the same way as the problem of leaks into net savings. In other words, the weights relevant to different endogenous items in the budget are a combination of their respective bases and leaks. If the relationship of a tax base to total income does not vary significantly with the kind of variations in income we are considering—and we are concerned with long-run equilibrium positions, not with short-run disequilibria—we can treat it as constant and have no problem. If the relationship of the bases to income is believed to change significantly in response to plausible changes in policy or other events, the same problems arise as with varying leaks: the constant employment budget may have to be abandoned in favour of a model that incorporates these effects. But measurement still remains an index number problem of a straightforward kind.

The same approach can be extended to an open economy with virtually no modification so long as there is an effective instrument (or set of instruments) for external adjustment, i.e. so long as the long-run rate of employment is not limited by an external constraint. For if that is so, the external instrument can be used to keep the foreign balance at zero, for any target value, in the long-run; which means that there is no endogenous foreign leak, and that the only relevant consideration is whether and how the use of the external instrument influences the leaks into net savings—for example, a fall in the exchange rate may generate inflation, which in turn may influence the rate of net savings.

If, for lack of an effective external instrument, the rate of employment is constrained, the choice of policies requires a more complex model. So long as the leaks are uniform (Cases A and B above), one can proceed by taking into account the leak into net savings only. One can still use the constant employment balance for purposes of measurement. But in formulating policy it will be necessary to plan the budget and measure the balance in it by reference to feasible (i.e. externally constrained) income, if that is less than constant employment income.

If the long-run net leaks are not uniform, but are constant from period to period, the appropriate procedure is to take into account the long-run leak into net imports as well as the leaks into net savings so as to produce a figure for long-run income consistent with the fiscal policy under consideration. And if the leaks change from one period to another, it is necessary to produce two figures using base- and end-period weights, following the procedure discussed earlier.

THE PROBLEMS IN PRACTICE

What Terry Ward and I found in practice when constructing and experimenting with our estimates of the constant employment budget was briefly as follows. (A fuller account is given in our study.)

Coverage and evidence on leaks

We could find no evidence that different fiscal instruments had different *long term* effects on private sector net saving, i.e. were associated with different leaks into the acquisition of financial assets in the long-run. But we saw *a priori* grounds for expecting that government lending and asset transactions (purchase and sales of land and company securities) would have an effect that was markedly smaller than that of other types of transaction and that varied with credit conditions. Our approach therefore was to exclude the latter types of transaction and to include all others unweighted. The value of the excluded items, and credit conditions, can be taken into account in judging what the private sector leak into net savings is likely to be.

The fact that we could find no evidence that the long-term leaks into net savings differ significantly from one budget item to another is not a dogmatic statement that we rule out the possibility of such differences, nor is it the result of intensive research into the question—which would be a difficult task. It means rather that, in the course of our work, which was primarily directed at modelling the fiscal system, and from our knowledge of other models, we came across no evidence of such differences, though we looked out for it. But two causes of significant changes in the leaks into net savings could be seen.

First, structural changes, meaning political changes which move agencies or activities between the private and public sectors, can have an important influence on the relative size of the financial balances of the two. The nationalization and de-nationalization of industries has caused enterprises, many of which are characteristically heavy borrowers, to be moved from the private sector to the public sector, and sometimes in the other direction. Similarly, changes in housing policy have meant that the share of house-building and the borrowing that goes with it that takes place in the private and public sectors has changed under different governments.

Second, changes in monetary policy are likely to influence the general long-term rate of private sector net savings, but there seems to be no evidence that this would produce a significant differential effect with respect to the leaks into net savings associated with different budget items. In this connection it may be noted that the monetarists, in their argument about 'crowding-out', appear to take the view rather categorically that the long-term net leaks do not differ from one budget item to another and will not be influenced by changes in fiscal policy. They should therefore find a measurement of discretionary fiscal policy along these lines rather straightforward.

The economic agencies covered are those comprised in the public sector, as conventionally defined.

Debt interest is included in our definition of the budget. The question arises, for how long a period should one accumulate an alternative debt history? That is to say, if the constant employment level of income chosen is substantially different from the actual level of income that obtained over the run of years for which the constant employment balance is calculated, the balances in the budget, and hence, progressively, the national debt, would have deviated from their actual values if the constant rate of employment had, in fact, been continuously maintained. The object, however, is not to build up a long, counter-factual history. It therefore seems appropriate not to accumulate an alternative debt history from one year to another, but only to allow for the difference in debt interest that would occur within a single year.

Composition and level of income and expenditure

We found from simulation runs that the estimates of the constant employment balance were influenced only slightly by variations in the composition of income and expenditure of the magnitude experienced since the war, including the recent depression; and that the rate of employment adopted in the constant employment estimates had an insignificant effect on the movement of the constant employment balance from year to year—though of course it did influence the absolute values.

Prices

The estimates were made at actual prices on the grounds that one is not concerned with, and does not know how to estimate, the rate of inflation that would have prevailed if the rate of employment had been different from what it was.

It has sometimes been suggested, since inflation became rapid, that the budget should be adjusted to allow for the 'inflation tax', meaning the extent to which private sector holdings of public sector debt have been diminished in value. Whatever the arguments in equity, this does not seem appropriate in the present context, partly because we are concerned to measure discretionary, not endogenous, changes, and partly because the effects on private sector net savings behaviour, though possibly strong, are highly uncertain. This being so, the preferable treatment (analogous to that applied to public sector asset transactions and lending) is to exclude the 'inflation tax' from the budget and to allow by one method or another for the effect of inflation on the rate of private sector net savings.

General

Our general impression was that the results one obtains are not very sensitive to the detailed assumptions and methods one uses in estimating the constant employment budget, an impression confirmed by the similarity of the movements shown by the Treasury's recently published estimates (Hartley and Bean, 1978) to the movements shown by ours.

CONCLUSION

I conclude that to measure fiscal policy is useful and feasible. Measurement would become problematical only if it became established that the changes in leaks into net savings and long-run changes in tax bases relative to GNP (i.e. the two sets of weights that are involved) associated with different budget items were so strong and perverse that, in comparing two periods (or policies in one period), base-weights and end-weights produced conflicting results. That day seems totally remote. At present there is no evidence that leaks into net savings differ significantly from item to item; and there is evidence that the tax bases do not vary substantially in relation to income if one abstracts from short-run disequilibria.

I find it regrettable that so little attention has been devoted to the measurement of the discretionary setting of monetary instruments, such as reserve ratios and open-market operatons. The obvious question is whether anything analogous to the constant employment balance can be produced with respect to monetary policy. The only person, to my knowledge, who appears to have addressed this question is George Perry of the Brookings Institution (see Perry, 1976). He suggests that the rate of interest be used to characterize monetary policy and that one might estimate a constant employment interest rate. He does not, however, attempt the exercise.

THE MEASUREMENT OF MONETARY POLICY*

C. A. E. Goodhart

1. DETERMINISTIC MODELS

Economists have generally tried to represent the complex real world by models that are implicitly assumed to capture its underlying structure perfectly. In other words, no uncertainty is formally attached to the coefficients in the behavioural equations (most of which are assumed to be zero); uncertainty enters explicitly only through an additive error term. Moreover, the expectation of that error is zero, so that for forecasting and simulation purposes most models become deterministic in form. Careful economists will, of course, be aware of the unreality of the implicit claim to perfect knowledge of the structure of the system; nevertheless, most forecasting takes place in the context of such deterministic models. We shall begin by discussing the measurement of monetary policy in such a context, then move on to take specific account of additive stochastic error, and end by considering the implications of uncertainty about the form (the coefficients) of the models themselves.

In a deterministic model there are, of course, no problems in measuring the effects of changing any policy instrument, *ceteris paribus*. The effects of some policy instruments may be small or even nil; readers will no doubt be able to think up examples for themselves. It is also possible that two nominally separate policy instruments may have virtually identical effects on the system, e.g. various forms of personal tax relief. Again, the exercise of one variable as an instrument may require a given path for another variable, and vice versa. For example, for any given path of a monetary aggregate there may be a unique consistent path for an interest rate and vice versa; it makes no difference in such deterministic conditions whether one expresses monetary policy in terms of monetary growth or interest rate movements.

Because they can in principle[1] solve their system of equations to read off the effects of a change in any policy instrument, *ceteris paribus*, model builders in general and forecasters in particular do not have much need of portmanteau measures of the thrust of policy. Of course such measured effects will vary from model to model. In some post-Keynesian models, monetary variables (whether movements in quantities, monetary aggregates, or in prices i.e. interest rates) have little effect. In other models, for example in the kind of rational expectations model analysed by Sargent and Wallace (1975, 1976) output (employment) will

*My thanks for prompting and helping with this paper are owed to Sir Alec Cairncross, to members of this series of seminars and to my colleagues at the Bank. The views and errors contained in it, however, remain my own personal responsibility and should not be attributed either to the Bank of England or to anyone else.

vary from its 'natural' level only if decision-makers are misguided by insufficient (incorrect) information: in this system the only policy open to the authorities, in anything but the very short term, is to inform the public about the rule of monetary growth that they *will* follow, which will then determine the rate of inflation. The differences between these supposed effects of monetary actions depend then on differences between the models themselves; that is, they are an aspect of model uncertainty: within each model measurement is conceptually simple.

Even so, there are some issues concerning measurement worth discussing in this context. These for the most part concern the balance between the various instruments, which I shall discuss mainly against the background of the extended neo-Keynesian models in common use. Among other things held constant within a deterministic model in order to measure the effect of any instrument change are the other possible instruments of policy. However, such instruments interact. Thus the choice, say, of a target monetary growth rate will have different effects on the economy depending on whether the PSBR is larger or smaller. Equally the effect of any fiscal stance will depend on the setting of the other instruments of policy.[2] Accordingly, even in a deterministic model, one cannot measure the thrust or stance of any one instrument in isolation without specifying the state of the other instruments and the initial conditions in the system.

The balance between the various instruments may matter considerably. For example, consider combinations of easier monetary/more restrictive fiscal policies compared with tighter monetary/easier fiscal policy packages having the same deterministic impact on output/employment. The first package would probably have in many models lower interest rates, a higher output of tradeables, a lower output of non-tradeables, a higher rate of inflation, less consumption, more investment, a stronger current account and a weaker capital account. Of course this is not to say that one or other package should be preferred on the basis of such model simulations alone. Lots of other factors should enter the judgement, including such considerations as the degree of model uncertainty attached to various policies (e.g., people may feel more confident about the value of the coefficients in the equations involving fiscal variables than they do about monetary effects), or the effects of the policies on income distribution, or the long-term stability of the various strategies, etc. Nevertheless, the point remains that in most models (though not, for example, in Sargent–Wallace type, rational-expectations models) one cannot measure the thrust of any single instrument in isolation.

So far it has been implicitly assumed that the authorities *can* undertake monetary policies of the traditional kind, i.e. can control monetary aggregates or interest rates. It is well known, however, that a small country that has an exchange rate objective (usually to peg it against another currency) can affect neither the level of its monetary aggregates nor its interest rates. Various frictions, including induced obstacles such as exchange controls, lessen the validity of this conclusion, and in any case medium-sized countries, such as the UK, may have a small influence on world monetary growth and world interest rates even in a fixed rate system.

Moreover, the balance of payments in the UK has often tended to weaken (strengthen) when the economy is cyclically strong (depressed), and this has tended to mean that the general direction of (monetary) policy for domestic purposes has normally accorded reasonably well with the needs of exchange rate policy. In so far as this was true, it would have allowed domestic monetary policy-makers an illusion of autonomy, in that they were able to feel that they were choosing to slow down the growth of the monetary aggregates or to raise interest rates in order to restrain an over-active economy just at the time when pursuit of an exchange rate policy would have had to involve a combination of policy changes and market reactions that would have led inevitably to just those monetary changes.

At the extreme, for a small open economy with a fixed exchange rate, monetary policy is limited to attempts to influence domestic credit expansion (DCE) and the level of reserves. There have been occasions when, owing to lack of reserves to sustain an exchange rate policy, this has approximately been the situation in the UK. More generally, even with a given exchange rate policy, there has been some latitude for autonomous policy actions. Of course, much the same considerations apply for fiscal policy. This raises the question of how far it is sensible or helpful to seek to measure the thrust or stance of either monetary or fiscal policies if both are constrained by a prior commitment to an exchange rate policy.

If, instead of an exchange rate policy, the authorities pursue a foreign exchange market intervention policy (which may be zero intervention—free-floating —but can also encompass non-zero intervention, for example to pay off public sector debt), then both monetary and fiscal policies are free of that immediate constraint. In view of the interaction between exchange rate movements and inflation, and the continuing objective of restraining inflation, it is now much less clear than it once seemed whether moving from an exchange rate policy to an intervention policy would necessarily provide the authorities in an open economy with a useful degree of extra autonomy to direct and control the thrust of domestic policies.

Not only are there several policy instruments, but there is also a range of objectives, in general more objectives than instruments. Although it may therefore be easy enough, within the context of a deterministic model, to *measure* the effects of changes in different instruments on the various objectives, e.g. employment, price stability, growth, the composition of output (investment and consumption), etc., it will not in general be possible to state normative preferences for using one instrument (or one package) rather than another without introducing implicitly or explicitly some preference function applying relative weights to the various objectives, and indeed within a dynamic system a function that can give relative weights to their respective achievement over time.

This problem of evaluating trade-offs arises less acutely in some models. For example, monetarists tend to argue that employment and growth will be determined by natural forces, so that all that the authorities can do is to control the rate of inflation by monetary measures. Some post-Keynesian economists believe that domestic labour costs are determined by non-economic factors, so that, apart from concern about the inflationary impact of changing terms of trade, the authorities can affect output through demand management without affecting the rate of inflation. In so far as trade-offs or potential conflicts between objectives *do* remain, it is not helpful to concentrate entirely on the interrelationship between one variable and one objective, whether that be monetary growth and inflation or fiscal policy and employment.

2. ADDITIVE STOCHASTIC UNCERTAINTY

With the expected value of the error term being zero, it is possible to use models consisting of systems of behavioural equations as if they were deterministic in form for forecasting and simulation purposes. *Inter alia*, this can mean that, for a given path of one variable (say a monetary aggregate), there may be a uniquely determined path for another variable (say an interest rate), and vice versa, so that policy could be expressed just as well in either form. If this relationship is behavioural in form (i.e. involves a behavioural equation, not just identities), such correspondence will cease when the error term takes on non-zero values. Although the mean expectation of error may be zero, the likelihood of the error term actually taking on a zero value is also infinitesimal.

Once allowance has to be made for unforeseen shocks, there ceases to be an exact correspondence between monetary movements and interest rates; a choice has to be made whether to express policy in terms of interest rates or monetary growth. The standard analysis of this question was developed by Poole (1970) based on a simple *IS/LM* model, assuming price constancy. He showed that the choice depended on the relative variance of the error term (the size of the disturbances to be expected) in the market for goods (the *IS* function) as compared with that in the market for money (the *LM* function). If the goods market was relatively unstable, holding the money stock constant caused interest rates to vary in such a way as to act as an automatic stabilizer. If the demand for money function was unstable, holding interest rates constant would sterilize the goods market against such financial disturbances.

A considerable part of the day-to-day debate on monetary policy is cast in these general terms, though rarely as elegantly as Poole put it. For example, when monetary growth diverges from its planned path, there will be those who will suggest that this is due to shifts in liquidity preference, to some change in the demand for money, at any rate to a disturbance originating purely within the financial system. Against this, others will point to comparisons of the relative stability of the relationship between money and incomes in the longer run, as compared with the relationship, say, between 'autonomous' and 'induced' expenditures (for example in the famous *AER* debate in 1965 between Friedman-Meiselman and Ando-Modigliani and others).

That debate continues. However, the original Poole analysis was seriously deficient in that it assumed constant prices. Introducing an inflationary process into the standard *IS/LM* model significantly shifts the likely balance of advantage towards fixing monetary policy in terms of the growth of the monetary aggregates. The reason for this can be illustrated in the simple model below.

$$O_t = f(r_t - \dot{p}_{e_t}, z_t, O_{t-1}) + e_1$$
$$\dot{p}_t = f(O_t - \bar{O}, \dot{p}_{e_t}) + e_2$$
$$\dot{p}_{e_t} = f(\dot{p}_t - \dot{p}_{e_{t-1}}) + e_3$$
$$M_t = p_t f(O_t, r_t) + e_4$$

where O is real output, $\bar{O}$ the natural (or full employment) level of output, r nominal interest rates, $\dot{p}_e$ the expected rate of inflation, z autonomous expenditures, p the price level, $\dot{p}$ the actual rate of inflation, and M the money stock. If the authorities try to peg r, the nominal interest rate, the system will be generally unstable. If they put r too low, O_t will rise relative to $\bar{O}_t$, raising p, and thereby feeding through to an upwards shift in inflationary expectations and a further fall in real interest rates. If the authorities instead peg M, the system will be stable. If nominal monetary growth is initially set too low to maintain the feasible level of real output, the fall in real output will depress inflation (and inflationary expectations), thereby allowing the rate of growth of real money balances and the economy to recover (though this recovery may for a time be hampered by the effect of expectations of lower rates of price increases on expenditures).

It may be suggested that the authorities could seek not to control nominal interest rates, but to control real interest rates instead (thereby largely restoring the choice between monetary control and real interest rate control to the same factors set out in Poole's original analysis–the relative variance of e_1 and e_4). The difficulty of this is mainly that price expectations cannot easily be discerned or measured and are not homogeneous. Furthermore, price expectations are very volatile. Accordingly, the authorities could not easily measure the movements in real interest rates.

Indeed, as inflation becomes both higher and more volatile, the ability to judge whether any level of interest rates is likely to prove attractive or discouraging to potential borrowers becomes harder. Even if we could measure price expectations adequately (and if these were homogeneous), the abstract concept of the real interest rate will probably not provide an adequate or sufficient indicator of conditions in financial markets. The concept leaves out such factors as the changing riskiness of borrowing, shifts in income gearing and debt gearing, liquidity problems, etc.; whereas the growth of the monetary aggregates does reflect how much the public and private sectors *have* chosen to borrow from the banking system. For all these reasons it is perhaps natural that the sharply worsening inflationary experience of the 1970s has led to a wide-spread move among monetary economists and central banks towards placing more emphasis on monitoring the growth of the monetary aggregates and less on trying to select an appropriate path for interest rates.

Most central banks try to hold the rate of growth of the monetary aggregates to their intended path by varying interest rates to that end—this is, for example, the case in the USA when the Federal Reserve Board adjusts the federal funds rate for the purpose of controlling the growth of M1[3]. A forecast is made of the likely growth of the economy over the next few months and the federal funds rate is then set so that the money supply should grow at the intended rate given the perceived growth in the economy. If, then, given this chosen federal funds rate, M1 grows faster than expected, this can only be due either to nominal incomes having grown faster than forecast or to an erratic error in the demand for money function.[4]

Thus, it has been argued, monetary developments, which are generally reported relatively quickly and accurately, might provide early useful information on developments in the real economy. In so far as unexpected variations in monetary growth reflected unexpected variations in the growth of nominal incomes, there would be a case for stabilizing the growth of the money stock and thereby also hoping to stabilize the growth of nominal incomes along its planned path. Professor B. Friedman has analysed the case for the adoption of intermediate monetary targets on exactly this basis, that they provide additional early information on the development of nominal incomes (Friedman, 1977).

This argument does not, I would contend, apply in the case of the UK. With weekly monetary data still in their running-in period, partly to allow estimates to be made of seasonal intra-monthly variations, we still have to depend for the time being on once-monthly snapshots of monetary conditions. The erratic, stochastic error in these single snapshots is relatively large. The process of collection, compilation and checking the data takes several weeks. It therefore takes several months before any trend divergence of monetary growth from its planned path can be clearly identified. By that time a range of more direct statistical indicators on the state of the economy, for example industrial output, retail sales, retail prices, car sales, trade balance, etc., will have become available.

In any case, in the short run, over a few months, movements in the monetary aggregates are likely to be influenced largely by the ebb and flow of sentiment in financial markets, e.g. temporary shifts in the pattern of investing the funds accruing to the contractual savings institutions. This is, perhaps, just another way of stating that in the short run—periods measured in terms of months rather than years—the extent of uncertainty and random variation in the money market is considerable.

Returning to Poole's original analysis, this would suggest that it would be wrong to place great weight and emphasis on short-term movements in the monetary aggregates. This point has indeed been emphasized by the monetary authorities (Bank of England, 1978). I shall suggest, however, in the next section that in the longer term the relationship between monetary developments and the growth of nominal incomes, especially of price inflation, is closer and more reliable. The long run is, however, no more than the summation of short runs. Although it will *not* generally be possible to state at any point of time that a current divergence of monetary growth from its planned path probably reflects a current divergence in the economy from its path, which might need correcting, none the less, a long continued undesired trend in monetary growth is—I would suggest—likely to be accompanied by an undesirable trend in the real economy.

This dichotomy between a looser short-term and a stronger longer-term relationship between money and incomes of course makes it tactically more difficult to know how soon and how strongly to alter course in response to any immediate monetary divergence. In some large part we try to obtain extra information to enable us to resolve this question. This information consists mainly of an analysis of the movements of the credit counterparts to monetary developments, i.e. the public sector borrowing requirement (PSBR), debt sales to the non-bank public, bank advances (which together form DCE) and external flows. These data enable a story to be constructed that can help to indicate why M3 departed from its planned course, and permit a more informed assessment to be made of whether this is likely to be a temporary blip or a more prolonged and serious trend.

In this section I have sought to review how the presence of additive stochastic errors affects the choice between monetary aggregates and interest rates as the main index of monetary policy, and also whether unforeseen developments in monetary growth could serve to provide early additional information on developments in the real economy. It is, possibly, worth ending with a slight *obiter dicta* by noting that the path of single aggregative indices of fiscal balance provides even less information on current economic developments. The divergence of the PSBR, for example, from its expected path during the course of the year provides by itself virtually no indication whatsoever of the concurrent path of the economy. The PSBR may be lower than expected because the economy is stronger than thought and tax revenues are higher, or because government expenditures (and thence the economy) are below their planned path. At least, with monetary variables there is some expectation that short-term divergencies (of M and Y) will have the same sign; with aggregate fiscal variables there is no such expectation. In this latter case, for purposes of assessing current developments it is essential to disaggregate, to review the separate developments of the various elements of expenditures and revenues. Indeed, for those watching the ongoing development of the economic system, the regular monthly data on the outcomes for the PSBR and CGBR are regarded as more important for their implications for financial markets and monetary developments than for any light that they might cast in themselves on 'real' economic developments.

3. MODEL UNCERTAINTY

Most economists appear to believe, more or less, in the model which they construct. Indeed, the present fashion in model-building is to incorporate expectation-generating functions into each model, whereby the modelled actors (e.g. labour, business) are put as believing that that particular model is correct. Blessed with knowledge of the true model of the economy, there is (as was noted in Section 1) no difficulty in measuring the effects of any policy instrument (which may be zero) on the ultimate economic objectives. However, the presence of additive stochastic errors, erratic disturbances, may (as was noted in Section 2) cause the economist to counsel greater (or less) reliance on one, or other, policy measure depending on the nature of the expected disturbances and the availability of information on their occurrence.

Unfortunately, there are many alternative models of the economy, and some of these—as has already been indicated—are contradictory rather than complementary; there is, for example, little in common between the CEPG model (Cripps, Fetherston and Godley, 1978; Fetherston, 1977) and Sargent (1976)-Barro (1976) rational expectations models. In the real world the authorities have to steer a course amid conflicting advice and differing perceptions of how the economic system works. There is currently a greater diversity of viewpoint—indeed, turmoil of ideas, theories and judgements—than at any time since the 1930s. In both these periods severe problems of economic management appeared (massive unemployment in the 1930s, recession with galloping inflation in the 1970s) which the authorities found it hard to remedy; in both periods the economics profession has been in, often unhappy, ferment with differing ideas and theories.

In this difficult context the authorities look for some reassurance that they are moving in the right general direction, and they also want to be able to communicate that reassurance to the general public, whose members will generally find it difficult to form a coherent picture of the economic system for themselves, the more so when the experts offer conflicting stories. In a sense the authorities have to apply weights to the various models/theories/perceptions offered to review which relationships are really trustworthy and over what time horizon, and then seek to try to communicate their control over such trustworthy relationships to the general public. Such a weighting system is inherently subjective. A proposition that might, however, receive fairly general assent is that the effects of monetary policy instruments are least certain (relative, for example, to fiscal measures) the shorter the time period considered, but become more reliable and better understood over longer time horizons.

In recent years, for example (that is, in the 1970s though not in the previous decade), alternative definitions of the money stock, in particular M1 and M3, have had plainly disparate short-term fluctuations. The movements of M1 can be reasonably well explained by variations in incomes and interest rates (see Coghlan, 1978). The movements of M3 have been subject to a more complex range of influences, including financial 'distortions' resulting from changing patterns of interest relativities, especially those in wholesale money markets and, perhaps at times—especially in 1972–3—supply-side disturbances. Although the problems of interpreting the movements in M3 are perhaps more severe, there is more supporting information wherewith to analyse and assess its developments—in particular the credit counterparts—and an instrument at hand—the 'corset' or Supplementary Special Deposit Scheme—to restrain untoward distortions resulting from perverse interest rate relativities. There is some additional information, in particular on financial conditions, to be gained by looking at the widest possible range of financial series, prices as well as quantities. It would, in my view, be wrong to infer that the authorities' actions in specifying a preferred (target) rate of growth for a single monetary aggregate implied that they thought that this would provide a wholly comprehensive and individually sufficient indicator of the stance of monetary policy whatever the latter might be taken to mean.

Furthermore, the links between changes in monetary conditions and in the real economy in the short run remain relatively poorly defined, though perhaps less so than in the 1960s. In recent years, following the shift towards greater exchange rate flexibility, the interrelationship between domestic monetary policies and exchange rate movements has become apparent—and one could argue that in the fixed exchange rate period there was no such thing as an autonomous monetary policy to measure anyhow. There has also been increasing attention paid to the effect of asset holdings on consumption. Even so, the estimation of the effects of monetary changes on the economy in the shorter run remains relatively uncertain, in particular perhaps the division of such effects into output and price responses.

In contrast, the short-run impact and multiplier effects of fiscal policies remain relatively clear-cut, though uncertainties about likely developments (and reasons for these) in savings and import propensities have increased. Possibly more importantly, however, such fiscal actions may also generate market and confidence reactions in the economy more broadly, which could affect the overall outcome. In part such reactions can be ascribed to an earlier market response to the possible longer-term implications of various fiscal strategies. These longer-term implications are more difficult to disentangle, but generally suggest that the short-term effects of fiscal actions may be eroded or even possibly reversed, in the longer term. Thus fiscal action, leading to a changed borrowing requirement, must affect the rate of acquisition and the balance of portfolios of financial assets by the private and overseas sectors. Increasingly over time, the initial once-for-all Keynesian-type impact will become overlaid by the longer continuing financial consequences. In particular, if monetary growth is held unchanged, the longer-term financial/wealth consequences of fiscal actions could lead to instability (see, for example, Christ, 1978). The longer-term consequences of changing fiscal actions while holding to a given monetary policy are, to say the least, uncertain.

Against this, one could well argue that it should be a strategic purpose to maintain co-ordination between fiscal and monetary policy, so that a changed fiscal policy *should* involve a changed monetary policy. However in the long run, many would contend, the economic system does move towards a closer approximation to a monetarist model in which output, productivity, growth, work and leisure are determined by real, or natural, forces, and in which the rate of growth of prices depends on the rate of growth of the monetary aggregates (and on this time scale it again should not matter greatly which monetary aggregate is taken as the index). This is not to say that over this time horizon fiscal policies will not matter; indeed, they would do so greatly, but rather for their structural and microeconomic effects on efficiency, risk-taking, the return to capital, etc. Thus in the long run the main direction of fiscal policies should be towards structural improvement, while monetary policies maintain macroeconomic stability, in particular price stability.

Even if this long-run position were agreed in theory—and many would not accept it—its practical importance depends on how long this long run may be. Perhaps the long run is becoming telescoped in time, as individuals and markets perceiving the longer-term implications (as they see them) of fiscal and monetary actions seek to anticipate them by their short-term response. Thus an expansionary fiscal action, accommodated by a more expansionary policy for monetary growth, could lead to a quick fall in the exchange rate and rise in inflation sufficient to negate much of that expansion; whereas an expansionary fiscal policy, unsupported by any change in monetary growth, might be largely crowded out.

The longer the time period under consideration, the relatively more clearly understood the macroeconomic effects of monetary policies, measured in terms of the growth of one or other definition of the monetary aggregates, become (relative to fiscal policies; indeed, the longer the time period the more important become the micro-economic and structural implications of fiscal policies relative to their macroeconomic implications). The schema outlined here is one in which fiscal actions have clear and strong short-term, but uncertain long-term, macroeconomic consequences, while monetary policies have uncertain short-term but relatively clear long-term consequences. Faced with a largely similar conclusion at the Brown Conference on Monetarism (Stein, 1976), Cagan noted that the Federal Reserve Board could act quickly, but was less deliberative and less subject to democratic pressures than was Congress; accordingly, he suggested (not entirely seriously) that the proper attribution of responsibility was for the Fed. to control fiscal policy and Congress to determine monetary policy—an *obiter dicta* that he, alas, cut out of his published note as discussant to the paper by Tobin and Buiter.

The gist of the above is that monetary policy, and in particular trends in monetary growth, should be viewed in a medium/long-term context (whereas fiscal changes have a more immediate impact effect). Such considerations, if they were accepted, should presumably influence the way in which the regular statistics are assessed and interpreted. The authorities have certainly tried to focus attention on longer-term monetary trends, rather than on the erratic month-to-month variations, and have had some limited success with this. Certainly it has been easy (possibly too easy, for there is a danger of oversimplification) to communicate to the public the general nature and importance of monetary targets. The problem has been rather to discourage excessive attention to short-run movements of little significance.

The response to this accusation (of excessive concern with short-term monetary movements) from outsiders has often been that they, and their colleagues, are perfectly aware of the slight importance of individual monetary observations. What they doubt—they add—is at times the willingness of the authorities to take the necessary actions to restore monetary growth to its preferred longer-term trend rate of growth and/or their ability to do so without inducing a major change in market conditions. Accordingly, any sign of a trend developing which is pushing growth above the upper limit may be taken by them as a sign of potentially serious market disturbances ahead.

It does seem somewhat easier to express and communicate monetary developments to the general public than to do this for fiscal policy. Although monetary developments are the counterpart of many influences, e.g. fiscal policy through the PSBR, debt management, bank lending, external flows, etc., the aggregate, compiled monetary series is simple, direct and easily understood. The articulation of the two parts of fiscal policy—tax changes and public expenditure changes—seems less well understood and indeed is less frequently discussed both in Parliament and elsewhere; as is well known, the problem with simply comparing revenue with expenditures and treating changes in the difference of these two main components—that is, in the public sector deficit—as a measure of the change in fiscal policy is that the latter is itself influenced by movements in both real incomes and prices. Trying to deal with this latter problem by estimating some 'full employment budget balance' has not been entirely successful; the resulting numbers are a complicated artificial construct, which vary depending on the intricacies of the calculation, and which are based on counterfactual assumptions (see Hartley and Bean, 1978). In addition, the result depends on the nature of the aggregate tax function, yet it is not clear that the *slope* of the function (which depends of course on the types of tax that happen to be levied) is necessarily relevant to assessing the overall fiscal stance at a particular time. In this respect monetary indicators have considerable relative advantages.

In the outline description of the paper that I was asked to write—a remit that

I am conscious of not fully meeting—the following question was asked: 'Are there "measures of monetary policy" comparable to those [e.g., the full employment budget deficit] available for fiscal policy and if not, why not?' In the course of writing this paper I have increasingly come to wonder whether this was a sensible question. In Section 1 I argued that it is not possible to measure the effects of any policy change without taking into account the state of other instruments of policy and initial conditions in the economy; moreover, even then, it would not be possible to make normative statements about alternative policy settings without being explicit about (subjective) preference functions. In Section 2 it was suggested that the weight to be attached to any potential instrument should depend both on the nature of the economic disturbances foreseen and the availability of information on these. In Section 3 it has been argued that uncertainty about the nature and workings of the economic system is such that the authorities have to base their actions on judgement about which relationships are likely to prove most reliable and trustworthy. Against this kind of background, the concept that there is some satisfactory single measuring rod of the stance of policy, whether for monetary or fiscal policies, seems unrealistic. This is not to say that it may not be sensible for certain purposes to adjust the budget deficit for cyclical factors (on to a full employment basis) to remove certain feed-back effects, (a possible distorting influence from which monetary aggregate series appear relatively immune). To suggest, however, that such artificial, and counterfactual, adjustments thereby provide a better measure, whether for positive or normative purposes, of the stance of fiscal policy than is available for monetary policies seems to me difficult to sustain.

THE ROLE OF EXPECTATIONS IN MONETARY
AND FISCAL POLICY

J. S. Flemming

This paper is divided into five sections. In the first I summarize the apparent effect of expectations on the effectiveness of monetary and fiscal measures in an entirely *ad hoc* and selectively empirical way. In the second I consider three examples of policies which themselves are based on hypothesized expectational effects, including the deliberate attempt to manipulate expectations. In the third I consider together the Keynesian idea that the problem for policy is to respond to autonomous expectational disturbances and the notion that policy makers' hands can be forced by anticipatory private sector action.

These sections are short and conventional. They emphasize that expectational problems are not new and have not been ignored; however, we will see that the treatment of expectations has been inadequate. In the last two sections I discuss a variety of approaches to the modelling of expectations with special reference to so-called 'rational expectations' (RE), the implications of RE and finally the policy and modelling implications of a more eclectic approach to expectations.

1. EXAMPLES OF THE APPARENT EFFECT OF EXPECTATIONS ON THE IMPACT OF POLICY

Expectations and the response of consumption to fiscal policy

A mechanical and backward-looking consumption function implies that the response of consumption to income tax changes would be lagged. A more forward-looking interpretation of the permanent income hypothesis would make the effect depend on the expected permanence of the change. Eisner (1969) has argued that the US income tax surcharge, which was announced as being temporary, and as being designed to stop the economy overheating without jeopardizing full employment, had very little impact on consumption for this reason.

This is an argument that should apply, if capital markets are good enough, to any explicitly counter-cyclical use of direct taxes, though I am not aware of UK data supporting the Eisner hypothesis. Indirect taxes are quite a different matter. If anticipated, indirect tax changes have many of the characteristics of a very radical monetary policy—they both alter intertemporal relative prices. The most famous example here is the effect on consumption of the (correct) expectation that Mr Jenkins would raise indirect taxes in his 1968 post-devaluation Budget.

Expectations and the response of investment to fiscal measures

Here again, the UK experience emphasizes the pseudo-monetary effect of expected changes in effective investment incentives. The announcement in 1964 of a future corporation tax rate that would reduce the real value of investment allowances accelerated investment plans, as have other temporary measures such as the temporary incentive for the building of hotels in London. In their study of the effects of fiscal policy on investment, Feldstein and Flemming (1971) found an effect of investment incentives so large, and with such short lags, as strongly to suggest a short-run effect much larger than any long-run effect would be, generous allowances being regarded as transitory.

Expectations and monetary policy

Expectations of monetary policy are reflected more in financial markets and the term structure than directly in expenditures. Here there are clearly major differences, depending on whether the policy instrument about which expectations may be formed is a quantity or an interest rate (see also Section 3 below). In 1970 the newly elected Conservative Government said it was concerned about money supply and would watch developments carefully, but would not yet act on interest rates. As a result interest rates were expected to rise and the money supply rose very rapidly.

The consequences of correctly anticipated quantity changes are less perverse. Interest rate changes may precede their explanatory quantity changes, but at least the move is in the right direction if the anticipated policy is sensible. Both effects complicate the estimation of the demand for money.

Expectations and the exchange rate or tariff changes

Under the fixed exchange rate regime the impact of anticipated changes of the parity on reserves was notorious. Experience with the temporary import surcharge has also identified substantial anticipatory effects both of their introduction and termination (Rees and Layard, 1972).

Anticipations and incomes policy

The possibility of influencing inflation expectations through price/wage policy is discussed in the next section. Here I want only to note the evidence that some unions accelerated their settlements in 1974-5 to get 'under the wire' of an expected restrictive policy. Similarly, settlements have been known to be deferred if it was believed that better terms could be obtained while the terms of an early settlement would be enforced for its full term.

2. POLICY DESIGNED TO TAKE ADVANTAGE OF EXPECTATIONS

Several, but by no means all, of the episodes referred to above were quite deliberate in the sense that policy-makers let their intentions be known with a view to eliciting appropriately anticipatory behaviour. Two other kinds of self-conscious expectational policy occur: in the management of the debt and in incomes policy.

Expectations in debt management

This is an area I do not understand, but one sometimes gets the impression that the Bank intervenes in the market to create flurries of activity and to engineer temporary periods of 'strength' into which to sell gilt-edged. The peculiar thing about this, if ever true, is that one should be able consistently to manipulate, and falsify, expectations every few months.

Wage/price policy as an influence on inflation expectations

Inflation expectations are liable to worsen the inflation/unemployment trade-off, and it is tempting to seek a means of influencing them directly. A number of people who admit that wage/price policies have adverse resource allocation effects believe that these may be more than offset by their impact on inflation expectations.

The appropriateness of this argument depends on whether, as a matter of fact, expectations are so influenced. Inasmuch as many people appear to believe that controls would work, it would seem that their adoption might at least influence expectations. Of course, if the spell is not to be broken something (else) must be done to justify the expectations—the controls will reduce the cost of the alternative unacknowledgedly effective instrument.

This is a plausible argument, at particular times, which is diametrically opposed to the rational expectations approach discussed below.

3. POLICY AS A RESPONSE TO SHIFTS OF EXPECTATIONS, POSSIBLY ABOUT POLICY

The macroeconomic policy problem as defined, implicitly, by Keynes was that of responding to shifts in aggregate demand caused by spontaneous revisions of expectations. Keynes emphasized the effects of such shifts as might occur in enterpreneurial expectations, which might influence investment and hence, through the multiplier, have a larger effect on aggregate demand. Recent work questions this analysis in two ways. It is suggested that spontaneous shifts of entrepreneurial expectations are unlikely, though they may shift in response to expectations of policy or political change. Thus the problem becomes the more general one of the policy response appropriate to the expectations of a policy change and is discussed further below.

The second argument (emphasized by R. E. Hall) is that, if consumption is related to forward-looking capitalization of future income streams, then expectations, and their revision, are as relevant for consumers as entrepreneurs. Although the proportionate magnitude of such consumer revisions is likely to be much smaller than entrepreneurs', the fact that consumption is a much larger proportion of GNP means that revisions of consumer expectations may well be as important as those of entrepreneurial expectations in their effect on aggregate demand.

If the main type of shifts in expectations relates to anticipation of policy, and if the main purpose of policy is to offset shifts in expectations, there is a possibility of instability, in policy at least. If entrepreneurs note that investment demand has declined slightly they may expect a response, e.g. of improved tax reliefs, and hold back investment until the relief materializes. If the policy response is reasonably swift no great harm ensues, but if it is delayed the economy may be more unstable than it would have been if there had been no possibility of a policy change.

This example of anticipation forcing the hand of the authorities is similar to that of a run on the foreign reserves under a fixed exchange rate regime forcing a devaluation. Both involve anticipations of a change in a 'price' fixed by the authorities. Anticipation of quantity changes may actually be stabilizing. Consider an economy in a floating-rate world in which the authorities may respond to unemployment by monetary expansion which many agents expect to lead to depreciation. In this case a rise in unemployment may lead to a spontaneous devaluation which will tend to restore employment even in the absence of any monetary expansion. Similarly, if monetary expansion rather than fiscal incentives were the expected response to an investment decline, anticipatory behaviour would depress interest rates and stimulate demand.

This is not an argument for monetary rather than fiscal stimulation, since an interest rate policy would be as vulnerable as a tax incentive policy—rather, it militates against policies involving direct manipulation of intertemporal prices.

4. APPROACHES TO THE MODELLING OF EXPECTATIONS

All of the discussion so far has served to highlight three propositions.

1. Several categories of expenditure and demand for financial assets depend on expectations about the future, and especially expectations of future policy.

2. Several important categories of expectations are influenced by current policy.

3. Therefore in designing policy it is important to be able to predict the impact of policy on expectations and on expenditures.

In this section I want to look at several possible methods of modelling these two links.

The standard procedure is to merge this problem in the general problem of lagged responses. Expenditures depend, with a lag, on expected taxes; expected taxes are a function of current and past taxes; therefore expenditure is a convoluted lag of current and past taxes. And this lag structure is estimated econometrically as though it were invariant over time. It thus fails to distinguish between tax changes announced as being permanent and those announced to be temporary.

This does not imply that forecasters may not adjust for such effects judgementally at the time and by a liberal use of dummy variables subsequently. But the basis of the judgement is informal, and no attempt is made to generalize on the basis of the dummies.

One fashionable alternative is to postulate rational expectations (RE). The government and private agents have the same (good) model of the economy; both recognize that the others are doing their best. Thus the Chancellor's next Budget will consist of the measures I would introduce if I were in his place, and I will anticipate those measures in my expenditures and speculations. Thus all he has to do is to identify the anticipated optimal policy and implement it. Given the common model, this process is not very difficult (in principle) and is not necessarily as vacuous as some RE proponents (e.g. Lucas, 1976) have argued.

The Lucas argument is that if the common model is good the private economy will, in the absence of discretionary policy, be subject only to serially uncorrelated random deviations from equilibrium. These deviations arise from the fact that certain types of contract, e.g. money wages, are fixed at time t to rule at time $t + 1$. If the economy is subject to random disturbance the equilibrium money wage will not be perfectly anticipated. However, monetary policy can correct for these mistakes only if the monetary authorities have an opportunity at time $t + \frac{1}{2}$ both to improve on the private agents' earlier forecasts and to influence monetary demand before time $t + 1$.

Fischer (1977) has shown that, if labour contracts run for more than one period and their renewal dates are symmetrically phased, then the case just made for compensating policy will exist—and I should emphasize that this money/wage example could be generalized.

The weakness of the RE approach is that the *common model does not exist, and therefore the models of different agents will typically be bad*. This follows from the fact that agents, including the authorities, use models of a form and structure that would be appropriate only if they were shared by all agents. In the absence of a common model, a good model must recognize that different agents entertain different models, that they therefore interpret experience differently, and that as they cannot all be right all the time some of them will revise the structure of their models.

There is clearly a problem of infinite regresses here if every agent attempts to model within his own model every other agent's modelling process. Were people to embark on this approach I would expect them either to go out of their minds or to converge on a rational expectations model quite quickly.

For practical purposes, however, I doubt whether many private agents could be described as entertaining such 'meta models'. The authorities, therefore, could probably build them without jeopardizing the sanity of anyone but themselves. Such a model could even be 'rationalized', in the sense that it initially attributed to various agents (firms, unions, households, gnomes) a variety of models specified in terms of function, and prior probability distributions on the coefficients.

The authorities could then calculate that if we do x, they will expect y while z will happen, so that they will revise their belief in such and such a way (which we can identify by applying Bayes theorem on their behalf), and then if we do x', z' will happen while people are expecting y' . . . and so on. In this way the authorities could still choose an optimal policy path and it would certainly not be as trivial as in the extreme RE case.

If one believed that Piaget was more relevant than Bayes to the modelling of housewives' and gnomes' learning processes, it might still be possible to construct a meta model along those lines—though econometricians would have to be re-educated first.

5. CONCLUSIONS

Although the previous section was rather critical of RE theory, there are at least three positive aspects of it.

1. It provides a very useful check on the internal consistency of any theory that purports to describe the behaviour of rational agents. One should ask of any such model whether the behaviour of any of its participants would be changed by giving them a copy of the article (or manual) in which it is described.

2. Lucas's criticism (1976) of policy simulation is valid in the terms of our hypothetical 'meta model' as well as the extreme RE case. If, say, a different monetary policy had been pursued in the 1950s, beliefs and expectations—and thus responses to all policies—would have been different in the 1960s.

3. When it is recognized that other agents are basing their responses to policy on their own forecasting models, two new types of intervention become feasible. (1) It is possible to try to persuade people intellectually of the falsity of models that the authorities believe to be false, and liable to induce their adherents to respond perversely to policy. (2) If the authorities have reason to believe that agents will respond to present policy by forming false expectations as to future policy, it may clearly pay to impose some limitations on the range of future policy choices in order to undermine perverse policy expectations.

Indeed, these two processes are complementary. Once the authorities have stated what they are doing now and expect to be doing in the future, it becomes desirable to be able to justify any deviations of future policy from that foreshadowed in terms of some intervening unpredictable occurrence. This is to move in the direction of the announcement of the authorities' 'response functions' and of the economic model on which they are based.

Thus the extensions I would like to see from the present monetary targetry would be to make the targets longer-run and contingent. At the same time it might be interesting to try to build what I have earlier called a meta model and to specify the expectations, and expectation-generating and revision mechanisms, of say 1960, so that one could undertake both past and prospective policy simulations.

However, any model that relied on modelling expectations on the basis of agents learning from experience would inevitably fail to capture those important aspects of expectations that relate to the content of the discussion that form the background from which any policy measures emerge.

Another weakness of the suggested approach is that the changes in agents' expectations formation processes within the period of a single forecasting exercise are likely to be very small. Thus in an optimization exercise they would have any effect on the chosen policy only if the objective function reflected the extent to which the terminal state of expectations would constrain future developments. In some ways the formulation of an appropriate objective function for this purpose would be a more radical departure than the modelling of expectations (see also the report of the Ball *Committee on Policy Optimisation* — Ball, 1978).

THE RELATIONSHIPS BETWEEN MONETARY
AND FISCAL POLICY

P. E. Middleton

This paper seeks to answer two questions which I was asked when invited to provide a paper for the seminar: (1) 'Where, if at all, are the monetary implications of fiscal policy assessed and reviewed?' and (2) 'Do these assessments affect fiscal decisions?' The scope originally suggested was wider than this, but much of the ground has been covered in speeches by the Governor of the Bank of England (1978), and Sir Douglas Wass (1978) and the Chancellor of the Exchequer (see Appendix 2). No attempt is made either to recapitulate the arguments or summarize the conclusions in this paper.

I shall concentrate on the way in which the Treasury examines the interaction between fiscal and monetary policy. This is done at a comparatively fine level of disaggregation and involves relationships between a large number of variables. Formal econometric models of the different sectors of the economy can play an important part in this sort of analysis, and for the past few years the Treasury has put a great deal of effort into developing models of domestic and international monetary markets. A description of the philosophy underlying these models and the way they relate to the macroeconomic forecasts forms the main part of this paper. Before describing them, however, it may be helpful to consider the broad outlines of the linkages between fiscal policy, monetary and external policy, since these shape the structure of the models we have developed and the relationship between them. The paper concludes with a brief look at the role and limitations of analysis based on the models in helping policy formulation.

LINKAGES BETWEEN FISCAL POLICY, MONETARY POLICY AND EXETERNAL POLICY

The government has an intermediate policy objective for the growth of the money supply, expressed in publicly stated guidelines for the growth of the monetary aggregates. These are expressed in terms of the behaviour of sterling M3 and domestic credit expansion. It is assumed that policy will continue to be based primarily on these aggregates, the properties of which are considered below.

STERLING M3 (£M3)

£M3, the wider definition of the money supply, consists of M1 plus all other sterling deposits (including time deposits) of UK residents in both the private and public sectors, including sterling certificates of deposit. It is relatively easy to define because it is confined to the banking system.

As a policy variable £M3 has the advantage of direct links with key areas of economic policy. The accounting relationship can be set out as follows:

  Public sector borrowing requirement
− Sales of public sector debt to the non-bank private sector
+ the increase in banks' lending in sterling to the private sector
− external finance of the public and banking sectors
− the increase in the banks' non-deposit liabilities
= the change in £M3

(These accounting relationships are set out in detail in Table 7.3 of *Financial Statistics*.)

There is thus a direct link with fiscal policy, through the size of the PSBR; with the authorities' open market operations; with bank lending to the private sector; and with external flows and exchange rate policy—the external adjustments are essentially the private sector's balance of payments on current and capital account.

DOMESTIC CREDIT EXPANSION − DCE

The ceilings to which we are officially committed by our agreement with the IMF relate to DCE. This is intended to provide a measure of domestically created money supply. DCE can be defined as the PSBR, *less* sales of public sector debt outside the banks, *plus* bank lending in sterling to the private and overseas sectors. The difference between DCE and £M3 is—broadly speaking—the balance of payments of the private sector. So, if a country is in balance of payments deficit, DCE will be greater than £M3 and vice versa.

The importance of DCE thus depends on the weight given to the external position. If the supply of domestically created money is kept below the amount that the public wants to hold it would induce inflows from overseas. By one route or another restricting DCE would contribute to a process that brings about improvements in the balance of payments on current and/or capital account. It is thus an important policy variable when monetary policy is directed primarily to external objectives. The use of £M3 as a target variable would have the disadvantage in these circumstances that a growth objective for it could be met in part—for a time at least—by increasing the external deficit. When the external position is as strong as it has been during 1977, DCE ceases to become an effective constraint.

It is not always easy to disentangle the direction of causality. A very strong external position creates good conditions for selling public sector debt and reduces the need for domestic bank lending; it thus brings about conditions in which DCE may be relatively low. On the other hand, if the growth of DCE is kept below the growth in the demand for money, the external position will tend to strengthen further.

In practice, both effects can operate at the same time and can interact with each other; but as long as we have specific objectives for the balance of payments and the exchange rate, DCE can provide useful information about the relation of monetary policy to these objectives.

THE PUBLIC SECTOR BORROWING REQUIREMENT

The relationship by identity between the borrowing requirement and £M3 and DCE points to an important link between fiscal policy and money supply. The PSBR is perhaps best seen as a measure of the public sector's need for finance, although it is not in fact a measure of the total amount that the public sector has to borrow in a given period, since, by convention, transactions of the Exchange Equalization Account that need financing (i.e. changes in foreign exchange reserves) are excluded, as are refinancings or repayments of existing debt. Changes in the reserves do not depend on government policies on public expenditure, tax rates and nationalized industries prices in the same way as those receipts and outgoings that contribute to the PSBR. The amount of existing debt that has to be rolled over in the period is also excluded; it depends on past rather than present receipts and outgoings, and on past debt management policies.

It would of course be wrong to assume from the identity relationship that a given increase in the PSBR would produce an increase of the same size in £M3, or that there is any close relationship, year by year, between them. Different public expenditure and tax measures, which have the same effect on the PSBR, can have very different effects on real demand and hence on private sector saving and investment and monetary conditions. The financial effects of fiscal policy also depend on how the authorities seek to finance the PSBR. Through their open market operations the monetary authorities are able to influence interest rates and the amount of liquidity in the economy so that, where the PSBR is financed by sales of gilts to the non-bank private sector, its expansionary effect on the money supply is much less than where it is financed by borrowing from the banking system.

However, as a general proposition, a big fiscal deficit will tend to lead to a rapid growth of money supply and/or to higher interest rates. Other things being equal, the higher the PSBR, the higher interest rates will have to be in order to achieve the sales of public sector debt to the non-bank sector and contain bank lending to the private sector in order to meet any monetary target. The rise in interest rates associated with a larger deficit and a given monetary policy would offset to some extent the effects of the fiscal expansion. It follows that it is essential to examine fiscal and monetary policy simultaneously and coordinate them as far as practicable.

THE EXTERNAL POSITION

The external position exercises a crucial influence on domestic monetary policy. Exchange rate policy is central to the ability of the authorities to control interest rates and influence the growth of the money supply. In a world of fixed exchange rates an independent monetary policy is impossible. Overseas interest rates play an important role in determining domestic monetary conditions and domestic interest rate levels. When the authorities are intervening to influence the exchange rate, external influences on the money supply can be substantial. The impact of these external flows is however extremely complex. Only transactions between non-residents and the non-bank private sector *directly* affect the money supply, although other flows may affect the exchange rate (to the extent that it is allowed to adjust) or interest rates (where the exchange rate is completely fixed), and hence may influence the demand for money. The full effect of external flows to the non-bank private sector will, however, depend on how they affect output and prices and hence the demand for money.

By contrast, a freely floating exchange rate gives the authorities a wider measure of freedom to control domestic interest rates and thus the domestic demand for money. With a freely floating exchange rate the direct effect of external flows on the monetary aggregates will be small—though not always negligible. Under these conditions monetary policy has a rapid impact on the rest of the economy through its effects on the exchange rate and thence through the effects of changes in the exchange rate on prices, the current account balance and the level of activity.

INSTRUMENTS OF MONETARY CONTROL

The growth of £M3 thus depends in large part on fiscal policy and the external position. Government can however exert a degree of control over the growth of the money supply by changes in the level and structure of interest rates or by quantitative restrictions on credit. Since the introduction of the policies associated with 'Competition and Credit Control' it has preferred the former, though circumstances have at times obliged it to use the latter through the imposition of a supplementary special deposits (SSD) scheme. SSDs act as a control on the growth of banks' interest-bearing eligible liabilities and so constrain the funds they have available for lending.

The structure of interest rates can, in the short run, influence the growth of the money supply as much as changes in their general level. This can be illustrated by the 'round-tripping' that took place in 1973. Companies then took advantage of lower interest rates on their overdraft facilities (related to bank base rates) than the interest rates they could earn on wholesale time deposits and certificates of deposit (related to money market rates) to borrow money and lend it back to the banks, thus inflating the money supply. This situation arose when monetary policy was tightened by calls for special deposits and banks re-acted by liability management—selling certificates of deposit in order to bid for reserve assets—rather than by reducing lending and raising base rates promptly. The authorities used SSD controls to avoid this perverse response, but now both they and the banks would view more rapid shifts in base rates to keep them in step with money market rates as a more appropriate way of avoiding the prob-lem. There are drawbacks to using SSDs—whether to deal with 'round-tripping' or excessive monetary growth resulting from other causes: they restrict compe-tition and encourage the development of parallel mechanisms for channelling funds through institutions not subject to SSD controls. Moreover, to the extent that they cause the personal and company sectors to reduce their bank deposits and holdings of certificates of deposit, and take up instead other assets which fall outside £M3 but are in practice equally liquid, it is questionable to what extent there is any underlying change in monetary conditions.

External factors can generally be seen as having a greater influence on short- than on long-term interest rates, for in a world where rates of inflation in differ-ent countries are likely to differ widely, people would find short-term assets denominated in different currencies much better substitutes than longer-term assets, because of the great difficulties in forecasting future exchange rates and rates of interest in different countries in the more distant future and the greater risk of capital loss on long-term assets if one's forecasts are wrong. Expectations about the future rate of exchange can play a major role in determining the level of UK interest rates (in relation to those prevailing in the rest of the world), particularly at the short end, and may affect the rate of growth of the money supply.

POLICY ANALYSIS

From the foregoing it will be clear that the pursuit of monetary guidelines has implications for many other areas of policy, and fiscal policy is only one of them. These may become evident through the operation of monetary instru-ments, especially the level and structure of interest rates, changes in the ex-change rate or other aspects of external policy such as exchange control, and constraints on fiscal policy.

Exactly how these all link up can be illustrated by returning to the question posed at the beginning of this paper: where are the monetary implications of fiscal policy assessed and reviewed? The answer is in the Treasury and the Bank, in order to assist the Chancellor of the Exchequer to select an appropriate mix of fiscal and monetary policies in relation to the government's broad objectives and other policies. The main occasion for such an assessment is of course the annual Budget, but there may be other occasions for review during the year that follow broadly the same process. This has three broad stages: (1) the preparation of base forecasts; (2) the analysis of policy changes; and (3) ministerial decisions on fiscal and monetary policy.

THE BASE FORECAST

In order to illustrate how the process takes place under current conditions, let us assume that the forecasters prepare a base forecast with the following characteristics:

— a given stance of monetary policy—either a certain growth in £M3 over the forecast period or some given assumption about velocity;
— the exchange rate floating freely—without official intervention;
— public expenditure and taxation based on existing policies.

How exactly these are determined is not relevant to this stage of the exposition. Treasury forecasts have four separate but closely related elements:

— world economic prospects;
— output, income and expenditure, including the current account of the balance of payments;
— domestic financial flows;
— external financial flows.

The preparation of the first, though an integral part of any forecast, need not be described in the present context. The second, prepared with the assistance of the National Income Forecast (NIF) model, is pretty well known; the model is published and updated regularly (see, for example, H.M. Treasury, 1978), and is used in various forms by outside agencies. The third and fourth make up the financial sector of the forecast; this is less familiar and is described below.

DOMESTIC MONETARY FLOWS

The Treasury and the Bank work closely together in the whole financial field, and the domestic financial forecast is produced jointly. The traditional procedure has been described by M.E. Hewitt (1977). It is based on the same assumptions as the NIF and the external forecast and uses a flow of funds approach to construct a forecast consistent with them.

This procedure has many advantages. Tracing flows of funds through a detailed matrix is a salutary discipline and is an essential component of any forecast when one considers how pervasive is government policy over the whole financial field.

Under this system, consistency between the real and financial forecasts depends essentially on the following.

1. Close collaboration at working level between the various forecasting teams as the forecasting round develops. Financial factors react on the National Income Forecast both through some of the modelled relationships and in the judgement that is applied to the output of the model in arriving at the forecast. Similarly, the National Income Forecast—especially saving and investment by the main sectors of the economy—reacts on the financial forecasts. The process is

one of regular but manual iteration—the crucial element is the close collaboration between the various forecasters and the judgements that they make.

2. Expectations and confidence play a very powerful role in the financial forecasts. There are of course great hazards in forecasting confidence. The financial flows reflecting the financial forecasters' view of confidence are however taken into account in the NIF in the way described above.

3. The assumptions are of course the same for all the forecasts. But those that concern monetary instruments are adjusted as the forecasting round proceeds. When we have a clearly stated monetary policy—such as that provided by the present guidelines for the growth of £M3—the level and structure of interest rates and the exchange rate are adjusted in the light of the picture shown by these intermediate stages in the forecasting process, so that in the final forecast the growth of the monetary aggregates is broadly in line with the policy. The extent of the adjustment in the case of the exchange rate also has to reflect other policy considerations. But this presents perhaps the most obvious example of iteration between the forecasts.

The process of manual iteration between the two parts of the monetary sector and between it and the real sector is exceedingly cumbersome and time-consuming if—as is usually the case—there are a number of variants, especially if no one variant is selected as a main case.

The Treasury has therefore put a great deal of its research effort in recent years into the development of fully computerized models of external and domestic financial flows. We have now reached the stage at which the capital flows model is fully programmed to iterate with the NIF model and a fully estimated model of domestic financial flows is being used in parallel with the flow of funds forecast.

THE MONETARY MODEL

The monetary model, which is described more fully in Appendix 1, is designed to be used with the external capital flows model to explore the relationship between domestic and external markets. It is not a reduced-form 'monetarist' model explaining nominal incomes and prices directly by the money supply, and possibly other variables such as fiscal policy: our model can do this only in conjunction with the NIF model.

A major reason for rejecting the reduced-form approach was that for policy purposes it is just as important to understand the channels through which monetary policy works as to get an overall estimate of its impact. We also wanted to develop a model that could be relatively easily adapted to deal with changes in the institutional structure. Reduced-form models take the money supply as exogenous and thus beg the question of how the money supply is actually determined.

Non-financial decisions of the private sector are contained within the NIF model. These relationships are influenced by financial factors such as interest rates and the availability of credit and provide *inter alia* the financial surplus of the private sector. The monetary model allocates these surpluses and deficits across financial markets, and in conjunction with the external capital flows model determines interest rates and the exchange rate in the process. Running the models together produces a simultaneous solution of real and monetary variables.

These financial surpluses must be allocated across the various markets in a way that satisfies balance sheet constraints. Each sector's financial surplus together with the increase in its liabilities must obviously equal its acquisition of financial assets. In practice this is achieved by making one asset a residual, determined by the accounting identity referred to above. This offers an embarrassment of choices: at the simplest level of aggregation we can model the demand for money or the demand for bonds but not both independently.

In principle both approaches should give similar results, but in practice differences emerge. Demand for money relationships traditionally reflect transactions theories neglecting speculative aspects, whereas theories of the demand for bonds are essentially speculative. We thought the speculative factors important enough to require an explicit model of the private sector demand for gilts. Given explicit models of bank lending to the private sector, National Savings and the like, the demand for money is then determined as the residual in the non-bank balance sheet identity.

To the extent that money is demand-determined or interest rates are fixed, such a specification of demand, albeit indirect, is all that is necessary to determine the quantity in circulation. However, the growth of the markets in wholesale bank liabilities and similar developments have given bankers much more scope over their liabilities and the interest rates offered on them. Similarly, the assessment of monetary stance in terms of quantities rather than rates makes supply factors more important and rates more endogenous. Of course, in the limiting case of a monetary target the supply is fixed and the demand for money determines the level and structure of interest rates.

THE INTERIM MONETARY SECTOR

In order to help with the simulation of policy options until the full monetary model became operational, we constructed an interim monetary sector. It was an early version of this model that was used for the purpose of the policy simulations described by Laury *et al.* (1978). Using the model has given us valuable experience in producing a computer solution of real and monetary variables. This is particularly important in the sort of freely floating regime that I postulated above. And we can now let the computer do much of the tiresome work of iterating between the exchange rate and the reserves to search out the exchange rate path consistent with the assumed policy on official intervention.

The interim monetary sector can also be useful in looking at variants to the main forecast, permitting them to be carried out more quickly, although judgemental modification may well still be required.

EXTERNAL CAPITAL FLOWS

We have also developed a fairly conventional structural model of capital flows, which both provides an overseas sector for the monetary model and completes the balance of payments in the NIF model. The approach is based on portfolio theory, and assumes that foreign and domestic assets are imperfect substitutes. According to this theory, the allocation of total portfolios between sterling and foreign currency assets depends on their relative rates of return and the risks of capital loss. The relevant rates of return are defined to include expected changes in exchange rates as well as interest rate differentials. Capital flows result from the adjustment of actual to desired stocks, in response to changes in relative yields and changes in wealth.

The most volatile capital flows, therefore, are related primarily to changes in interest rates and exchange rate expectations. The main behavioural relationships are at a fairly high level of aggregation. A separate sub-model disaggregates these flows into the categories required by the monetary model.

Exchange rate expectations are modelled explicitly—a feature that is crucial to the flexible use of the whole model under different exchange rate regimes. This is, of course, a difficult area, and one in which judgement and intuition necessarily play an important role. We have therefore deliberately developed a considerable degree of flexibility in the treatment of expectations.

A distinction is drawn between:

– longer-run expectations about the exchange rate on the part of those engaged in foreign exchange transactions (this is best thought of as their *equilibrium* rate) and
– the view they take in the short run: their *expected rate* one quarter ahead.

The equilibrium rate may be determined either by relative competitiveness or by relative money supplies adjusted for trend differences in real growth, or by some combination of the two. The expected rate takes account of what has actually been happening to the spot rate, and allows for an extrapolative element in the formation of expectations. We can also allow expectations to be affected by the visible balance, relative to the trade balances of the rest of the OECD. And these various influences on expectations can be combined together in any way we desire. The usual procedure in forecasting is to look at the implications of a range of assumptions about expectations, and how they are formed. The formulation used in the final forecast typically reflects a range of factors.

Our attempts to test these various formulations of expectations over the recent past suggest that functions based on relative money supplies tend to perform rather better than those based on, for example, competitiveness or the visible balance. It seems plausible that one of the more important ways in which the money supply may affect the economy in the short run is through its effect on confidence. Furthermore, fluctuations in monetary growth may be expected to lead to capital flows that will affect the exchange rate directly.

EXCHANGE RATE DETERMINATION

The development of a capital flows model has enabled us to experiment with different approaches to predicting the exchange rate in preparing forecasts and setting up variants. The old approach was to fix the path of the exchange rate either in real or nominal terms, and consider the implications for the monetary aggregates, the reserves and the economy in general. An alternative approach— still scarcely beyond the development stage—is to make assumptions about the change in the reserves, and the growth of the money supply, and let the model 'solve' for the exchange rate and interest rates. To give some of the flavour of how the capital account model works in conjunction with all the other models referred to, I will round off this section on the external side by briefly describing how we would forecast a freely floating exchange rate in line with the assumptions in the section describing the Base Forecast above.

Many balance of payments flows in the short run are *relatively* insensitive to the current exchange rate. The current account is largely determined by past movements in competitiveness, by domestic demand and world trade. To a lesser extent, some capital flows can also be regarded as fairly insensitive to the exchange rate in the short run. But 'short-term' capital movements, on the other hand, depend crucially on market operators' assessment of the profits to be made from holding sterling, a major determinant of which is the expected change in the exchange rate.

Changes in the actual exchange rate clear the foreign exchange market by changing the expected return on holding sterling. Short-term capital flows are thus induced to offset the surplus or deficit on other balance of payments transactions. If 'underlying' balance of payments flows are in surplus, then the exchange rate must appreciate sufficiently to persuade those undertaking foreign exchange transactions that the prospects for future gains are at least somewhat less than they were, and so trigger an outflow of short-term funds. How much the exchange rate has to move to achieve this result depends both on the way in which speculators from their expectations and on the responsiveness of capital flows to changes in exchange rate expectations. Clearly, modelling expectations adequately is crucial to this approach. At the same time, however, it is obviously the case that the resulting exchange rate path will also depend on anything and everything that in a fixed-rate world would be reflected in movements in the reserves.

THE ANALYSIS OF POLICY CHANGES

A base forecast gives a quantitative estimate of the economic conjuncture and its prospects for the development of the economy on given assumptions. While forecasting is necessarily subject to great uncertainties, this base forecast does provide a starting point for defining the options. A further important role is to help policy formulation by carrying out simulations to assess the impact of changes in policy.

Different fiscal packages can be examined in conjunction with varying assumptions about monetary policy and policy in the foreign exchange markets. It would, for example, be possible to show the implications for the economy of a given fiscal boost on the assumption that velocity remains as in the base case, on the assumption of a more relaxed monetary policy—say, with interest rates unchanged—or on the assumption of the same growth in the money supply in nominal terms as in the base forecast, and with the application of different sorts of monetary instruments. Different sorts of fiscal package—different combinations of tax and expenditure measures—would have different monetary effects. So would different attitudes towards intervention in the foreign exchange market. And all these combinations will have different implications for the real economy.

All this, however, is only part of a complex process in which the costs and benefits of different fiscal packages are assessed, taking into account also the implications for wage bargaining, industry, social objectives and many other issues. These were discussed in the speech by Sir Douglas Wass to which I referred earlier.

MINISTERIAL DECISIONS

It must also be emphasized that, after all the analytical work that I have described is done, ministers are provided with only the most general guide to the appropriate combination of monetary, fiscal and other policies in the circumstances foreseen. There are a number of reasons why this is so.

There is a large margin of error in the forecasts and related simulations. This is particularly true of many of the inputs to the forecast of £M3 growth. The current account and the PSBR, with large quantities on each side of the account, are very difficult to forecast accurately. Moreover, financial markets are by their nature subject to sudden moods which just cannot be predicted. The most we can do is point to the direction of movement—we cannot be confident that we have their extent or timing right.

Economic analysis is only as good as the underlying relationships in the models and the judgement applied by those who use them. Ministers take account of our analytical work, but we do not urge them to accept it as gospel or as containing an accuracy that it cannot possess. There is little danger in practice of their doing so because they have throughout the year the benefit of an expanding quantity of other forecasts and other analyses of suggested policy options some of which are based on very different models. It is also extremely difficult to find reliable and uncontroversial measures of either the stance of fiscal policy or the stance of monetary policy a subject that Mr Goodhart deals with elsewhere in this volume.

The Treasury will of course give its considered advice to the Chancellor on the range of fiscal and monetary policy options that seem possible. But the Treasury is not the only source of advice; other ministers and other organizations also become involved. As I have been talking mainly about the financial field, I should perhaps make the obvious point that the governor of the Bank of England will formulate his own advice across the whole area of policy, both domestic and overseas. Though there is a fair amount of co-ordination between the Treasury and the Bank to make sure that there is a common assessment of the prospects, the opinions and advice that are given are by no means always identical. The Bank contributes its special knowledge of financial institutions and its experience as a direct operator in the financial markets on behalf of the Treasury. The Treasury's particular slant in relation to this is integrating those policies with the rest of the government's policy in general, with industrial policy, incomes policy and macroeconomic policy as a whole.

Ministers are essentially in the business of assessing the risks inherent in the different options facing them. Monetary and fiscal policy are both intermediate objectives, and may be assigned different weights at different times even given the same priorities for the primary objectives to which they relate. Moreover, primary objectives and the weight that ministers put on them have a political dimension in its widest sense. The choice between the importance attached to counter-inflation, growth, employment and external objectives cannot be determined by economic analysis alone. But this analysis can, and does, help illustrate the possible risks and constraints on different courses of action.

APPENDIX 1

THE TREASURY MONETARY MODEL: A SHORT ACCOUNT

For the last three years a research programme has been under way within HM Treasury directed towards the construction of a model of the UK monetary sector. The model has been designed to assist in the joint Treasury/Bank of England financial flows forecast (NIF) model (see, for example, H.M. Treasury, 1978). Such iteration produces a general equilibrium solution of real and monetary variables. Among other things, this makes it easier to analyse formally the effects of monetary and fiscal policy. This paper gives a brief description of the model, its formal structure, characteristics and implications. A more detailed technical account is provided in Spencer and Mowl (1978).

The monetary model can be used with a model of external capital flows—as described in outline by Beenstock and Bell (1979) or in detail by Lomax and Denham (1978)—to explore the relationship between domestic and external markets. It should be stressed at the outset that the model is not a reduced-form 'monetarist' model, explaining nominal incomes and prices directly by the money supply, and possibly other variables such as fiscal policy. Our model can do this only in conjunction with the NIF or some similar apparatus.

A major reason for rejecting the reduced-form approach was that we felt it just as important to understand the channels through which monetary policy worked as to get an overall estimate of its impact. We also wanted to develop a model that could be relatively easily adapted to deal with changes in the institutional structure. Reduced-form models take the money supply as exogenous and thus beg the question of how the money supply is actually determined; moreover, these methods are not directly applicable to open economies such as the UK. Informal monetarist analysis, however, does offer a check on the overall shape of any forecast provided jointly by the NIF and a financial model such as that described here.

Our forecasting methods are based upon the concept that monetary and non-monetary instruments are traded by various sectors through markets in which interest rates move to equate supply with demand. Thus a specification of behaviour in these markets allows interest rates and quantities including the monetary aggregates to be determined simultaneously.

These markets are represented by the rows of the matrix of Table 7.1. The columns similarly represent the financial balance sheets of different sectors which must sum to measures of financial wealth. The level of sectoral and asset aggregation is higher than that used in the financial forecast.

Looking at the matrix via the liabilities of each sector in turn, the liabilities of the public sector include notes and coin (row 1), reserve assets (row 3), and a 'gilts' aggregate (row 5). Most of the monetary instruments are supplied as bank liabilities which are divided into retail deposits (row 8), essentially those yielding a zero rate of return or one related to base rate, and parallel money deposits (row 9), those offering a market related rate such as certificates of deposit (CDs). Bank assets include the liabilities of the public sector, of which reserve assets are important, and also advances to the overseas and non-bank private sectors (row 7). Discount houses are in some ways similar to banks but their call money liabilities have reserve asset status and these are subject to different regulations. Since we base the model of bank behaviour on the reserve asset and other conventions followed by the commercial banks, we treat the discount market and 'other banks' (Bank of England and Giro) as separate sectors. The framework is completed by the balance sheets of the private and overseas sectors.

Non-bank behaviour and the demand for money

The non-financial decisions of the private sector are contained within the NIF model. These relationships are influenced by financial factors such as interest rates and the availability of credit, and determine, *inter alia*, the financial surplus of the private sector. The monetary model allocates these across financial

TABLE 7.1

Balance Sheet of the Treasury Model of the UK Monetary Sector

Financial instruments	Public sector (PU)	12½% banks† (CB)	Other banks‡ (OB)	Discount houses (DH)	Non-bank private (PR)	Overseas (OS)	Nominal interest rates
1. Notes and coin	$CASH_{PU}$	$CASH_{CB}$			$CASH_{PR}$		zero
2. Banks balances at Bank of England		$BBAL$	$BBAL$				zero
3. Interest-bearing reserve assets (Treasury and local authority bills, call money)	$RESV$	$RESV_{CB}$	$RESV_{OB}.$	$RESV_{DH}$	$RESV_{PR}$	$RESV_{OS}$	Treasury bill rate
4. Special deposits		$SDEP$	$SDEP$				Treasury bill rate
5. Other marketable government debt (mainly gilts)	$GILT$	$GILT_{CB}$	$GILT_{OB}$	$GILT_{DH}$	$GILT_{PR}$	$GILT_{OS}$	Rate on 2½% consols
6. Non-marketable government debt	$NMKT$				$NMKT_{PR}$	$NMKT_{OS}$	Various
7. Banks' £ lending	$LEND_{PU}$	$LEND_{CB}$	$LEND_{OB}$	$LEND_{DH}$	$LEND_{DR}$	$LEND_{OS}$	Mark-up on base rate
8. £ sight and time deposits ('retail' deposits)	$BDEP_{PU}$	$BDEP_{CB}$	$BDEP_{OB}$	$BDEP$	$BDEP_{PR}$	$BDEP_{OS}$	Base rate related

	PU	CB	OB	DH	PR	OS	
9. Parallel money:							
(a) CDs + inter-bank		$CDEP_{CB}$	$CDEP_{OB}$	$CDEP_{DH}$	$CDEP_{PR}$	$CDEP_{OS}$	3-month LA deposit rate
(b) local authority temporary debt	$LATD$	$LATD_{CB}$	$LATD_{OB}$	$LATD_{DH}$	$LATD_{PR}$	$LATD_{OS}$	
10. Net foreign currency liabilities	$SWIP_{PU}$	$SWIP_{CB}$		$SWIP_{DH}$	$SWIP_{PR}$	$SWIP_{OS}$	Covered Euro-dollar rate
11. Foreign exchange reserves	FX					FX	US Treasury bill rate
12. Net government indebtedness to Bank of England	$GINDBD$		$GINDBD$				
13. Miscellaneous liabilities	$MISC_{PU}$	$MISC_{CB}$	$MISC_{OB}$	$MISC_{DH}$	$MISC_{PR}$	$MISC_{OS}$	
Total financial assets	NW_{PU}	NW_{CB}	NW_{OB}	NW_{DH}	NW_{PR}	NW_{OS}	
Total financial assets							
Less liabilities							
= financial net worth							

† Those banks subject to 12½ per cent reserve requirement.
‡ Bank of England Banking Department and Giro

markets and in conjunction with the capital flows model determines interest rates and the exchange rate in the process. Running all the models together produces the desired simultaneous solution of real and monetary variables.

The equations are of the stock adjustment type, in which assets and liabilities are adjusted over time towards long-run values that depend upon wealth, income and relative interest rates. It is assumed that persons and non-bank companies take rates in these markets as independent of their decisions, and in this section we analyse their decisions assuming that rates are fixed. Their 'decision tree' is shown in Figure 7.1. Bank lending is determined, given bank rates, by a compromise of demand and supply. The estimated equations reflect both influences. Cumulating financial surpluses and capital revaluations give an estimate of net financial wealth. Adding on bank lending and other liabilities gives a measure of gross wealth.

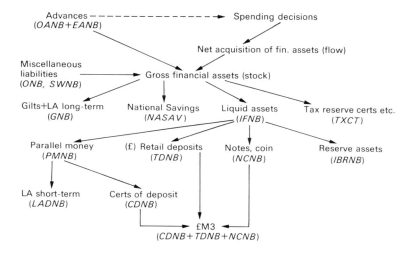

Fig. 7.1. Flow diagram of non-bank decisions.

As the figure shows, these funds must be invested in gilts, National Savings, tax reserve certificates and liquid assets. Econometric equations have been developed to handle the demand for gilts and National Savings. The gilts equation is based on a speculative demand theory in which investors look at the yield gap between long and short interest rates and compare this with expected capital gains or losses. Various formulations of expectations have been tried, and much of our present research effort is devoted to this area. The demand for National Savings is more straightforward; we explain it by interest differentials and income flows.

Tax reserve certificates and the like are handled judgementally and liquid assets emerge as a budget residual. A system of portfolio allocation equations disaggregates liquid assets into reserve assets, local authority deposits, CDs, retail bank deposits and cash. The aggregate is dominated by the last three of these items which are the components of £M3. So the demand for money is determined indirectly, essentially as the result of decisions relating to financial surplus, bank lending and investment in gilts. This is a feature the model shares with the financial flows forecast.

In principle, this approach should give similar results to alternatives that model the demand for money directly, considering the demand for gilts to be the residual. However, in practice different results can emerge. Theories of the demand for bonds are by nature speculative, neglecting the transactions motive for holding money. On the other hand, most estimates of the demand for money have been based on the transactions demand, thereby sweeping speculative factors under the carpet. We thought the speculative factors important enough to require an explicit model of the demand for gilts. Consequently, the performance of the model in this area depends critically upon the success with which we handle the expectational factors affecting gilt sales.

Bank behaviour, policy reaction functions and the supply of money

To the extent that money is demand-determined, a specification of demand is all that is necessary to determine the quantity in circulation. It is undoubtedly true that historically money has been largely demand-determined. Bankers had little scope for changing their deposit rates or other terms to vary the inflow of deposits and the authorities usually saw their role in the bond market as one of steadying interest rates. However, recent developments associated with the growth of the parallel money markets in the 1960s and 1970s and the move to 'Competition and Credit Control' (CCC) in September 1971 have necessitated the modelling of supply factors—particularly for the wider aggregates which include wholesale deposits. A useful and up-to-date discussion of these developments is to be found in Barge and Wise (1977).

We look first at the decisions of a typical commercial bank and in particular at its degree of control over its monetary liabilities. These are set out in Figure 7.2. Banks act as oligopolists in advances and 'retail' deposits markets, setting their rates in line with MLR and market rates. The model allows for lags in this relationship. As described earlier, advances then result as a compromise between demand and supply. Banks have little scope for affecting retail deposits through non-price terms, and in the model they are taken by the banks as exogenous.

Together with a judgemental assumption about non-deposit liabilities, retail deposits and advances leave a residual amount of finance available for investment in, or to be obtained from, other markets. We term this residual 'investible funds'. It is a key model variable, since it is largely beyond the banks' immediate control and any fluctuations in these funds must be financed in other markets.

Traditionally, movements in deposits and advances have been financed by precautionary holdings of notes and coin and reserve or near-reserve assets. The latter include gilts and local authority deposits. However, the development of an active market in their certificates of deposit has enabled banks to place large quantities of these liabilities at their own initiative. This is an important feature of current banking practice and plays a similarly important part in the model. It enables banks to run down their precautionary reserves to minimal levels, relying upon such 'liability-side liquidity' in order to meet an outflow of funds. Since all

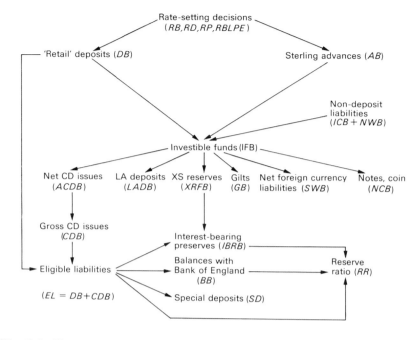

Fig. 7.2. Flow diagram of bank decisions. 'Investible funds' equals non-deposit liabilities plus retail deposits net of required reserves and special deposits, minus bank advances. 'Net certificate of deposit issues' equals the total issue minus an allowance for required reserves and special deposits.

banks are likely to be experiencing an outflow at the same time, over-reliance on this form of liquidity will be costly. The likelihood of these costs must be weighed against the known cost of the alternative—holdings of excess reserve assets.

In the model excess reserves are inversely proportional to the cost of holding reserve assets rather than higher-yielding Local authority (LA) deposits or CDs. So if the initial Treasury bill–LA deposit rate differential is high the banks will rely on issuing CDs, keeping reserves at the minimum (12½ per cent of eligible liabilities) as in 1972–5. If, as has been the case since 1975, the differential is negligible, the banks will maintain excess reserves adequate to cope with any likelihood. This is a key feature of the model as is demonstrated in the next section. The central line of Figure 7.2 shows the choices open to the banks in these markets.

A part of all deposits (12½ per cent) is not available for lending because it has to be invested in reserve assets; some may also be held in special deposits. Furthermore, both retail and wholesale deposits are handled *net* of these reserve assets and special deposits. The net figures are grossed up to obtain total eligible liabilities, special deposits and balances at the Bank of England. Together with the equation for excess reserves, this determines total reserve assets. These relationships are illustrated in the lower half of Figure 7.2.

The discount market is usually handled judgementally, since the frequency with which the 'rules of the game' have changed in this area precludes econometric modelling. Given the importance of reserve asset creation by these institutions, we have however built in some *ad hoc* feedbacks in some simulations.

The supply side of the model is completed by a set of reaction functions for the monetary authorities. Since one of the aims of the project is to analyse the effect of different policies, these are imposed rather than estimated. The model is most easily set up if the authorities fix all rates on central government debt, so that the only endogenous rates are parallel money market and bank rates. However, we usually allow all rates to 'float' in order to clear markets, given fixed supplies. It is equally possible to give the authorities money supply or other targets which they attempt to meet by varying rates on or supplies of their debt.

The parallel money market includes local authority debt, but this is not used as a policy variable, so that rates in this market can be influenced only indirectly by policy. Special deposit calls mainly work through the responses of banks in this market. The supplementary special deposit scheme ('the corset') also works through this market. Owing to a lack of data on its operation, banks' reactions to the scheme are imposed rather than estimated.

Minimum lending rate plays only a minor role in the model. It is usually linked through 'the formula' to the Treasury bill tender rate. If the formula is suspended, changes have a weak influence on bank rates and even this link is questionable empirically. It is likely however that breathing life into the discount market will give this policy instrument more bite.

Some characteristics and implications

The main interactions in the model can be illustrated by an examination of how the model reacts to an external stimulus such as a reduction in the PSBR. We suppose in this example that this is matched by a financial deficit on the part of the private sector. In the short run this will be financed mainly by a rundown of liquid assets, especially retain bank deposits. There will also be a tendency for bank borrowing to rise.

We have seen that the banks' reaction to such outflows will depend critically on their initial reserve ratios. Reductions in investible funds mainly increase CD issues, which drive rates against the banks. These rate changes moderate the sales of CDs, encouraging a rundown of reserves instead. In the model this response to rates is non-linear, so that if initially short-term interest rate differentials are low and reserve assets excessive the overall effect of the outflow will be to reduce bank reserve ratios. There will be a rise in the general level of rates, producing a secondary fall in the demand for money. On the other hand, if differentials are high and the scope for reserve asset reductions limited, then the outflow will almost exclusively be met by CD issues. A much larger rise in CD rates will occur, and this rate will tend to rise relative to other rates, especially if these are being fixed by the authorities.

In this instance the secondary rate effects may lead to a perverse overall response of the monetary aggregates. The CD rate leads other rates, increasing the demand for CDs and other 'wholesale' components of M3. To the extent that these funds come out of gilts and other public sector liabilities, that is the end of the story. However, as presently specified, bank rates tend to fall behind market rates so that much of the finance comes from bank advances and retail deposits. If this is the case, the banks' collective bidding for CDs will largely be self-defeating; indeed, the reserve assets required on CD issues financed by bank loans can reduce the net finance available to them. In the model these processes can be unstable in the absence of remedial action by the authorities. They are not unlike the 'round-tripping' actually seen during 1973 and 1974.

One clear implication is that Treasury bill rates should not be allowed to get too far out of line with other short rates, otherwise banks will rely on CD issues when the system is squeezed, making it likely that special deposit calls and other attempts at control have to be reversed or a 'corset' imposed to avoid round-tripping and other perversities.

APPENDIX 2

REMARKS ON MONETARY POLICY   Denis Healey*

The Governor of the Bank of England and the Permanent Secretary of the Treasury have already had something to say from their own vantage points about the way we now see monetary policy. Let me add my contribution as the minister on whom ultimate responsibility must lie.

I am often asked why, now that sterling is so strong and our reserves are so high, we do not tell the IMF to go hang and forget about monetary policy. My answer is the same as I used to give as Secretary of State for Defence to those who asked why we still based our security on NATO although there has not been a European war for thirty years. It is like asking why do we not dismantle the dam because we have not had a flood since it was put up.

Monetary policy and targets are important tools of economic management. They are not just a device forced on us in 1976 by our creditors. Unless we continue to publish sensible targets and are seen to be taking them seriously, we shall find it difficult to finance our domestic deficit without increasing interest rates to levels that choke off investment, and even more difficult to maintain our credit abroad so that we can prevent debt repayment from imposing unnecessary restraint on our domestic growth and arrange to refinance some of our overseas debts.

I do not think anyone would now dispute that, when the last Conservative Government allowed the money supply to expand in 1972 and 1973 to well over twice the increase in money national income, it created inflationary pressures that lasted well into our period of office. By the same token, the present government was right to keep the growth of sterling M3 below the intended growth of money national income over the last four years so as to get the relationship between money supply and money national income back to where it was in the early years of this decade. If we are to prevent the money supply from once

*An extract from a speech by the then Chancellor of the Exchequer to the Labour Economic Finance and Taxation Association in February 1978.

again increasing inflationary pressures we must not allow its growth to get again significantly out of line with the intended growth of money national income.

The publication of monetary targets can bring stability to the markets by making the government's intentions clearer in this respect. That is why, over the last four years, the Americans, the Germans, the British and the French have in turn all adopted some form of target for one or more of the monetary aggregates. All of us have found it worth while.

We have also learnt from experience that control of the monetary aggregates in relation to published targets is not as straightforward as it might seem at first sight, and that monetary policy cannot be the only weapon of economic management. As the Governor said last week [Bank of England, 1978], monetary policy and monetary targets should not be seen as ends in themselves, but like fiscal policy and incomes policy, as a useful means towards wider ends of economic policy—the conquest of inflation, the achievement of growth and the reduction of unemployment.

Moreover, it is not easy to decide what is the best measure of monetary growth or precisely what relationship it should have to the growth of money national incomes. The mechanistic rules of thumb in which some self-styled monetarists believe just do not seem to apply in real life.

Germany, for example, has in recent years consistently had the lowest level of inflation among the major countries. This is an enviable achievement, which owes much to the fact that she uses monetary policy with flexibility. For example, [in 1977] the growth in her central bank money—the measure Germany uses for money supply—was 9 per cent as against the 8 per cent target she set; but contrary to some monetarist theories, her GDP growth, instead of being higher, was under half what she expected when she set the target. Moreover, between November 1977 and January 1978, her central bank money rose at a 15.5 per cent annual rate. Instead of attempting to compensate for this increase by fixing a lower target for 1978, as some theorists would demand, the Bundesbank has once again fixed a target of 8 per cent, although the forecast of money GDP is only 5½ per cent. Its main reason for this more generous target is to permit expansion to offset the recent lack of growth in the economy and the upward pressure on the Deutschemark.

I know that it is impossible to draw a precise analogy between Germany's situation and ours since the two financial systems are different. Nevertheless, the German experience argues strongly against a mechanistic view of the relationship between monetary growth, inflation and output, and argues even more strongly against being obsessed by temporary bulges in the money supply. . . .

In the United States there has developed a malignant interaction between the regular publication of money supply figures and market expectations about the response of the central bank to those figures. This has done real damage to the operation of America's monetary policy in recent years. Germany has been successful in avoiding this neurotic interaction and, partly as a result, has been able to use monetary targets flexibly so as to avoid compounding economic stagnation with a restrictive monetary policy.

This must also be our objective in Britain. As you know, we are now considering whether to adopt rolling targets for the money supply[1] so as to avoid being hag-ridden by the cumulative figure on a particular date at the end of the banking year. This would enable us to make a more intelligent and more realistic use of monetary targets without either tightening or relaxing monetary policy as a whole. No one can doubt that we take the control of the monetary aggregates seriously after our decision in October 1977 to risk some loss of price competitiveness through an increase in the exchange rate of sterling, rather than risk an excessive increase in our money supply through inflows of foreign currency.

MONETARY AND FISCAL POLICY IN THE NATIONAL INSTITUTE MODEL*

National Institute of Economic and Social Research

This paper describes some recent work carried out in order to improve the monetary and fiscal sectors of the National Institute quarterly econometric model. It is very much a description of work in progress; here, we deal only with a preliminary and incomplete version of the monetary sector and with personal direct taxation. Some simulations with the extended model, incorporating this work, are also discussed.

THE MONETARY SECTOR

Introduction

We have adopted what might be called a 'general equilibrium' approach to modelling the financial system, which builds up an explanation of the broadly defined money stock (M3) from simple models of the portfolio behaviour of the banking system and the response of the public to the government's borrowing operations. The bulk of econometric research into financial behaviour in this country has been confined to the demand for money. The 'supply side' of the system has been largely ignored. A number of economists in recent years have questioned whether the money market (at least on a definition of the money stock which includes wholesale deposits) is always sufficiently close to equilibrium to validate the procedure of relating the quantity of money actually observed to income and interest rates and interpreting the result as a demand for money function. More fundamentally, unless the money stock is purely demand-determined (in which case it is not a particularly interesting variable since it does not affect anything), such functions do not explain, in a causal sense, how changes in money stock occur; they cannot, for example, cast any light on the important linkages between the money supply and fiscal policy and between the money supply and the balance of payments. Our final reason for not limiting ourselves to the estimation of a single equation for money demand is that the effect of a change in the money supply on the real economy is likely to depend critically on how that change came about; and in order to model the

*The research on the monetary sector was carried out by David Savage with, in the early stages, Penelope Rowlatt; that on personal taxation by R. W. R. Price. The simulations were carried out by Paul Ormerod, and the paper edited by Michael Surrey. Fuller accounts of the research work (including empirical results) are given in Savage (1978) and Price (1978a). A description of the full model in which these new sectors were embedded is contained in NIESR (1977).

causal linkages between the monetary and real sectors of the economy within the framework of a model such as that of the National Institute, it is necessary to disaggregate money into its constituent credit flows.

The institutional framework

We first briefly survey some institutional characteristics of the UK monetary system which we believe have an important bearing on the way in which the sector should be modelled. We are conscious of the fact that there has often been a wide gap between assumptions made by econometricians in their attempts to model the monetary system and the analyses of institutionally minded economists more closely involved in the operation of financial markets, and we were anxious that our efforts should pay due regard to the framework of rules, conventions and habits within which decisions are made.

We begin with the banks' balance sheet identity, the basis of which is the application to the banking system of the simple accounting concept of equality between assets and liabilities. The liabilities of the banking system consist mainly of deposits received from UK residents and non-residents, but also include certain non-deposit liabilities such as banks' share capital. The assets side of the balance sheet can be written in two alternative ways, depending on whether the banks' assets are analysed by sector of liability or type of asset. The two balance sheet identities for the banking sector (*excluding* the Discount Market) may be written in flow terms as:

$$\Delta RDEP + \Delta WDEP + \Delta OSDEP + \Delta DDEP + \Delta NDL \equiv \Delta BLPUB + \Delta BLPRIV$$
$$+ \Delta BLOS + \Delta BLD \qquad (8.1a)$$

$$\Delta RDEP + \Delta WDEP + \Delta OSDEP + \Delta DDEP + \Delta NDL \equiv \Delta CB + \Delta R$$
$$+ \Delta SD + \Delta SEC + \Delta ADV \qquad (8.1b)$$

where

RDEP	$\equiv$ retail deposits of UK residents
WDEP	$\equiv$ wholesale deposits of UK residents
OSDEP	$\equiv$ deposits of overseas residents
DDEP	$\equiv$ deposits of discount houses
NDL	$\equiv$ non-deposit liabilities (net)
BLPUB	$\equiv$ bank lending to public sector
BLPRIV	$\equiv$ bank lending to non-bank private sector
BLOS	$\equiv$ bank lending to overseas sector
BLD	$\equiv$ bank lending to discount houses
CB	$\equiv$ notes and coin held by the banking system
R	$\equiv$ banks' reserve assets
SD	$\equiv$ special deposits
SEC	$\equiv$ banks' investments in non-reserve assets
ADV	$\equiv$ advances

CB and *SD* are liabilities of the Bank of England Banking Department and are included in *BLPUB*. Designated reserve assets are: balances with the Bank of England, which are also a liability of the Bank of England Banking Department and included in *BLPUB*; money at call, a liability of the discount market and included in *BLD*; short-term debt issued by the public sector as borrower, which is included in *BLPUB*; and 'top quality' commerical bills, which are a liability of the non-bank private sector and appear in *BLPRIV*.

On the liabilities side of the balance sheet, the distinction between retail and wholesale deposits is crucial to discussion of the portfolio behaviour of banks. Retail deposits are deposits that are received through the banks' networks of local branches, yield a zero or uncompetitive rate of interest, and are held primarily to take advantage of banks' money transmission services. More specifically, they may be defined as including not only current accounts, but also seven-day and savings accounts, which, although they cannot be used for making payments, are almost entirely small savings from the personal sector and are extremely liquid. Prior to the introduction of Competition and Credit Control the rate offered on seven-day and savings deposits was fixed by cartel. Although each bank has had more freedom to determine its own rate since 1972, the authorities have the right to intervene to protect the competitive positions of the National Savings Bank and the building societies.

Wholesale deposits are large deposits by companies and financial institutions which yield a rate of interest similar to money market rates and are held for speculative motives. They consist of large sums (over £10,000) received through the banks' networks and the inter-bank market and the banks' issue of negotiable certificates of deposit.

Turning to the assets side of the balance sheet, under the Competition and Credit Control system banks are legally required to hold at least 12½ per cent of their eligible liabilities (sterling deposits less funds deployed with other banks) in the form of reserve assets. This requirement replaced the traditional liquidity constraints that banks' liquid assets should not fall below 30 per cent of deposits (28 per cent after 1963) and that, within this total, cash should make up at least 8 per cent.

In elementary textbooks, the reserve asset base is often treated as an intermediate policy target, set by the central bank at a particular value in order to achieve some desired level of the money stock. On this assumption, the base becomes exogenous and a mechanical money multiplier model of the determination of the money supply is applicable. The assumption of an exogenous monetary base has also in the past been frequently adopted by econometric model-builders.

In practice, the reserve base is not exogenously determined. There are a number of ways in which the banking system can increase its holdings of reserve assets in order, for example, to accommodate an expansion in the private sector's demand for credit.

1. *Balances with the Bank of England.* There is an agreement that the clearing banks should hold 1½ per cent of their eligible liabilities with the Bank of England. Such balances are non-interest-bearing and therefore not reserve assets which are attractive to banks.

2. *Money at call.* One possibility is that banks sell certificates of deposit to the discount houses and then, in return, lend them, as money at call, the finance with which to pay for them. In terms of identity (8.1b) this transaction would increase both *DDEP* and *R* by the same amount. It would leave banks' eligible liabilities unaffected (in the calculation of which certificates of deposit held by the discount market are netted out). The scope for 'manufacturing' reserve assets in this way has been limited since July 1973, when new arrangements were introduced for controlling the discount market's assets.[1]

3. *Treasury bills, local authority bills and government stock with a life shorter than a year.* By raising their rates of interest on wholesale deposits the banks can encourage the private and overseas sectors to substitute wholesale deposits for short-term government debt, thus increasing *WDEP* (or *OSDEP*) and *R* by the same amount as in (8.1b).

4. *'Top quality' commercial bills.* The ability of the banks to expand their reserve base in a similar fashion by purchasing commercial bills is limited by an agreement that they should count as reserve assets only up to 2 per cent of eligible liabilities.

It is not our intention to deny that the authorities could, in principle, directly control the monetary base if they so wished;[2] it is sufficient for our purpose that such a policy has never been attempted in the United Kingdom, even since the introduction of monetary targets in 1976. The instruments used to control the money supply have been the level of interest rates, controls on bank lending and, less commonly, the level of public borrowing and the exchange rate.

In addition to the reserve asset constraint, the lending policies of banks have on occasions been subjected to controls of various kinds.

1. Quantitative ceilings were imposed from time to time between 1955 and 1971. They were officially abandoned when Competition and Credit Control was implemented.

2. Qualitative requests, the usual objective of which has been to channel lending to priority sectors, were also used during the 1950s and 1960s and, unlike quantitative ceilings, are extant.

3. Calls for special deposits have been made since July 1958. When a call is made, each bank is required to lodge a certain percentage of its eligible deposits with the Bank of England. It is, however, possible for banks to accomplish the necessary portfolio adjustment by running down their investments in government bonds (SEC), thus avoiding any reduction in advances. Calls for special deposits have at times been accompanied by a request from the Bank of England that the adjustment in assets should be made by reducing advances rather than investments, but, by definition, the special deposit call is not then a substitute

for direct instruction to the banks. Most researchers have concluded that special deposits have been largely ineffective as a determinant of lending.

4. The Supplementary Special Deposits Scheme (popularly titled 'the corset') was first introduced in November 1973. This scheme operates by requiring banks to lodge with the Bank of England a non-interest-bearing special deposit if their interest-bearing eligible deposits exceed a specified ceiling. Once the ceiling has been reached, the scheme makes it unprofitable for banks to finance an expansion in lending by bidding for wholesale deposits.

A final institutional consideration that should be taken into account in the construction of a model of banks' portfolios is that the public sector's residual financing needs have to be met by borrowing from the banks. The process is essentially very simple. Any excess of public spending over revenue (including receipts from the sale of public debt to the private and overseas sectors) is held by the public in the form of bank deposits. The banks, in turn, use these funds to purchase government debt. The banks' role in this process of providing residual finance for the public sector need not, of course, be entirely passive; by adjusting the interest rates they offer on wholesale deposits they can encourage substitution between their deposits and government debt, which affects the residual financing requirement.

A description of the model

It is convenient to modify identify (8.1a) in two respects. First, while it was useful in the previous section to treat the discount market separately from the banking sector because of its role as a supplier of reserve assets, the banking system is now defined as inclusive of the discount market. With this consolidation, $\Delta DDEP$ and ΔBLD disappear from the identity and $\Delta BLPUB$ is redefined to include public sector borrowing financed by the discount houses. Second, the distinction between retail and wholesale deposits is replaced by the distinction between sterling sight deposits ($SDEP$) and time deposits ($TDEP$). This is solely for reasons of data availability. $TDEP$ includes seven-day and savings deposits, which, as we argued earlier, it would be more appropriate to aggregate with current accounts.

The banks' balance sheet identity can be rewritten as:

$$\Delta SDEP + \Delta TDEP + \Delta OSDEP + \Delta NDL \equiv \Delta BLPUB + \Delta BLPRIV + \Delta BLOS.$$

$$(8.1c)$$

We breathe behavioural life into this accounting identity by means of the following assumptions.

1. The banking sector as a whole has little scope for influencing the total supply of sight deposits by altering either the price or the non-price terms it offers to customers. Accordingly, $\Delta SDEP$ is assumed to be exogenous to the banking system and to be determined purely by factors affecting people's desire to hold balances for transactions purposes, such as real incomes, prices and rates of interest.

2. $\Delta TDEP$ is regarded as the residual item in the identity, it being assumed that banks accommodate their balance sheets by adjusting the rates of interest they offer on wholesale deposits.

3. Bank lending to the public sector is treated as the residual source of public sector finance. The public sector borrowing requirement may be financed by sales of gilt-edged, Treasury bills, National Savings and other government debt to the British public ($\Delta PRLP$), borrowing from the rest of the world, including the running down of foreign exchange reserves ($\Delta OSLP$), issuing legal tender (ΔCUR) and borrowing from the domestic banking system:

$$PSBR \equiv \Delta PRLP + \Delta OSLP + \Delta CUR + \Delta BLPUB. \qquad (8.2)$$

This accounting identity can be equally well reversed to show the various financial flows accompanying any change in bank lending to the public sector:

$$\Delta BLPUB \equiv PSBR - \Delta PRLP - \Delta OSLP - \Delta CUR.$$

This identity shows that bank lending to the public sector depends, in an accounting sense, on the size of public sector borrowing, the ability of the authorities to sell debt to the non-bank private sector, and the impact on the foreign exchange market—and the reserves position—of a balance of payments deficit (or surplus).

To obtain $BLPUB$ as the residual of (8.2) it is necessary to explain $\Delta PRLP$ and ΔCUR. $PSBR$ and $OSLP$ are taken as given from the rest of the National Institute model.[3]

$\Delta PRLP$ is explained by a model of portfolio behaviour. Taking the stock of net financial assets of the non-bank private sector as a whole, the possible substitutes for government debt are notes and coin, bank deposits, bank advances (a negative item in the calculation of the stock of financial assets), and overseas investments. The share of the stock of financial wealth that the non-bank public choose to hold in the form of government debt would thus be expected to depend on the relation between yields on government debt and rates of interest on bank time deposits, the availability of bank loans and the relation between bank borrowing rates and yields on government debt, and the relation between yields on government debt and yields on overseas assets. In addition, a number of other variables would be expected to have effects on the public's portfolio allocation of their financial balances. In particular, expectations of interest rates, and of resulting capital gains and losses, are known to be of considerable importance in the gilt-edged market. Also, changes in the level of economic activity would be expected to induce substitution between public debt and bank deposits by affecting the demand for transactions balances.

CUR is taken to be purely demand-determined; in other words, it is assumed that the Bank of England does not attempt to influence the supply of currency but passively issues legal tender to satisfy the demands of firms and individuals. It would be expected that the volume of market transactions conducted in cash terms would be related to the level of consumers' expenditure on goods and services. Rates of interest may also influence the public's demand for currency: bank time deposits are probably the chief interest-bearing substitute for legal tender. Finally, it is necessary to make some attempt to allow for secular change in institutional payments, practices and habits (the increase in the length of the payments period, vertical integration, the evolution of the credit card system, and so on), which has been responsible for a progressive substitution of bank deposits for notes and coin.

4. The statutory reserve asset ratio is assumed not to be a binding constraint on banks' lending policies, and the volume of bank advances to the private sector is taken to be demand-determined, except during periods when lending ceilings or 'the corset' were operative. The determinants of demand would be expected to include: the level of economic activity, the rates of interest charged on loans, the cost and the availability of alternative sources of finance, and the ability of firms and individuals to self-finance.

5. The remaining, less important, items in the banks' balance sheet identity— $\Delta OSDEP$, $\Delta BLOS$ and ΔNDL—are at the present stage of the model's development treated as exogenous.

This very simple model of banks' behaviour, with its extreme assumption that banks manage only the liabilities side of their balance sheets and allow their assets to go their own way, is offered not as a 'realistic' model of the working of the banking system, but rather as an attempt to caricature the working of the system in a way that enables a relatively simple statistical representation to be made.

In our discussion of the model so far we have taken all rates of interest as given. The rates that have featured in our description of the non-bank public's demand function for sight deposits, currency, government debt and bank advances are:

— *Rates on public sector debt.* The yield on 2½ per cent government consolidated stock is taken to be representative of rates of return on long-term government debt and the yield on Treasury bills representative of rates at the shorter end.

— *Rates on bank time deposits.* The rate on seven-day deposits with the London clearing banks is taken as representative of rates on retail time deposits and the rate on three-month sterling certificates of deposit as representative of rates on wholesale time deposits.

— *Rates on bank loans*, which are approximated by the London Clearing Banks' base lending rate, plus the maximum mark up.

The central interest rate in the model is the Treasury bill rate, which is treated as a policy instrument. We attempt to explain its behaviour in terms of trends in world interest rates and the response of the authorities to economic developments. Given the path of short-term rates, the rate on long-term public debt may be obtained in the conventional way from a term structure relationship.

Before Competition and Credit Control, primary banks had little room to vary their borrowing and lending rates relative to Bank rate. Since 1972, banks have had more freedom to determine their own rates, although from time to time there has been official pressure to keep rates down. Rates on retail time deposits tend to be 'sticky', and are assumed to follow with lag movements in the general level of short-term market rates, the certificate of deposit rate being employed as a representative short-term rate. The rate on certificates of deposit is assumed to be set in relation to the rate of return on reserve assets—that is, the Treasury bill rate—and the demand for advances. The rate charged on loans is, in turn, related to the marginal cost of funds, the certificate of deposit rate.

When an equation is omitted in a system subject to accounting identities it is important to examine its implied form. The 'missing equation' in our model is the demand for time deposits. The quantity of time deposits in the model is implicitly determined by the public sector borrowing requirement, reserve flows and the public's demands for government debt, narrow money and bank loans. It would be unreasonable to assume that the public will passively accept the quantity of time deposits that are brought into being, on the 'supply side' of the monetary system, so to speak, by these various credit flows. If, for example, an increase in loan demand initially puts into recipients' hands balances in excess of the amount that they wish to keep, one would expect the rate of interest on wholesale deposits to rise. Disequilibria in the market for deposits cannot, however, be modelled at all easily, and our function for the certificate of deposit rate is extremely simple.

Bank lending to the private sector

We decomposed total bank advances into loans to industrial and commercial companies, loans to the personal sector for house purchase, other personal sector loans and loans to other financial institutions. This disaggregation was suggested both by the set of variables predicted by the National Institute and available for use as explanatory variables, and by the role of bank-lending flows in explaining real variables in the National Institute model. Relationships were estimated for the first three of these categories; borrowing by other financial institutions, which is quantitatively not very important, has not as yet been modelled.

The equations are of the conventional stock adjustment form, the assumed determinants of the desired stock of advances being:

1. *An appropriate economic activity variable.* This was taken to be the growth of manufacturing output in the equation for loans to industrial and commercial companies, investment in private dwellings in the equation for loans for house purchase, and real personal disposable income in the equation for other personal sector loans.

2. *The rate of interest charged on bank loans.*

3. *The rate of interest charged on alternative sources of finance.* The rate on

building society mortgage advances was the obvious choice for the housing loans equation. The yield on three-month local authority deposits was included in the other two functions. This rate may play a dual role: as well as a proxy for rates charged by other financial institutions for short-term credit, it may be representative of rates of return on short-term financial assets. *Ceteris paribus*, a higher yield on short-term investments might induce firms and businesses to increase bank borrowing by discouraging them from financing their current expenditure by selling financial assets and encouraging them to take out loans to increase their holdings of such assets.

4. *The net acquisition of financial assets by the sector*. An increase in internal liquidity would be expected to reduce the volume of bank borrowing by enabling firms and individuals to maintain a similar standard of current consumption with less reliance on credit.

Unfortunately, the period since 1972 does not offer sufficient observations for reasonable regression analysis, and dummy variables were included in the demand functions, estimated for the period since 1963, to take into account the effects of Competition and Credit Control and lending requests.

The two interest rate variables did not perform particularly well when included separately in the equations. The differential between rates was found to fare rather better in the equations for loans to companies and loans for house purchase, while the rate on loans by itself was found to perform best in the equation for other personal loans.

Perhaps the most unsatisfactory feature of the results was the very slow rate of adjustment implied by the estimated coefficients on the lagged stock of advances. Indeed, the estimated coefficient on the lagged stock in the equation for company loans was consistently positive, which renders the partial adjustment model economically meaningless: it is therefore constrained to equal zero. Other studies have also tended to find surprisingly long lags, which can possibly be rationalized by the argument that official intervention in the market for loans and non-price rationing by branch managers have generally prevented rapid adjustments towards equilibrium.

The public's demand for notes and coin and sight deposits

The non-bank private sector's holdings of currency and sight deposits are explained in the model by demand functions for M1 (the sum of currency and sight deposits) and for currency.

The familiar theoretical specification of the function for M1 is that the transactions demand for money depends on the level of real income, the price level, and a representative short-term rate of interest (the rate on three-month local authority deposits). The dynamic specification follows the example of Hendry (Hendry and Mizon, 1978). While the short-run lag structure is freely estimated, the function has the 'steady-state' property of a unit elasticity of M1 with respect to nominal income and the long-run property that the ratio of M1 to nominal income varies inversely with the level of interest rates.

The demand function for currency also makes use of Hendry's approach to dynamics. The model assumes that there is a 'steady-state' elasticity of unity of currency with respect to consumers' expenditure and that the ratio of currency to consumers' expenditure declines over time because of institutional change. We were unable to uncover any perceptible interest rate effects.

Sales of public debt to the non-bank private sector

We found it extremely difficult to model the public's demand for public debt and we have some misgivings about the equations. We disaggregated total debt sales into 'long and short' debt (defined as British government securities, local authority debt, public corporation stocks and Treasury bills) and National Savings.

The share of the stock of financial wealth that is held in the form of long and short debt is positively related to the yield on 2½ per cent government consolidated stock and the yield on Treasury bills, and negatively related to the average rate of interest on bank time deposits. The equation is estimated with net sales of debt as the dependent variable; under the assumption that the stock demand is homogeneous with respect to wealth, the interest rates have been scaled by the non-bank private sector's stock of financial assets. The equation does less than justice to the theoretical specification outlined earlier: the only substitution possibility allowed for is between government securities and bank deposits, and no account is taken of the transactions motive for holding money balances in preference to government debt.

The equation for National Savings is conceptually similar, but incorporates a more complex dynamic structure. The rate on National Savings Certificates is employed as the 'own' rate of return and the rate on short-term local authority debt as the competitive rate. The equation contains an 'error feedback mechanism', according to which sales of National Savings respond to the discrepancy between the desired share of National Savings in personal sector portfolios, which is assumed to depend on the levels of the interest rates, and the actual share. Attempts to incorporate partial adjustment or error adjustment mechanisms into the relationship for long and short debt yielded less acceptable results than a simple discrete lag formulation.

Interest rates

It is assumed that in the absence of government intervention in the bill market, external flows would tend to bring the level of the Treasury bill rate in the UK into equality with short-term rates prevailing in the rest of the world, after allowing for any anticipated change in the value of the exchange rate. More specifically, the rate is assumed to depend on the (uncovered) US Treasury bill rate (with its coefficient constrained to unity) and the balance on visible trade, on the assumption that a good trade balance inspires confidence in the pound, and vice versa. The period during which the trade balance is assumed to influence exchange rate expectations is limited to the period of floating, that is since the end of 1971. The level of foreign exchange reserves and a 'monetary targets' variable are also included in the regression on the assumption that the authorities will tend to push short-term rates above those prevailing abroad—either by manipulation of the balance of demand and supply of bills or by direct instruction by the Bank of England to the discount houses to alter their bid price—if the stock of reserves falls to low levels or if the rate of growth of the money supply is deemed excessive.

The function for the consol rate is consistent with the standard expectations model of the term structure of interest rates. The estimated relationship satisfies the maxims that movements in long rates lag behind movements in short rates and are of smaller amplitude, and that long rates are more sensitive than short rates to expectations of price changes.

The rate on sterling certificates of deposit is related to the Treasury bill yield (with its coefficient constrained to unity) and the lagged volume of bank lending to the private sector. The certificate of deposit rate in turn determines banks' lending and seven-day deposit rates, with the standard partial adjustment mechanism being used to represent the well-known 'stickiness' of prime rates.

DIRECT TAXATION

Since a major purpose of macro-models is to evaluate and advise on budgetary policy, the model should be able to simulate the effects of changes in the various tax instruments. Also, while the Treasury publishes estimates of the effects of tax changes, alternative estimates may be necessary to take account of alternative earnings and personal income forecasts. Moreover, since the 1977 Finance Act, income tax forecasts have to incorporate the effects of annual indexation of personal allowances under 'unchanged policy' assumptions. Official estimates of the amounts of tax yield involved in this are not available in advance, so a forecasting model must be self-reliant.

The built-in properties of the tax system have come to be recognised, in recent years, as of equal importance to the operation of stabilization policy as discretionary tax rate changes. The aggregate marginal rate of income tax has consistently increased in the last fifteen years or so (see Price, 1978b), and this has obvious repercussions for the multiplier, and hence for the 'built-in stability' of the revenue system; also, fiscal drag has become an increasingly important factor in determining budgetary strategy as nominal incomes have risen: it affects both the overall tax burden and the 'mix' of direct and indirect taxes. The model is therefore designed to identify changes in marginal and average rates of tax, the difference between which determines the elasticity of the tax yield and hence fiscal drag.

There are a number of conceptually distinct stages involved in deriving a model of income tax. The first involves the derivation of a series of tax functions relating to cross-sections of income earners identified in the Inland Revenue's *Survey of Personal Incomes*. The second concerns the process of aggregation by which these functions are translated into terms applicable to total tax revenue; aggregate personal income as defined in the national accounts contains items that are not included in the statutory tax base. The third step is to account for the effects of changes in the various budgetary instruments; so that the model can incorporate budget changes in its forecasts, so that it can allow for index-ation, and so that it can be used to simulate budget changes in the past. The fourth and final stage is to convert what is, up to this point, a model of annual tax accruals on to a quarterly payments basis.

The basic model derived from cross-section personal income data

The difference between modelling the income tax liabilities of the personal sector and an activity such as consumption or savings is that the latter is be-havioural and the former institutional. The rates and allowances applicable to individual tax payers are known, and can be reduced to a mathematical formula. The difficulty is one of aggregation: describing the operation of allowances and rates for a mass of individuals. There are a number of ways of proceeding. One is to estimate a time series function with aggregate personal income tax defined as a function of discretionary tax changes and personal income (or, which is much the same, tax yield adjusted for discretionary changes defined as a function of personal income). We would expect the aggregate elasticity to be a declining function of income, because of the concentration of incomes below the thres-hold for upper rates of tax; this would rule out a logarithmic specification. But we would also expect a rising aggregate marginal rate of tax rather than a con-stant marginal rate because of the effect of people moving across the tax threshold from a zero to a positive marginal rate. It proved possible to fit quite acceptable equations displaying such characteristics. But the approach was rejected because of the poor forecasting performance of the generated equations and because a time-series methodology is not well suited to describing a constantly changing and developing institution such as the tax system.

An alternative approach is to build a model of aggregate tax liabilities from individual tax returns or disaggregated income groups. The drawback of such models is, of course, their size. A third approach, which retains a good deal of the versatility of the disaggregated methodology, in terms of its ability to simu-late the effects of changes in tax parameters on built-in flexibility, progressive-ness, etc., is a cross-section one, which is used here.[4] Basically, the model is derived from the Inland Revenue's *Survey of Personal Incomes* (*SPI*), which con-tains tax and income data by range of total income. From this we can calculate the *average* tax paid by people within each income group, and determine how such average tax liabilities change as average incomes change.

From the *SPI* we have, for each income range i, an estimate of the average tax paid per person, $x_i = T_i/N_i$, where T_i is the total tax paid by persons in income band i, and N_i is the number of persons in that band. The average income per person is $y_i = Y_i/N_i$, where Y_i is the total income in band i. We can then regress x_i against y_i to determine how tax liabilities change with income, *on average*. Each taxpayer will, of course, have his own individual tax function; but at any point on the gross income scale there will be an array of taxpayers with different allowances and different tax liabilities. This methodology therefore entails an averaging of the component individual tax schedules. Unlike the curve facing an individual, whose marginal rate of tax moves in discrete jumps as he moves either across the tax threshold or into higher rate bands, the aggregate average tax schedule yields a continuously rising marginal rate of tax, since at any point in the range of gross incomes there will be some people within a particular rate band and others moving from one rate band to the next.

From regression analysis, the best proxy for the type of progressiveness to be expected from the income tax system turned out to be:

$$x_i^t = \beta_{0t} + \beta_{1t}y_i + \beta_{2t}y_i^2 + \beta_{3t}y_i^3 + \beta_{4t}y_i^4. \tag{8.3}$$

The estimated equations yield an increasing marginal rate of tax, an increasing average rate and an elasticity that is substantially declining, though fairly flat in the middle income ranges.

The translation of the cross-section model into an aggregate forecasting model

As it stands, equation (8.3) gives us the tax liabilities—and hence the average and marginal rates of tax—applicable to recipients of a particular gross income. Aggregate marginal and average rates of tax may, however, be derived from the tax functions by a process of weighting the rates applicable to each bracket i by the proportion of total income in that bracket. Taking the average rate schedule (equation (8.3) divided through by y_i), we derive an aggregate average rate function as:

$$ar_t^t = \sum_{i=1}^{n} (x_i^t/y_{it})w_{it}, \text{ where } w_{it} = Y_{it} / \sum_{i=1}^{n} Y_{it}$$

$$= \beta_0 \sum_{i=1}^{n} y_{it}^{-1} w_{it} + \beta_{1t} + \beta_{2t} \sum_{i=1}^{n} y_{it} w_{it} + \beta_{3t} \sum_{i=1}^{n} y_{it}^2 w_{it} + \beta_{4t} \sum_{i=1}^{n} y_{it}^3 w_{it}$$

$$\tag{8.4}$$

where ar_t^t = the average rate of tax under the tax function actually operative in year t (superscript) calculated at the level of income in year t (subscript).

On the condition that the income weights (and hence the income distribution) are constant, equation (8.4) can be generalized to give the average rate that tax function t would generate at the level of income in any year $t+j$. Individual incomes in bracket i will rise, *pari passu*, with gross income, giving an average rate of tax of:

$$art_{t+j} = \left(\beta_{0t} \sum_{i=1}^{n} y_{it}^{-1} w_{it}\right) g_{t+j}^{-1} + \beta_{1t} + \left(\beta_{2t} \sum_{i=1}^{n} y_{it} w_{it}\right) g_{t+j}$$

$$+ \left(\beta_{3t} \sum_{i=1}^{n} y_{it}^2 w_{it}\right) g_{t+j}^2 + \left(\beta_{4t} \sum_{i=1}^{n} y_{it}^3 w_{it}\right) g_{t+j}^3 \tag{8.5}$$

This gives, for each tax schedule t, an average rate function which operates against an index of income based in each year t. For practical purposes, however, we need a set of coefficients operating against a common index. Defining a common index, $G_t = y_t/y_{1970}$, the average rate which tax function t would generate in year $t+j$ is derived as:

$$art_{t+j} = \left(G_t \beta_{0t} \sum_{i=1}^{n} y_{it}^{-1} w_{it}\right) G_{t+j}^{-1} + \beta_{1t} +$$

$$+ \left(G_t^{-1} \beta_{2t} \sum_{i=1}^{n} y_{it} w_{it}\right) G_{t+j} \left(G_t^{-2} \beta_{3t} \sum_{i=1}^{n} y_{it}^2 w_{it}\right) G_{t+j}^2 +$$

$$+ \left(G_t^{-3} \beta_{3t} \sum_{i=1}^{n} y_{it}^3 w_{it}\right) G_{t+j}^3$$

$$= TC0_t \, G_{t+j}^{-1} + TC1_t + TC2_t \, G_{t+j} + TC3_t \, G_{t+j}^2 + TC4_t \, G_{t+j}^3 \tag{8.6}$$

say, since the bracketed terms are constants ('tax coefficients').

The definition of y needs some discussion. The national accounts definition of personal income includes imputed income: rent attributed to owner occupation, and employers' contributions to national insurance funds. These do not form part of the tax base. Moreover, even netting these items out, gross income as defined in the *SPI* is only approximately 80 per cent of personal income. Some types of income, like most current grants, are untaxed, while others are subject to different amounts of 'erosion', i.e. offsets and deductions allowed before taxable income is obtained. Allowing for these untaxed elements, the average rate of tax derived directly from the *SPI* would have to be reduced by about 20 per cent to gain the true average rate on personal income.

However, there is a stronger consideration. The aggregate tax functions derived above do not, as they stand, allow for the different marginal rates of tax on different types of income, except in so far as those with a zero marginal rate are explicitly excluded from the tax base. For this reason, the definition of Y should be as near to the definition of the tax base as is possible to derive from the national income accounts. On the other hand, since the various income components of the tax base are themselves subject to widely different marginal rates of tax, there is the problem of how an aggregate equation deals with this. In the long run, the composition of income may be constant enough to validate the use of an aggregate marginal rate of tax, but in the short run, and for simulation purposes, different marginal rates must be taken into account. This the model does by adjusting the definition of Y to take account of marginal rates on particular types of income which are above or below the average. For instance, while for one reason or another only about half of the unearned income identified in the national accounts finds its way into the tax base, such income is subject to twice the average marginal rate. For this reason, the whole of personal income from dividends and interest (*NPIPER*) is included in the definition of income. Correspondingly, a part of wages and salaries, pensions (which are subject to a relatively low marginal tax rate), are netted out. The full definition of the operative income base is then:

$$YG = 0.97(WS + FP) + ECPRI + 0.42\ RETPENS + NPIPER$$
$$+ (IRSEPER - IR - SACC) \tag{8.7}$$

where

WS	= wages and salaries
FP	= forces pay
ECPRI	= employers' contributions to private funds (i.e. total employers' contributions less the contributions of employers to national insurance funds[5])
RETPENS	= statutory retirement pensions (the only element of current grants included)
NPIPER	= income from dividends and net interest
IRSEPER	= income from rent and self employment
IR	= imputed rents
SACC	= stock appreciation and capital consumption

Tax yield (accruals) is then derived as $art_{t+j}\ YG_{t+j}$.

The instruments identified here are the principal allowances and rates:

Allowances
(1) the married person allowance (*MPA*)
(2) the single person's allowance, and wife's earned income relief (which are identical) (*SPA*)
(3) the age allowance (*AGEA*)
(4) child allowance (phased out over the period 1977/8-1979/80 (*CHA*).

Rates
(1) the basic rate of tax on earned income (*SRT*)
(2) (from (1978/9) the reduction from the standard rate (*RED*) allowed through the reduced rate of tax
(3) a composite of higher tax rates (*URT*).

The basic procedure is to treat a change in allowances as having an effect on taxable income equal to the change in allowance times the number of people claiming such allowances; the effect on tax yield is then this change times the marginal rate of tax. More precisely, a tax function $f_t(y_i)$, as described in equation

(8.3), would be expected to change with subsequent budgetary intervention to give a new function $f_{t+1}(y_i)$; i.e.,

$$x_i^{t+1} = f_t[y_i(1 - da_{it+1})] = [f_t(1 - da_{it+1})]y_i = f_{t+1}(y_i) \qquad (8.8)$$

where da_{it+1} is the proportional change in allowances introduced in the budget in year $t+1$; i.e. $(a_{it+1} - a_{it})/a_{it}$.

In practice, of course, it is unwieldy and difficult to allocate allowance changes on a cross-section basis. Instead, using the available information provided on the total amount of allowances set against tax, we evaluate the aggregate proportional change in taxable income and proceed as if this were the same for all income brackets i. This aggregate change is estimated as:

$$dA_{t+1} = \sum_{k=1}^{4} \frac{ALLOWS_{kt}}{YG_t} \cdot \frac{(A_{kt+1} - A_{kt})}{A_t} \qquad (8.9)$$

where

dA_{t+1} = the aggregate percentage change in taxable income caused by a change in allowances in budgetary year $t+1$

$ALLOWS_k$ = the total amount of allowances set against tax, being the sum of the four types of allowance (k) described above.

Tax rate changes are treated as follows. Since approximately 93 per cent of the tax yield is the product of the basic rate of income tax (ignoring, for the moment, reduced rates of tax), a 1 per cent increase in the basic rate can be taken as increasing yield by 0.93 per cent; an average 1 per cent increase in upper rates can be correspondingly taken as increasing yield by 0.07 per cent. Following the introduction of a 25 per cent reduced rate band, account must be taken of the fact that a third of the income liable to the basic rate is subject to this lower rate. The tax coefficients are thus adjusted by the following factor:

$$DR_{t+1} = 0.93\frac{(SRT_{t+1} - 0.312RED)}{SRT_t} + 0.07\frac{UR_{t+1}}{UR_t} \qquad (8.10)$$

where *RED* is the *difference* between the basic and reduced rate.

Incorporating both allowance and rate changes, a new aggregate tax function can be derived directly from equation (8.6) as:

$$ar_{t+j}^{t+1} = (DR_{t+1} TC0_t) G_{t+j}^{-1} + \{[DR_{t+1}(1 - dA_{t+1})] TC1_t\} +$$

$$+ \{[DR_{t+1}(1 - dA_{t+1})^2] TC2_t\} G_{t+j} + \{[DR_{t+1}(1 - dA_{t+1})^3] TC3_t\}G_{t+j}^2$$

$$+ \{[DR_{t+1}(1 - dA_{t+1})^4] TC4\}G_{t+j}^3$$

$$= TC0_{t+1} G_{t+j}^{-1} + TC1_{t+1} + TC2_{t+j} G_{t+j} + TC3_t G_{t+j}^2 + TC4_t G_{t+j}^3. \qquad (8.11)$$

This generates the average rate of tax accruing in year $t+j$ from the new tax function $t+1$.

Indexation is accomplished as defined in the 1977 Finance Act, i.e. by up-rating allowances by the percentage change in the consumer price index between the fourth quarters of year t and year $t-1$.

The quarterly payments model

As they stand, the tax functions refer to annual tax accruals. Payments of income tax by the personal sector, on a quarterly basis, are derived as follows.

Each tax function operates unchanged for the whole of the financial year; but the average rate of tax changes through the year because of the continuous growth of incomes. Re-expressed on a quarterly basis, the average rate accruing under tax function t (superscript) in quarter q of year t (subscript) is:

$$ar_{tq}^t = f_t(G_{tq}) \qquad (8.12)$$

where $G_{tq} = YG_{tq}/(YG_{1970}/4)$, this quarterly version of G being based on the average value of YG in 1970, to give a quarterly index series that is directly consistent with the annual one.

Tax payments (*TXPER*) are then derived by splitting tax accruals into two components: those that relate to income on which tax is deducted at source— Schedule E (PAYE) and ACT—and those that relate to income on which there is a lag in payment—roughly speaking, Schedule D and (formerly) surtax. This income split is defined as *IRSEPER* and the rest of personal income. Payments of tax on the former are taken as lagged five quarters (a lag based on institutional rather than econometric considerations).

Simulations of fiscal and monetary policy

Table 8.1 shows some results of simulating fiscal and monetary policy changes with the expanded National Institute model.[6] Fiscal policy is represented by a step change of £100 million per quarter (at 1970 prices) in public authorities current expenditure, and monetary policy by a once-for-all two point change in the Treasury bill rate.

In simulation 1, earnings are exogenous (so there is no 'augmented Phillips Curve' effect) and the exchange rate is fixed. The fiscal expansion raises gross domestic product throughout, though after four years the effect is negligible. This is primarily because, in the NIESR model, an increase in demand and capacity utilization raises export prices which, with the exchange rate fixed, reduces the volume of exports. The current balance deterioration puts upwards pressure on interest rates.

This (1) reduces the value of personal wealth and thus moderates the rise in consumers' expenditure, and (2) leads to some increase in the sales of public sector debt to the non-bank private sector. This increase is, however, insufficient to finance the whole of the increase in the PSBR, and so there is some increase on the money supply.

TABLE 8.1

Simulation 1: Public authorities' current expenditure increased by £100m per quarter at 1970 prices: earnings and exchange rate exogenous

Quarter	QCE	QEX	QM	QGDP	AV	CPI	ER	MS	PSBR	CB
1	4	1	16	67	–	–	–	0.2	–90	–15
4	17	–5	39	75	–	–	–	0.5	–90	–45
8	13	–19	33	45	–	–	–	0.2	–105	–59
12	10	–38	26	23	–	0.1	–	0.1	–150	–80
16	6	–58	19	4	–	0.1	–	0.4	–213	–116

Simulation 2: as (1) but with earnings endogenous

Quarter	QCE	QEX	QM	QGDP	AV	CPI	ER	MS	PSBR	CB
1	7	1	16	68	0.1	–	–	0.2	–90	–16
4	17	–5	41	75	0.2	–	–	0.5	–90	–47
8	18	–23	38	42	0.8	0.3	–	0.2	–106	–65
12	9	–51	30	3	1.1	0.6	–	0.1	–151	–92
16	2	–73	19	–19	1.4	0.8	–	0.4	–229	–130

Simulation 3: as (1) but with exchange rate endogenous

Quarter	QCE	QEX	QM	QGDP	AV	CPI	ER	MS	PSBR	CB
1	4	1	16	68	–	–	–	0.2	–90	–15
4	13	–	32	80	–	–	–0.7	0.6	–92	–49
8	–3	4	23	67	–	0.3	–1.3	0.4	–104	–66
12	–17	3	16	55	–	0.5	–2.0	0.6	–144	–81
16	–28	–3	13	43	–	0.7	–2.5	1.3	–192	–72

Simulation 4: as (1) but with earnings and exchange rate endogenous

Quarter	QCE	QEX	QM	QGDP	AV	CPI	ER	MS	PSBR	CB
1	7	1	16	68	0.1	–	–	0.2	–90	–16
4	14	–	33	81	0.3	0.1	–0.8	0.6	–93	–52
8	1	3	26	68	1.0	0.7	–1.7	0.5	–106	–77
12	–24	–1	16	43	1.7	1.4	–2.8	0.8	–147	–106
16	–46	–5	12	24	2.5	2.1	–3.4	1.2	–206	–83

Simulation 5: Treasury bill rate residual increased by 2 points per quarter: earnings and exchange rate endogenous

Quarter	QCE	QEX	QM	QGDP	AV	CPI	ER	MS	PSBR	CB
1	–5	–3	10	–4	–0.1	–	1.1	–	15	12
4	–14	–15	–12	–43	–0.1	–0.2	0.1	–4.7	12	–4
8	–51	–15	–28	–59	–0.1	0.1	–0.3	–9.7	25	23
12	–68	–21	–33	–76	–	0.1	–	–13.9	11	43
16	–84	–19	–38	–76	–0.3	–	0.7	–18.9	–7	69

Notes

QCE   = consumers' expenditure at 1970 prices (£m)
QEX   = exports of goods and services at 1970 prices (£m)
QM   = imports of goods and services at 1970 prices (£m)
QGDP = gross domestic product at factor cost at 1970 prices (£m)

Simulation 2 again assumes a fixed exchange rate regime but now has average earnings determined by an expectations-augmented Phillips Curve. The effect is to exaggerate the general shape of the first simulation. The delayed rise in prices both worsens exports further and, by raising the savings ratio, further moderates the rise in private consumption.

In simulations 3 and 4 a floating exchange rate is assumed and the two average earnings regimes are examined. In both cases, the fall in the exchange rate following a fiscal expansion virtually stabilizes the volume of exports at the base level. The rise in imports, however, still gives a deterioration in the current balance. This is less than under a fixed exchange rate, however, and so interest rates rise less and the increase in the money supply is greater. The most noticeable difference between the first pair of simulations and the second pair is that the floating rate makes fiscal policy more effective (in terms of real GDP), but only at the cost of a higher price level and lower personal consumption.

Simulation 5 sketches the effect of a rise in interest rates. There is a reduction in GDP: private housing investment is cut and, more important, the reduction in the value of personal wealth has a marked effect on consumers' expenditure. The higher level of interest rates pushes the exchange rate up temporarily while capital stocks adjust to the new level of interest rates, but there is also a permanent increase reflecting the improvement in the current balance. The money supply falls quite sharply, reflecting the size of the change in the Treasury bill rate (2 points is 23 per cent of the average rate over the base-run period).

The simulations, then, accord broadly with *a priori* expectations about the effects of changes in fiscal and monetary policy. But perhaps their most significant feature is the crucial nature of the specification of the model at large— for example, the dependence of the results on the inclusion of wealth in the consumption function, and of capacity utilization effects on export prices. Given the differences between the various econometric models of the UK currently in operation, it seems unlikely that any of them can give more than the broadest indications of the relative efficacy of fiscal and monetary policy.

AV = average weekly earnings (%)
CPI = consumer price index
ER = IMF exchange rate (%)
MS = money stock, M3 definition (%)
PSBR = public sector borrowing requirement (£m)
CB = current balance of payments (£m)

All variables are deviations from the levels of the control solution. Initial conditions are 1972(I).

A minus sign in the *PSBR* column indicates an increase in the deficit.

THE RELATIONSHIP BETWEEN FISCAL AND MONETARY POLICY IN THE LONDON BUSINESS SCHOOL MODEL

A. P. Budd and T. Burns

The main purpose of this paper is to outline the relationship between fiscal and monetary policy in the London Business School (LBS) model. The conclusions are as follows.

1. The relationship between fiscal and monetary policy is a very close one, and under a floating exchange rate the prime determinant of monetary variations is changes in fiscal policy.

2. Changes in the monetary aggregates are an 'efficient' estimate of overall policy stance because, unlike the budget deficit, the required adjustments for output variations and external financing are automatically contained in the monetary measure.

3. If we wish to compute a measure of fiscal 'stance' from the behaviour of the actual fiscal deficit the adjustments have to be made in relation to the behaviour of the private sector rather than in relation to the determination of the tax and benefit system. The two most important adjustments relate to the position of output relative to its trend and the underlying inflation rate.

4. If the fiscal, and by implication monetary, 'stance' is expansionary relative to the underlying inflation rate, this will induce a fall in the exchange rate and a higher inflation rate than otherwise would have been the case. Equilibrium will be restored by the private sector surplus adjusting to the new higher fiscal deficit. The output effects of the change in fiscal policy will be transitory.

5. Fiscal policy should be set in relation to the target inflation rate. The first step is to compute the appropriate monetary growth given the underlying growth rate. Then the appropriate fiscal policy is the one that is consistent with required monetary growth on the assumption that interest rates will be determined by world rates and expected rates of depreciation.

1. THE MEANING OF FISCAL AND MONETARY POLICY

The definition of fiscal policy that we use in the LBS system is straightforward; it means the level of public expenditure and the structure of all tax rates and charges. The meaning of 'unchanged fiscal policy' is more complicated in these days of cash limits, partial indexation of income tax allowances, 'temporary' national insurance surcharges and automatic adjustment of social security payments. We have tended to extend the meaning of unchanged fiscal policy to include the indexation of specific indirect taxes; but we always make such assumptions explicit.

It is one thing to define fiscal policy at any time; it is another to attempt to provide some indicator that allows useful comparisons to be made between the 'stance' of fiscal policy at two different dates. Our chosen definition is that fiscal policy is expansionary if it is attempting more than to offset changes in private sector demand and is deflationary if it is not attempting to offset changes.

The definition of monetary policy presents far greater problems in defining policy but it is easier to judge policy 'stance'. We have taken the approach that monetary policy relates to the target growth of the nominal money stock. On this view there is an immediate problem in attempting to distinguish monetary policy from fiscal policy as they are jointly determined; the actual relationship between the two depends on the stage of the cycle and the rate of inflation. Apart from fiscal policy, the most important instruments are interest rate policy and exchange rate policy, but these are capable of being controlled only in the very short run. Interest rates over a period of time are dependent upon world interest rates and expectations about the movement of exchange rates, while the exchange rate can be controlled only as long as the system can bear the reserve loss or gain. We define monetary 'stance' in relation to the behaviour of the real money stock. Monetary policy is easy where the real money supply is growing faster than the underlying growth of output, i.e., where the nominal money supply is expanding faster than the underlying growth of output plus the existing inflation rate. Similarly, it is tight when monetary growth is below the rate of inflation plus the growth rate.

In the remainder of this paper we first of all investigate the parts of the LBS model relating to the supply of money. In Section 3 we examine the way in which the factors affecting the demand for money and the adjustment mechanism are involved in exchange rate determination. Several simulations are presented in Section 4 in order to obtain the impact of price changes and output changes upon the fiscal deficit and private sector surplus and to examine the process of exchange rate adjustment to a fiscal stimulus. Finally, we draw some conclusions on the basis of these simulations.

2. THE SUPPLY OF MONEY

The general approach to money in the LBS model can be presented in terms of factors affecting supply, factors affecting demand, and the adjustment mechanism which moves the market towards equilibrium. Basically we attempt to use the approach of determining M3 via banks' assets in order to obtain some notion of the 'supply' of money. The demand for money function is contained within the exchange rate function, and adjustment between demand and supply is brought about by changes in the exchange rate inducing changes in the level of nominal income.

The determination of the supply of money via the assets of the banks begins with the identity that the change in money supply is domestic credit expansion

(DCE) minus external financing minus the change in non-deposit liabilities. An empirical relationship that we have occasionally used to estimate this is as follows:

$$\Delta M3 = -2.964 + 0.53\ DCE + 0.31\ DCE_{-1} + 0.50\ BAL + 0.47\ BAL_{-1} \quad (9.1)$$
$$\quad\ (3.83)\quad (0.05)\qquad (0.06)\qquad\quad (0.20)\qquad (0.17)$$
$$\bar{R}^2 = 0.8, DW = 1.8, SE = 179$$

where $\Delta M3$ is the change in money supply, and BAL is the current account of the balance of payments. This can be interpreted as meaning that non-deposit liabilities are about 16 per cent of the change in money supply and that the current account serves as a useful proxy for external financing during the historical period. Under a clean floating system external financing should be close to zero, and we usually set the term on the balance of payments to zero when attempting to capture this effect. Later in this section we outline some attempts that we have made to model external financing directly in terms of financial factors.

The next stage is to divide DCE between the borrowing requirement, lending by banks to the private sector and private sector purchases of public sector debt:

$$DCE = \text{borrowing requirement} + \text{lending by banks to the private}$$
$$\text{sector} - \text{private sector purchases of public sector debt.}$$

In a closed economy the right-hand side would be identically equal to increases in private sector cash *plus* bank lending to the private sector *plus* bank lending to the government.

The borrowing requirement (BRG) is determined by fiscal policy and the level of output in current prices. We aggregate the two remaining items on the right-hand side and define 'net lending' as DCE *minus BRG*. The estimated equation takes the form:

$$\frac{DCE-BRG}{GDP\$} = \underset{(0.0875)}{0.3892} \frac{KII\$}{GDP\$} - \underset{(0.0466)}{0.1407} \sum_{t=i}^{n} \frac{DCE-BRG}{GDP\$}$$

$$+ \underset{(0.2503)}{0.6669} \frac{GDP}{GDPT} - \underset{(0.2414)}{0.684} - \underset{(0.00015)}{0.000497}\ (RLB + 27.5). \quad (9.2)$$

$$\bar{R}^2 = 0.62,\ DW = 1.59, SE = 0.0254$$

The estimation period is 1963(I) to 1976(IV). *BRG* is the borrowing requirement, *GDP\$* is the current value of *GDP, KII\$* is the level of stocks, *GDPT* is trend *GDP* and *RLB* is bank rate. This equation together with the simultaneous determination of the borrowing requirement determines DCE.

The equation has replaced earlier systems, in which 'net lending' was disaggregated into private sector purchases of public sector debt, bank lending to the personal sector and bank lending to the public sector. This was discontinued as the components display some complementary behaviour; on occasions bank lending is expanded to finance gilt purchases. Furthermore, those variables were not used elsewhere in the model (although it might have been useful to incorporate them into equations determining interest payment flows between sectors). The stock variable is important as it implies stable long-run behaviour between the stock of bank lending relative to GDP and the stock of public sector debt relative to GDP. The general idea is that, for a given level of the borrowing requirement, DCE is larger the higher the ratio of inventory to GDP, the higher the pressure on capacity and the lower is Bank rate.

Another version of this equation includes external financing as an argument. The logic of this is that, when the exchange rate is under pressure, sentiment moves away from gilt sales and firms borrow from the banks to undertake leading and lagging. It is not correct to assume that in the short term external financing automatically reduces the money supply; that is true for a *given* level of DCE, but as we can see DCE is itself affected by external financing. An equation reflecting this, estimated over 1963(II) to 1977(III), is:

$$\frac{DCE - BRG}{GDP\$} = \underset{(0.08)}{0.50} \frac{KII\$}{GDP\$} - \underset{(0.08)}{0.15} \sum_{i=1}^{n} \frac{DCE - BRG}{GDP\$}$$

$$+ \underset{(0.25)}{0.39} \frac{GDP}{GDPT} - \underset{(0.00011)}{0.00045} \, (RLB + 27.5)$$

$$- \underset{(0.243)}{0.467} - \underset{(0.128)}{0.483} \, \Delta RES \tag{9.3}$$

$$\bar{R}^2 = 0.72, DW = 1.59, SE = 0.02$$

where ΔRES is a measure of reserve changes defined as the difference between DCE and the change in money supply.

This implies that in the short-run half of external financing is reflected in an increase in DCE; in the long run this is not so because the stock term dominates the relationship. The level of Bank rate is determined as follows:

$$RLB = \underset{(2.1552)}{50.1953} - \underset{(88.7353)}{348.0557} \frac{BAL}{GDP\$} + 2.3974 \cdot \frac{1}{4} \sum_{i=0}^{3} \left\{ \left[\left(\frac{PC}{PC_{-1}} \right)^4 - 1 \right] \cdot 100 \right\}_{t-i}$$

$$- 0.885 \cdot \frac{1}{4} \cdot \sum_{i=0}^{3} \left\{ \left[\left(\frac{EER}{EER_{-1}} \right)^4 - 1 \right] \cdot 100 \right\}_{t-i} \tag{9.4}$$

$$\bar{R}^2 = 0.731, DW = 0.47, SE = 11.978$$

where the estimation period is 1958(II)–1976(II) and RLB is Bank rate, BAL is the current balance, PC is the consumer expenditure deflator and EER is the effective exchange rate. The equation was originally designed to represent a reaction function in which the authorities increase Bank rate in response to poor balance of payments figures, high inflation and falls in the exchange rate.

It is possible that, rather than reflecting a reaction function, this may be a slightly mis-specified relationship whereby interest rates are determined by the world interest rate and the expected exchange rate change. If we take the notion that the covered interest rate differential tends to zero, then:

$$r_{uk} = r_w + (e_s - e_f) \tag{9.5}$$

where r_{uk} is the UK short-term interest rate, r_w is the world short-term interest rate and $(e_s - e_f)$ is the gap between the forward and spot exchange rate (defined over the relevant time period). If we assume that world interest rates are determined by world inflationary expectations, then

$$r_w = \theta + \dot{p}^e_w \tag{9.6}$$

where $\dot{p}^e_w$ is the expected inflation rate in the world as a whole. If the gap between the spot and forward exchange rates is determined by the inflation gap between the UK and the world, the balance of payments and previous exchange rate movements

$$(e_s - e_f) = (\dot{p}^e_{uk} - \dot{p}^e_w) - \alpha_1 BAL - \alpha_2 \dot{e}_{-1} \tag{9.7}$$

where $\dot{p}^e_{uk}$ is the expected inflation rate in the UK and $\dot{e}$ is the change in the exchange rate, then, substituting (9.6) and (9.7) into (9.5) gives the arguments in euqation (9.4).

If this is the correct interpretation of equation (9.4) it is of major significance, as it suggests that short-term interest rates are basically determined by world financial flows rather than being capable of manipulation in order to achieve various combinations of monetary and fiscal policy.

The modelling of the long-term interest rate has not yet been completed. Our feeling here again is that this is largely market-determined; i.e., it is the market's view of future short-term interest rates. Clearly, the authorities do have the power at times to change this in order to vary sales of gilt-edged stock, but this power is ultimately limited by portfolio considerations.

Some general points may be made about this system. First, as is clear, it is highly aggregated as regards sectors, monetary assets and non-monetary financial assets. The personal and company sectors are considered jointly, and no distinction is made between purchases of public sector debt and changes in bank borrowing. Further, there is no distinction between cash, current accounts and deposit accounts. As far as the banks' assets are concerned, there are no distinctions between different types of government financial assets. There is therefore no distinction between reserve and non-reserve assets. Finally, as far as the monetary system is concerned there is only one interest rate—Bank rate. However, there is an equation linking Bank rate with long-term interest rates (represented by the yield on consols).

These simplifications inevitably mean that many aspects of monetary behaviour, particularly in the short run, have not been modelled. We cannot directly incorporate changes in special deposits, for example, and we will not normally pick up movements between certificates of deposit and Treasury bills by the private sector which can have so marked an effect on M3.

There is some built-in stability in the link between the money supply and the exchange rate. A rapid growth of the money supply will lead to some combination of balance of payments deficits, fall in the exchange rate and acceleration of inflation. The authorities will in turn raise interest rates, and will thereby slow the growth of the money supply.

The implication of this model and the equation whereby cumulative net lending bears a stable relationship to current price GNP is that movements in the borrowing requirement are the dominant factor behind changes in money supply. Changes in interest rates lead to a once-and-for-all change in the cumulative net lending–output ratio, but long-term efforts to fund a borrowing requirement to achieve a given inconsistent money supply target would require constantly increasing or falling interest rates.

3. THE DEMAND FOR MONEY AND THE ADJUSTMENT MECHANISM

The equation used for forecasting exchange rates can, as we have said, be interpreted as representing the demand for money and the adjustment process for equating the demand for and supply of money. The approach emphasizes the relationship between the equilibrium quantity of money in the UK and the quantity of money in the rest of the world.

The background ideas can be expressed in a number of simple equations. It should be emphasized that the equations presented for price determination, for example, are deliberate simplifications of certain long-run properties of the model. They represent the spirit of a far more complex set of structural equations which are actually used in forecasts and simulations. The complete system is described in more detail in Ball, Burns and Warburton (1978).

Starting from the assumption that the demand for real money balances in the domestic economy is determined by real incomes, we have

$$\frac{M_d^d}{P_d} = K_0 \, Y_d^{\alpha_1} \tag{9.8}$$

$$\frac{M_w^d}{P_w} = K_1 \, Y_w^{\beta_1} \tag{9.9}$$

where

M^d = demand for nominal money
P = prices index
Y = level of real income

and the subscripts d and w refer to domestic and world. The determination of prices distinguishes between traded and non-traded goods. The former are assumed to be set in competitive markets and are therefore equal to world prices in terms of a common currency; the prices of non-traded goods depend on the relative productivity in the traded and non-traded goods sector. The overall price level in each country therefore depends on the relative productivity of traded and non-traded goods and on the ratio of traded output to non-traded output.

The equations are as follows.

$$P_d = P_T \cdot \Pi_T/\Pi = \Theta P_T \tag{9.10}$$

$$P_w = \Theta_w P_{Tw} \tag{9.11}$$

where Π = productivity in the economy as a whole, the subscript T refers to the traded goods sector and Θ is the ratio of productivity in the traded goods sector relative to the economy as a whole.

Purchasing power parity for traded goods is represented by

$$P_T = \frac{P_{Tw}}{E} \tag{9.12}$$

Dividing (9.8) by (9.9) and eliminating the price variables gives us an equilibrium or long-term relationship for the exchange rate:

$$\frac{M_d^d \cdot E}{M_w^d} = k \frac{Y_d^{\alpha_1}}{Y_w^{\beta_1}} \cdot \frac{\theta}{\theta_w} \text{ where } k = K_0/K_1 . \tag{9.13}$$

Equation (9.13) determines the share of the UK's money stock, expressed in international currency units, in the world money stock. It is related to the real income ratio, where real incomes are weighted by the income elasticities of demand for real balances, and the ratio of the productivity factors.

This equation can be used in its simplest form as an exchange rate function. In practice we include other variables: the flow of OPEC sterling balances, and the cumulative sum of the current account of the balance of payments. The estimated equation is

$$\ln \frac{EER \cdot KM3\pounds}{KM3W} = \begin{array}{c} -4.631 + 1.081 \, (\ln \dfrac{GDP}{WIP} - 0.004 \, TIME) \\ (0.415) \, (0.9453) \end{array}$$
$$\begin{array}{c} + 0.0000198 \, CBAL + 0.00017 \, OIL \\ (0.0000036) \qquad (0.000034) \end{array} \tag{9.14}$$

$$\bar{R}^2 = 0.949, DW = 0.54, SE = 0.0512$$

where the estimation period is 1963(I)–1977(IV). *EER* denotes the effective exchange rate and *KM3£* the stock of nominal money in the UK on an M3 definition. *KM3W* is a measure of world money defined as the weighted index of M3 figures for the six largest OECD countries, and *CBAL* is the current balance of payments cumulated from 1963. The variable *OIL* represents the change in the holdings of sterling balances by the OPEC countries, which is required to take out the special characteristics of sterling demand of oil producers. *GDP/WIP* is an index of the ratio of the UK gross domestic product to an index of world industrial production, where no account has been taken at this stage of differences in the elasticity of demand for real balances between the UK and the other major countries included in the world index. The time trend reflects the growing disparity in the productivity ratios described in the theoretical specification. The long-term trend in the ratio has been independently determined as described in Burns, Lobban and Warburton (1977).

Equation (9.14) is a combination of the demand for money function and the adjustment mechanism. For any given level of real income the exchange rate moves to equilibrate the demand and supply for nominal money. An exogenous increase in the supply of money will lower the exchange rate, which in turn will raise the level of domestic prices until the level of real balances is restored to the equilibrium level.

Equation (9.14) suffers from heavy serial correlation, partly owing to the absence of the appropriate lag adjustment and partly because the time period includes periods of heavy exchange intervention by the authorities. We have been experimenting with a specification incorporating better specified lagged distributions and external financing behaviour. This takes the form of

$$\Delta E = \alpha_0 - \alpha_1 (\Delta M_3 - \Delta M_w) + \alpha_2 (\Delta Y - \Delta Y_w) + \alpha_3 \left(\frac{E^*}{E}\right)_{-1} \quad (9.15)$$

where E^* is the long-term equilibrium value of the exchange rate. This is in the form suggested by Davidson *et al.* (1978), where α_1 and α_2 give the short-run effects of the changes in money supply relative to output and the term (E^*/E) measures the initial disequilibrium.

The long-term equilibrium rate has been obtained from a version of (9.14):

$$\ln \frac{EER \cdot KM3\pounds}{KM3W} = \underset{(0.054)}{-5.84} + \underset{(0.06)}{1.20} \left(\ln \frac{GDP}{WIP} - 0.004 \, TIME\right) \quad (9.16)$$

where the relative effects of the OPEC sterling balances and cumulative current account have been omitted.

In estimation, the change in the money supply has been replaced by domestic credit expansion and equations are presented for the exchange rate, the level of official financing and the sum of the two to represent total exchange rate pressure. Examples of equations estimated over the period from 1971(I) to 1977(III) are as follows:

$$\sum_{i=0}^{-3} \frac{BOF}{KM3} = \underset{(0.016)}{0.037} - \underset{(0.09)}{0.77} (\Delta_4 \ln DC - \Delta_4 \ln KM3W - \Delta_4 \ln GDP + \Delta_4 \ln WIP)$$
$$+ 0.885 \, OIL - 0.079 \, DVI + 0.378 \ln\left(\frac{E^*}{E}\right)_{-4} \quad (9.17)$$

$$\bar{R}^2 = 0.84, DW = 0.813, SE = 0.029$$

$$\Delta_4 \ln EER = -0.05 - 0.50 \, (\Delta_4 \ln DC - \Delta_4 \ln KM3W - \Delta_4 \ln GDP + \Delta_4 \ln WIP)$$
$$\quad (0.005) \; (0.06) \tag{9.18}$$
$$+ \, 2.37 \, OIL - 0.072 \, DVI + 0.212 \ln \left(\frac{E^*}{E}\right)_{-4}$$
$$\quad (0.02) \qquad (0.020) \qquad (0.117)$$
$$\bar{R}_2 = 0.895, DW = 1.36, SE = 0.02$$

$$\sum_{i=0}^{-3} \frac{BOF}{KM3} + \Delta_4 \ln EER = -0.017 - 1.277 \, (\Delta_4 \ln DC - \Delta_4 \ln KM3W$$
$$- \, \Delta_4 \ln GDP + \Delta \ln WIP) + 3.58 \, OIL - 0.163 \, DVI + 0.535 \left(\frac{EER^*}{EER}\right)_{-4}$$
$$\quad (0.45) \qquad (0.044) \qquad (0.251)$$
$$\bar{R}^2 = 0.878, DW = 0.97, SE = 0.04 \tag{9.19}$$

where

BOF = balance for official financing
DC = stock of domestic credit
EER^*= calculated values from equation (9.16)

This suggests that, historically, the effect of any excess monetary growth or initial disequilibrium tends to be shared between exchange rate changes and official financing. The authorities have moved to dampen the impact of monetary policies upon the exchange rate with consequent effects upon the reserves. The coefficient in equation (9.19) suggests some short-term over-reaction of the foreign exchange market, although the stabilizing term suggests a fairly rapid correction.

In this system there is substantial 'crowding-out' resulting from the operation of a strong effect of inflation upon private sector expenditure. In the LBS model this comes through the behaviour of the savings ratio. Again, this is described in detail in Ball, Burns and Warburton (1978), but the key feature is that the savings ratio is related to the growth of nominal disposable income and the existing liquid assets–income ratio. In this form it has strong similarities to the revised version of the New Cambridge equation, where the net acquisition of financial assets by the private sector is related to the growth of nominal income. The impact of an increase in the inflation rate via savings is therefore very strong.

Another source of evidence results from our attempts to estimate relationships between output changes and changes in the real stock of money balances for a number of countries. The variables are graphed in Figure 9.1 and the results are shown as Table 9.1.

The basic specification of the relationship is

$$\Delta_4 \ln Q = \alpha_0 + \alpha_1 \Delta_4 \ln \left(\frac{KM}{P}\right)_{-i} + \alpha_2 \Delta_4 \ln WIP + \alpha_3 \ln \left(\frac{KM}{P}\right)_{-4} - \alpha_4 Q_{-4} \tag{9.20}$$

where Q is industrial production, KM is the broadly defined money supply, WIP is industrial production of the rest of the world and P is the price level.

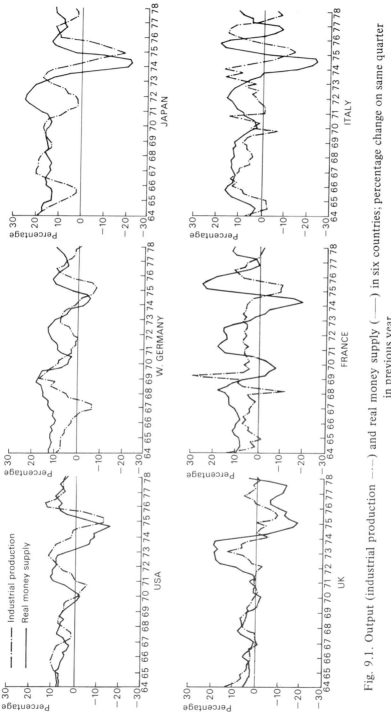

Fig. 9.1. Output (industrial production - - -) and real money supply (———) in six countries; percentage change on same quarter in previous year.

TABLE 9.1.
Output and Real Money Supply in Six Countries†

Country	Starting date	i	α_1	α_2	α_3	α_4	$\bar{R}^2$	DW	SE
USA	1964 (III)	2	0.58 (0.12)	0.21 (0.11)	−0.27 (0.09)	0.28 (0.10)	0.73	0.45	0.03
Japan	1964 (IV)	2½	0.60 (0.09)	0.22 (0.16)	−0.30 (0.11)	0.20 (0.08)	0.65	0.20	0.05
Germany	1964 (IV)	2½	0.74 (0.21)	0.06 (0.14)	−0.37 (0.13)	0.21 (0.06)	0.72	0.41	0.03
France				0.48 (0.11)	−0.22 (0.09)	0.15 (0.05)	0.77	0.59	0.03
Italy	1964 (IV)	3	0.28 (0.12)	0.30 (0.17)	−0.40 (0.15)	0.24 (0.09)	0.71	0.73	0.04
UK	1964 (IV)	2½	0.18 (0.04)	0.41 (0.07)	−0.09 (0.09)	−0.004 (0.050)	0.76	0.85	0.02

† All equations are estimated to 1977 (IV) and are of the form

$$\Delta_4 \ln_i Q = \alpha_0 + \alpha_1 \Delta_4 \ln\left(\frac{KM}{P}\right)_{-i} + \alpha_2 \Delta_4 \ln WIP + \alpha_3 \ln\left(\frac{KM}{P}\right)_{-4} + \alpha_4 Q_{-4}$$

The specification is again taken from Hendry *et al.* (1978). The coefficient α_1 describes the short-run relationship between output and real money stock movements, while the level terms form a stock adjustment mechanism that guarantees the long-run relationship in the form:

$$Q = \frac{\alpha_0}{\alpha_4} + \frac{\alpha_3}{\alpha_4}\left(\frac{KM}{P}\right). \qquad (9.21)$$

In all cases except France, changes in the real money stock have powerful lagged effects upon output, and the disequilibrium terms are also important except in the UK. Much of the variance over the period in the real money stock is due to changes in the inflation rate, and the results are consistent with the approach that an increase in the inflation rate relative to monetary growth has a sharp impact upon output movements.

4. SIMULATIONS

The preceding sections have described the supply of and demand for money in the LBS model. The supply of money depends principally on the borrowing requirement (and therefore on fiscal policy), the stage of the business cycle and the rate of inflation; the demand for money depends principally on the level of relative output and on productivity trends. Adjustments between the two are produced by changes in the exchange rate which in turn generate changes in the domestic price level. In this section we explore some properties of the LBS model in terms of changes in fiscal and monetary policy. We have included the results of three simulations. Simulations (1) and (2) examine the partial effects of changes in the rate of inflation and level of output separately upon the major sector flows. Simulation (3) traces the impact of changes in fiscal policy upon monetary behaviour, output and inflation.

The first two simulations are particularly relevant to the question of 'adjusted' fiscal and monetary policy. It is widely agreed that, for a given set of fiscal instruments, the budget deficit depends on the level of output. It is also clear that simple examination of the size of the fiscal deficit (or of its ratio to GNP) does not reveal whether fiscal policy is tight or lax. However, we strongly question the view that budget deficits adjusted for output tell us (1) whether fiscal policy is tight or lax or (2) whether it is appropriate to the government's objectives. In particular, we stress the role of inflation in the spending decisions of the personal sector. The higher the rate of inflation, the larger will be the personal sector surplus and the smaller will be the level of 'net lending' (DCE minus the borrowing requirement). An apparently tight fiscal policy may in effect be too slack if inflation is falling rapidly.

In these simulations inflation has only a small direct effect on the borrowing requirement. This is because we assume that both direct and indirect taxes are indexed. As a result, the buoyancy of the revenue is almost equal to the buoyancy of expenditure. (Implicitly, there are no cash limits.)

Simulation (1)–increase in inflation rate by 1 per cent per annum

The first simulation shows the impact of raising the inflation rate by 1 per cent per annum. This is done by fixing the world price level to rise progressively by 0.25 per cent faster per quarter than in the base run. Output is constrained to be unchanged with any shortfall or excess expenditure being artificially allocated to exports. The exchange rate is left unchanged. The results are summarized in Table 9.2 for the key variables. They suggest the following.

1. It takes three and a half years for the faster inflation in world prices to be fully reflected in increases in consumer prices; by then the four-quarter change in *PC* is 1 per cent.

2. Consumer spending falls as the savings ratio rises. By year 4, when the inflation rate has risen by 1 per cent per annum, the effect is an increase of 0.5 per cent in the savings ratio, rising to over 0.6 per cent.

3. The private sector surplus rises by 0.25 per cent of GNP once the inflation rate increase has settled down at 1 per cent per annum.

4. The borrowing requirement automatically rises by less than 0.1 per cent of GNP as the growth of expenditure only slightly outgrows tax receipts. (N.B. direct and indirect taxes are indexed.)

5. Net lending (DCE minus the borrowing requirement) is lower, reflecting higher nominal interest rates and lower stock-building, as the company sector deficit increases.

TABLE 9.2

Simulation 1 – A 1% Increase in the Inflation Rate

		C £m70	IF £m70	II £m70	X £m70	M £m70	PC %Δ	FJ/ PROP	FC/ PROP	BAL £m	BRG £m	DCE £m	M3$ £m	SJ$/ PROP	NLG/ PROP
1976	1	− 2	0	0	1	0	0	0	0	− 9	1	0	− 4	0	0
	2	− 7	0	0	2	− 3	0.2	0	−0.1	− 7	12	3	− 1	0.1	0
	3	−14	0	0	6	− 4	0.3	0.1	−0.1	− 5	14	4	0	0.1	0
	4	−21	0	0	9	− 7	0.5	0.1	−0.1	5	18	0	3	0.2	−0.1
1977	1	−27	0	0	11	− 9	0.7	0.2	−0.1	12	29	2	9	0.2	0
	2	−28	0	−1	11	−10	0.9	0.2	−0.1	22	32	−6	12	0.3	−0.1
	3	−25	−1	0	12	− 7	1.0	0.2	−0.1	18	28	15	27	0.3	0
	4	−32	−1	0	13	−11	1.2	0.2	−0.1	22	33	−1	21	0.3	−0.1
1978	1	−36	−1	0	14	−12	1.4	0.3	−0.1	14	35	0	15	0.3	−0.1
	2	−43	−1	0	17	−15	1.7	0.3	−0.1	33	36	8	26	0.4	−0.1
	3	−45	−1	0	18	−15	1.9	0.3	−0.1	40	40	8	41	0.4	−0.1
	4	−49	−1	1	20	−16	2.1	0.3	−0.1	41	44	19	52	0.4	−0.1
1979	1	−53	−1	0	19	−20	2.3	0.4	−0.1	47	53	11	56	0.4	−0.2
	2	−57	−1	1	23	−18	2.6	0.4	−0.2	54	50	12	58	0.5	−0.1
	3	−61	−1	0	24	−21	2.9	0.4	−0.2	71	58	20	75	0.5	−0.1
	4	−63	−1	0	24	−22	3.1	0.4	−0.2	61	65	31	89	0.5	−0.1

		C £m70	IF £m70	II £m70	X £m70	M £m70	PC %Δ	FJ/ PROP	FC/ PROP	BAL £m	BRG £m	DCE £m	M3$ £m	SJ$/ PROP	NLG/ PROP
1980	1	-65	-1	0	25	-23	3.4	0.5	-0.2	67	65	32	92	0.5	-0.1
	2	-70	-1	0	28	-24	3.7	0.5	-0.2	85	64	27	97	0.6	-0.1
	3	-69	-1	0	27	-25	3.9	0.5	-0.2	87	70	20	104	0.6	-0.1
	4	-73	-1	-1	27	-27	4.2	0.5	-0.2	99	75	16	104	0.6	-0.1
1981	1	-72	-1	-1	27	-28	4.4	0.5	-0.2	121	72	0	111	0.6	-0.1
	2	-74	-1	-1	29	-27	4.7	0.5	-0.3	133	47	-22	108	0.6	-0.1
	3	-73	-1	-2	28	-27	4.9	0.5	-0.3	132	50	-5	120	0.6	-0.1
	4	-75	-1	-2	28	-29	5.1	0.5	-0.3	114	52	0	115	0.6	-0.1
1982	1	-74	-1	-3	26	-31	5.4	0.5	-0.3	112	50	1	112	0.6	-0.1
	2	-79	-1	-3	29	-32	5.7	0.5	-0.3	129	40	3	121	0.6	-0.1
	3	-80	-1	-4	29	-34	5.9	0.5	-0.3	142	37	-10	128	0.6	-0.1
	4	-82	-1	-4	30	-35	6.1	0.6	-0.3	130	39	-17	118	0.6	-0.1
1983	1	-82	-1	-5	30	-35	6.3	0.6	-0.3	140	33	-24	112	0.7	-0.2
	2	-86	-1	-5	32	-37	6.6	0.6	-0.3	153	20	-28	118	0.7	-0.2
	3	-87	-2	-5	32	-38	6.8	0.6	-0.3	159	18	-33	125	0.7	-0.2
	4	-87	-2	-5	32	-38	7.1	0.6	-0.4	134	28	-28	121	0.7	-0.2

TABLE 9.3

Simulation 2 – A 1% Increase in Output

		BRG £m	TYA £m	TEA £m	YGTP £m	YGRA £m	G$ £m	EDBA £m	ESAB £m	EGGA £m	ENIH £m	FG £m	FG/PROP	DCE £m	NLG/PROP
1976	1	−30	23	4	6	5	12	−2	−2	−8	9	28	0.2	155	0.8
	2	−19	26	7	7	7	13	−5	−1	−4	10	24	0.2	132	0.6
	3	−87	26	11	9	8	13	−8	0	1	12	89	0.4	108	0.7
	4	−94	27	14	9	8	9	−11	0	1	13	99	0.4	129	0.8
1977	1	−102	48	15	9	8	7	−14	0	−1	15	104	0.4	110	0.8
	2	−123	63	17	9	8	10	−19	0	−2	17	122	0.4	88	0.7
	3	−147	75	23	10	9	13	−23	0	−4	19	148	0.5	91	0.8
	4	−159	65	23	8	8	3	−28	−1	−7	16	155	0.5	42	0.7
1978	1	−166	62	20	8	7	2	−33	−1	−8	16	158	0.5	10	0.6
	2	−159	61	22	9	8	6	−38	−1	−7	18	161	0.5	0	0.5
	3	−169	62	26	10	9	11	−42	0	−4	20	164	0.5	−28	0.4
	4	−161	56	28	11	10	13	−47	0	−3	20	163	0.5	−22	0.4
1979	1	−158	50	24	10	9	10	−53	0	−5	19	162	0.5	−41	0.3
	2	−174	56	28	12	11	15	−59	0	−3	21	175	0.5	−56	0.3
	3	−191	64	30	12	11	18	−65	1	−2	23	188	0.6	−77	0.3
	4	−204	67	33	12	11	19	−72	0	−3	23	202	0.6	−84	0.3

	BRG £m	TYA £m	TEA £m	YGTP £m	YGRA £m	G$ £m	EDBA £m	ESAB £m	EGGA £m	ENIH £m	FG £m	FG/ PROP	DCE £m	NLG/ PROP
1980 1	-211	56	29	11	10	10	-79	-1	-9	21	207	0.6	-96	0.3
2	-221	62	27	12	11	11	-88	0	-8	22	221	0.6	-96	0.3
3	-234	68	26	12	11	12	-96	0	-9	23	235	0.6	-103	0.3
4	-243	63	28	12	11	10	-105	-1	-10	23	245	0.6	-134	0.3
1981 1	-253	66	26	13	12	15	-115	0	-9	26	254	0.6	-158	0.2
2	-270	63	26	13	12	9	-126	-1	-11	24	270	0.6	-163	0.2
3	-286	58	26	13	12	8	-135	-1	-13	25	279	0.6	-176	0.2
4	-296	58	28	13	12	9	-145	-1	-11	25	289	0.6	-190	0.2
1982 1	-298	69	23	14	13	14	-155	0	-11	27	301	0.6	-188	0.2
2	-311	70	25	16	14	18	-165	0	-9	28	313	0.6	-198	0.2
3	-322	73	26	16	15	21	-175	0	-8	30	324	0.7	-222	0.2
4	-338	73	31	16	15	21	-185	0	-7	30	338	0.7	-243	0.2
1983 1	-347	71	27	17	15	20	-196	0	-8	31	346	0.7	-247	0.2
2	-363	77	28	17	16	24	-207	0	-7	32	362	0.7	-263	0.2
3	-371	75	29	18	16	23	-217	0	-7	32	372	0.7	-281	0.2
4	-379	59	27	15	14	9	-228	-1	-14	28	383	0.7	-279	0.2

Simulation (2)—increase in output by 1 per cent

The second simulation considers the case of a 1 per cent increase in output brought about by an exogenous increase in exports. The exchange rate is fixed. The aim of this simulation is to investigate the impact of a 1 per cent change in the level of output upon the borrowing requirement and the amount of net lending (that is, bank lending to the private sector less sales of public sector debt). The results of the relevant variables are presented in Table 9.3. They suggest the following.

1. By year 2 the public sector deficit is reduced by 0.44 per cent of current price GDP and falls steadily to over 0.6 per cent of GDP, reflecting the decline in interest rates.

2. Net lending as a proportion of GDP begins by being 0.7 per cent higher than in the control as output expands. Over time this effect is reduced as the stock term in the net lending equation (9.2) comes into effect.

3. The result is that initially DCE is higher than in the control; the downward effects upon the borrowing requirement are offset by an expansion of net lending. After two years the effect upon DCE turns negative as the borrowing requirement reduction increases and the net lending effect is reduced.

Simulation (3)—reduction in income tax of £100m. per quarter in 1970 prices

This simulation is taken from the paper by Ball, Burns and Warburton (1978) and shows the results relative to the control of a £100 million reduction in income tax in real terms, that is to say at 1970 prices. The results, displayed here in Table 9.4, are discussed more fully in the original paper. Briefly they can be summarised as follows.

1. The impact upon the borrowing requirement of the measure is about 1 per cent of GNP.

2. The money supply grows by 16 per cent in eight years. The exchange rate falls and prices rise by a similar amount.

3. The savings ratio falls by over 1 per cent.

The general effect of the policy change under these assumptions is that there is a modest rise over the first two years in both real consumption and output, but later output is not far from its initial level and consumption is actually lower than in the control. The major impact is upon the inflation rate, as the extra borrowing leads to monetary expansion and exchange rate depreciation.

5. IMPLICATION OF SIMULATIONS

The first group of simulations has important implications for fiscal policy. Both variations in the inflation rate and in the level of output have important influences upon private sector demand and the financing of the budget deficit.

If output falls relative to trend, either because of higher private saving or because of a reduction of exports, then deficit financing becomes easier as public debt sales rise relative to bank lending. At the same time the fiscal deficit automatically increases with a reduction in output owing to the operation of automatic stabilizers. Of course, there is no reason why the induced impact upon the fiscal deficit should exactly equal the increase in the ability of the private sector to finance it. This is the major drawback to any attempt to use the constant employment budget deficit as an indicator of fiscal stance. It tells us the extent to which an observed change in the budget deficit between two dates is due to non-discretionary changes and provides some guide as to whether the government was trying to change the fiscal deficit over and above the autonomous changes built into the fiscal system. But it tells us nothing about whether the changes automatically offset movements in net lending.

According to the simulations, a change in the underlying inflation rate has a major impact upon the private sector surplus. We would expect to have a higher private sector surplus in an economy with a higher underlying inflation rate. By implication, the same stance of fiscal policy in the higher inflation economy would involve a higher fiscal deficit.

This suggests that, if we are trying to compute an adjusted fiscal deficit that gives a guide to fiscal stance, it is necessary to adjust the actual fiscal deficit for movements in both output and inflation. The estimates given are that for every 1 per cent addition to the inflation rate we would expect the private sector to be in surplus by an extra 0.25 per cent; hence, if the aim is to finance the existing rate of inflation, it is necessary that the fiscal deficit rise by 0.25 per cent. Similarly, we have the estimate that for every 1 per cent output is below trend net lending will be about 0.6 per cent of GDP lower; i.e., a given fiscal deficit will generate a smaller DCE. Applying these estimates, we can adjust the observed fiscal deficit to obtain the equivalent demand effect if inflation was zero and output was on trend.

The fact that higher inflation generates a larger private sector surplus has led some commentators to conclude that budget deficits are self-financing. In other words, it is argued that large deficits do not cause a problem when there is rapid inflation since the large private sector surpluses 'mop up' the gilts. This view confuses a number of separate issues. It is of course true that *ex post* all deficits are financed, but in any given period this may represent major disequilibrium in one sector or another (including the overseas sector). The major objection to the argument is that it implicitly treats inflation as exogenous. If the government pursues policies that result in rapid inflation, part of the adjustment process will come through large private sector surpluses. The remedy for inflation will include policies that reduce the fiscal deficit, even if the excessive deficits are, apparently, being financed without difficulty.

An attempt to calculate an adjusted budget deficit is undertaken in Greenwell's *Monetary Bulletin*, (Greenwell *et al*., 1978). Because of measurement problems no attempt was made to allow for the impact of changes in output,

TABLE 9.4 (a) Simulation 1: Direct tax cut of £100m, export price function (14), expenditure on the gross domestic product and flow of funds (difference)

		GDP	C	IF	INP	II	G	X	M	FCA	BRG	FG	FC	FJ	FO
76	1	6.76	17.14	0.05	0.00	1.52	0.00	0.24	7.47	4.71	201.32	-201.30	-0.03	173.57	27.77
76	2	16.48	38.78	0.15	0.05	4.20	0.00	0.93	16.92	10.65	208.96	-208.17	-2.23	141.27	69.12
76	3	15.55	32.48	0.24	0.21	4.97	0.00	2.19	15.41	8.92	219.08	-219.73	-18.31	154.97	83.07
76	4	17.58	33.33	0.36	0.60	5.21	0.00	4.11	16.27	9.16	239.60	-239.36	-34.32	158.82	114.85
77	1	11.35	10.79	0.02	0.86	2.77	0.00	6.66	5.93	2.96	292.53	-292.88	-36.16	231.31	97.72
77	2	11.04	11.30	-0.56	1.16	1.61	0.00	8.57	6.77	3.10	306.06	-307.99	-23.98	274.44	57.53
77	3	15.44	22.18	-0.93	1.63	1.82	0.00	9.42	10.95	6.09	307.45	-308.28	-22.40	258.13	72.55
77	4	14.27	16.64	-1.52	1.77	2.15	0.00	10.48	8.91	4.57	330.98	-330.04	-36.78	281.51	85.31
78	1	14.21	10.17	-1.70	2.14	2.02	0.00	11.47	4.95	2.79	339.55	-339.60	-60.96	296.53	104.03
78	2	4.87	-14.75	-2.04	2.25	1.16	0.00	11.71	-4.73	-4.05	358.41	-359.40	-68.57	351.91	76.07
78	3	5.19	-19.33	-2.45	2.48	0.38	0.00	12.68	-8.59	-5.31	384.15	-382.06	-58.13	410.03	30.14
78	4	2.42	-29.67	-2.97	2.63	0.16	0.00	13.85	-12.91	-8.15	401.64	-399.79	-71.10	449.14	21.74
79	1	1.25	-33.25	-3.36	2.71	0.84	0.00	15.15	-12.73	-9.13	428.51	-429.61	-73.35	471.04	31.91
79	2	1.38	-35.88	-3.57	2.77	2.73	0.00	16.94	-11.30	-9.86	441.11	-441.61	-72.02	489.69	23.95
79	3	2.34	-42.46	-3.41	2.77	3.51	0.00	19.37	-13.67	-11.66	467.17	-467.59	-62.04	535.39	-5.76
79	4	2.72	-49.68	-3.15	2.77	4.70	0.00	21.76	-15.43	-13.65	492.01	-493.27	-85.30	567.58	10.97
80	1	4.61	-55.89	-3.26	2.59	4.45	0.00	23.80	-20.15	-15.35	521.69	-524.29	-96.47	632.64	-11.87
80	2	3.08	-59.93	-3.66	2.32	6.22	0.00	25.10	-18.89	-16.46	541.80	-542.42	-97.96	682.95	-42.56
80	3	5.65	-53.53	-3.84	2.41	6.64	0.00	25.49	-16.18	-14.70	564.33	-563.15	-118.91	734.60	-52.55
80	4	5.16	-53.13	-3.94	2.63	6.52	0.00	25.14	-15.99	-14.59	596.89	-595.56	-146.69	790.28	-48.02
81	1	8.32	-43.81	-3.83	2.92	6.61	0.00	25.28	-12.04	-12.04	615.63	-614.59	-143.33	842.31	-84.39
81	2	9.90	-41.65	-3.49	3.17	6.77	0.00	26.24	-10.60	-11.44	576.07	-575.10	-173.20	847.51	-99.22
81	3	11.35	-36.21	-2.82	3.49	6.30	0.00	26.03	-8.09	-9.95	570.64	-570.94	-183.92	846.36	-91.50
81	4	11.75	-38.50	-1.95	3.95	5.57	0.00	26.02	-10.02	-10.58	599.01	-599.17	-228.70	860.47	-32.60
82	1	10.45	-39.17	-1.33	4.36	4.53	0.00	25.31	-10.36	-10.76	611.64	-611.60	-248.43	878.33	-18.31
82	2	6.69	-49.81	-1.13	4.71	2.45	0.00	24.92	-16.58	-13.68	622.45	-622.61	-227.29	922.55	-72.63
82	3	6.53	-46.27	-1.56	4.79	0.87	0.00	24.89	-15.89	-12.71	630.02	-628.28	-236.37	966.79	-102.15
82	4	6.66	-46.87	-2.14	4.89	-0.55	0.00	24.51	-18.83	-12.87	652.62	-653.36	-267.17	1005.65	-85.14
83	1	7.68	-36.10	-2.87	4.77	0.07	0.00	23.40	-13.26	-9.92	656.67	-656.21	-264.50	1019.59	-98.85
83	2	5.83	-38.03	-3.14	4.72	0.52	0.00	22.41	-13.63	-10.45	645.11	-645.10	-246.20	981.03	-89.69
83	3	5.50	-36.69	-3.22	4.54	0.25	0.00	20.89	-14.18	-10.08	642.64	-642.27	-265.59	1002.23	-94.38
83	4	2.35	-43.05	-3.19	4.40	-0.05	0.00	19.66	-17.15	-11.85	672.06	-674.23	-323.89	1043.33	-45.24

TABLE 9.4 (b) *Direct tax cut of £100m, export price function (14), personal incomes, employment and consumption (% difference)*

		YD	YD$_I$	LAJ	AEM	YMS	YJG	YJO	TJYP	ENIH	LE*	LL*	CND	CD	SJS
76	1	1.033	1.029	-0.835	0.059	0.060	0.001	0.160	-4.641	0.059	0.00	0.00	0.203	0.117	0.70
76	2	1.218	1.088	-0.869	0.227	0.237	0.122	0.454	-4.327	0.213	1.69	-1.39	0.439	0.421	0.55
76	3	1.493	1.064	-0.989	0.462	0.487	0.428	0.770	-3.993	0.448	5.78	-4.77	0.336	0.650	0.60
76	4	1.937	1.063	-1.267	0.877	0.921	0.864	1.274	-3.561	0.857	9.64	-7.95	0.336	0.740	0.59
77	1	2.493	1.036	-1.592	1.414	1.483	1.459	1.802	-3.407	1.424	13.99	-11.54	0.052	0.842	0.77
77	2	3.075	1.132	-1.919	1.967	2.066	1.932	2.305	-2.777	1.871	15.10	-12.46	0.055	0.956	0.85
77	3	3.394	1.179	-2.007	2.366	2.431	2.194	2.587	-2.376	2.210	13.71	-11.32	0.188	0.829	0.83
77	4	3.948	1.164	-2.308	2.875	2.940	2.741	3.225	-1.772	2.661	13.61	-11.23	0.130	0.771	0.86
78	1	4.414	1.146	-2.512	3.358	3.419	3.254	3.714	-1.058	3.087	12.71	-10.49	0.056	0.713	0.92
78	2	4.958	1.000	-2.756	3.857	3.921	3.937	4.297	-0.593	3.841	13.34	-11.01	-0.240	0.659	1.02
78	3	5.515	1.012	-2.973	4.453	4.520	4.471	4.821	0.038	4.423	11.82	-9.76	-0.294	0.607	1.06
78	4	6.053	0.953	-3.162	4.990	5.036	5.077	5.461	0.666	4.933	9.29	-7.67	-0.406	0.528	1.10
79	1	6.590	0.957	-3.338	5.524	5.556	5.607	6.065	1.221	5.444	6.41	-5.29	-0.434	0.416	1.15
79	2	7.119	0.931	-3.500	6.051	6.068	6.128	6.650	1.746	5.948	3.28	-2.71	-0.457	0.342	1.15
79	3	7.745	0.967	-3.725	6.731	6.745	6.717	7.232	2.323	6.600	2.44	-2.01	-0.524	0.300	1.25
79	4	8.375	0.962	-3.947	7.311	7.321	7.347	8.036	2.929	7.171	1.75	-1.44	-0.599	0.252	1.31
80	1	8.980	1.018	-4.111	7.905	7.916	7.945	8.669	3.597	7.756	1.80	-1.49	-0.671	0.197	1.41
80	2	9.593	0.959	-4.261	8.498	8.513	8.556	9.361	4.190	8.346	2.59	-2.13	-0.719	0.176	1.39
80	3	10.062	0.958	-4.277	8.990	9.006	9.005	9.844	4.722	8.824	2.98	-2.45	-0.645	0.122	1.32
80	4	10.609	0.975	-4.358	9.473	9.493	9.526	10.599	5.242	9.307	3.73	-3.07	-0.641	0.114	1.33
81	1	11.137	1.078	-4.398	10.013	10.036	9.935	11.170	5.897	9.848	4.28	-3.52	-0.535	0.138	1.33
81	2	11.587	1.050	-4.385	10.448	10.475	10.412	11.691	6.388	10.284	5.10	-4.20	-0.510	0.215	1.29
81	3	11.944	1.029	-4.319	10.841	10.876	10.803	11.998	6.892	10.668	6.63	-5.46	-0.447	0.273	1.23
81	4	12.455	1.047	-4.395	11.281	11.322	11.292	12.638	7.293	11.106	7.88	-6.50	-0.474	0.322	1.27
82	1	12.970	1.081	-4.454	11.806	11.854	11.761	13.168	7.976	11.630	9.34	-7.70	-0.485	0.349	1.31
82	2	13.524	1.026	-4.536	12.329	12.379	12.364	13.816	8.486	12.147	9.78	-8.07	-0.610	0.401	1.36
82	3	13.985	1.034	-4.540	12.812	12.859	12.806	14.207	8.961	12.619	9.02	-7.44	-0.570	0.405	1.33
82	4	14.488	1.063	-4.589	13.282	13.324	13.299	14.921	9.513	13.074	7.90	-6.52	-0.573	0.390	1.36
83	1	14.962	1.164	-4.595	13.783	13.818	13.640	15.428	10.097	13.560	6.73	-5.55	-0.448	0.370	1.36
83	2	15.372	1.098	-4.570	14.153	14.185	14.111	16.012	10.496	13.920	6.08	-5.01	-0.466	0.386	1.32
83	3	15.734	1.083	-4.517	14.528	14.559	14.496	16.334	10.918	14.287	5.87	-4.83	-0.450	0.396	1.29
83	4	16.231	1.078	-4.583	14.958	14.988	14.998	17.049	11.394	14.705	5.62	-4.62	-0.523	0.416	1.35

*difference

TABLE 9.4 (c) Simulation 1: Direct tax cut of £100m, export price function (14), prices and costs
(% difference)

		PGDP	EER	PC	PIF	PG	PX	PM	TREF	PMAN	PXGM	PIMO	AEM	PRDM	ULCM
76	1	-0.017	-0.261	0.004	0.092	0.044	0.088	0.218	-0.048	0.273	0.090	0.060	0.059	0.058	-0.002
76	2	0.054	-0.703	0.128	0.339	0.204	0.318	0.615	0.027	0.752	0.328	0.237	0.227	0.133	0.092
76	3	0.269	-1.279	0.425	0.300	0.460	0.685	1.167	0.312	1.356	0.706	0.544	0.462	0.106	0.355
76	4	0.590	-2.201	0.865	0.725	0.885	1.276	2.078	0.698	2.436	1.308	1.048	0.877	0.104	0.772
77	1	1.158	-2.905	1.442	1.397	1.462	1.963	2.814	1.106	3.160	2.026	1.657	1.414	0.031	1.389
77	2	1.765	-3.091	1.922	1.835	1.974	2.424	3.015	1.498	3.309	2.544	2.123	1.967	0.025	1.952
77	3	2.004	-3.765	2.189	2.256	2.317	2.884	3.723	1.770	4.131	3.001	2.540	2.366	0.066	2.283
77	4	2.504	-4.353	2.751	2.794	2.897	3.373	4.401	2.286	4.794	3.602	3.104	2.875	0.057	2.811
78	1	2.972	-5.036	3.231	3.303	3.471	4.058	5.255	2.591	5.607	4.254	3.645	3.358	0.059	3.323
78	2	3.577	-5.666	3.919	3.845	4.002	4.637	5.862	3.364	6.203	4.889	4.196	3.857	-0.021	3.894
78	3	4.151	-6.097	4.458	4.360	4.562	5.175	6.395	3.876	6.763	5.480	4.757	4.463	-0.011	4.502
78	4	4.676	-6.553	5.053	4.876	5.075	5.707	6.962	4.606	7.368	6.065	5.307	4.990	-0.022	5.044
79	1	5.230	-7.022	5.580	5.448	5.599	6.240	7.493	4.908	7.926	6.640	5.850	5.524	-0.019	5.567
79	2	5.746	-7.446	6.132	6.015	6.106	6.715	7.984	5.604	8.437	7.164	6.351	6.051	-0.004	6.049
79	3	6.390	-7.860	6.713	6.622	6.813	7.197	8.375	6.270	8.639	7.644	7.009	6.731	0.007	6.728
79	4	6.982	-8.319	7.341	7.177	7.397	7.762	8.908	6.935	9.186	8.251	7.593	7.311	0.013	7.299
80	1	7.571	-8.805	7.882	7.710	7.980	8.341	9.468	7.244	9.769	8.853	8.193	7.905	0.027	7.929
80	2	8.203	-9.108	8.552	8.270	8.579	8.831	9.859	8.141	10.136	9.375	8.734	8.498	0.012	8.487
80	3	8.684	-9.447	9.018	8.735	9.065	9.264	10.278	8.542	10.547	9.811	9.196	8.990	0.030	8.951
80	4	9.174	-9.862	9.541	9.233	9.658	9.543	10.781	9.104	11.057	10.309	9.692	9.473	0.023	9.437
81	1	9.709	-10.212	9.952	9.757	10.089	10.235	11.216	9.170	11.491	10.820	10.197	10.013	0.044	9.955
81	2	10.129	-10.519	10.427	10.178	10.524	10.643	11.622	9.873	11.877	11.245	10.626	10.448	0.052	10.381
81	3	10.515	-10.853	10.804	10.567	10.923	11.031	12.011	10.211	12.300	11.646	11.026	10.841	0.055	10.777
81	4	10.927	-11.309	11.290	11.009	11.374	11.518	12.598	10.743	12.881	12.152	11.499	11.281	0.052	11.266
82	1	11.450	-11.810	11.762	11.535	11.911	12.080	13.206	10.888	13.524	12.738	12.046	11.806	0.036	11.762
82	2	11.996	-12.192	12.371	12.049	12.438	12.590	13.685	11.788	14.021	13.272	12.568	12.329	0.006	12.313
82	3	12.470	-12.473	12.818	12.507	12.918	13.020	14.090	12.183	14.389	13.732	13.035	12.812	0.008	12.793
82	4	12.924	-12.821	13.285	12.948	13.384	13.482	14.540	12.697	14.847	14.212	13.512	13.282	0.014	13.284
83	1	13.429	-13.075	13.639	13.417	13.879	13.913	14.865	12.661	15.187	14.671	13.972	13.783	0.026	13.756
83	2	13.795	-13.387	14.119	13.806	14.265	14.288	15.304	13.427	15.604	15.050	14.359	14.153	0.015	14.127
83	3	14.165	-13.697	14.494	14.179	14.647	14.668	15.710	13.759	16.021	15.434	14.743	14.528	0.013	14.517
83	4	14.599	-14.097	14.991	14.620	15.091	15.146	16.230	14.354	16.563	15.930	15.210	14.958	-0.008	14.967

TABLE 9.4 (d) *Simulation 1: Direct tax cut of £100m, export price function (14), monetary sector and interest rates (difference)*

		BAL	BALI	BALY	BRG	DCE	MJS	KMJS*	RLB	RS	RL	GDPS*	BRG	KII*	YCT –
76	1	−27.77	−8.62	−19.15	201.32	203.54	108.03	0.288	0.59	0.06	0.06	0.039	0.78	0.008	−0.30
76	2	−69.12	−10.17	−58.95	208.96	204.97	171.66	0.725	1.67	0.17	0.17	0.192	0.76	0.032	3.45
76	3	−83.07	−5.78	−77.29	219.08	198.67	168.76	1.122	3.14	0.33	0.31	0.399	0.77	0.059	4.62
76	4	−114.85	0.17	−115.02	239.60	191.53	163.03	1.529	5.30	0.55	0.53	0.735	0.79	0.087	4.70
77	1	−97.72	7.61	−105.34	292.53	200.90	165.79	1.933	7.15	0.74	0.72	1.253	0.91	0.101	14.82
77	2	−57.53	8.68	−66.22	306.06	206.93	171.89	2.278	7.57	0.79	0.76	1.858	0.90	0.109	38.56
77	3	−72.55	16.67	−89.22	307.45	220.97	181.21	2.660	7.89	0.82	0.79	2.133	0.93	0.119	41.10
77	4	−85.31	50.35	−135.66	330.98	245.14	198.37	3.178	8.06	0.84	0.81	2.627	1.04	0.130	45.75
78	1	−104.03	57.01	−161.04	339.55	259.11	213.25	3.613	7.66	0.80	0.77	3.092	1.05	0.141	52.47
78	2	−76.07	66.48	−142.55	358.41	259.02	217.51	4.023	8.11	0.84	0.81	3.618	1.04	0.146	76.89
78	3	−30.14	77.81	−107.95	384.15	264.85	220.85	4.412	8.14	0.84	0.81	4.195	1.04	0.148	98.94
78	4	−21.74	83.66	−105.40	401.64	281.88	231.43	4.808	7.95	0.83	0.79	4.696	1.03	0.148	121.20
79	1	−31.91	88.79	−120.70	428.51	307.84	250.46	5.216	7.97	0.83	0.80	5.241	1.04	0.152	141.84
79	2	−23.95	93.25	−117.20	441.11	345.21	278.31	5.660	7.28	0.76	0.73	5.758	1.02	0.166	170.22
79	3	5.76	96.82	−91.06	467.17	374.22	305.25	6.112	7.12	0.74	0.71	6.410	0.99	0.186	209.10
79	4	−10.97	95.74	−106.71	492.01	398.99	327.37	6.577	7.08	0.73	0.71	7.004	1.02	0.211	242.18
80	1	11.87	102.55	−90.68	521.69	400.43	335.78	7.045	7.18	0.74	0.72	7.609	1.04	0.235	280.93
80	2	42.56	104.48	−61.92	541.80	441.86	358.22	7.532	6.90	0.72	0.69	8.229	1.00	0.267	333.09
80	3	52.55	108.31	−55.76	564.33	465.05	383.32	8.055	6.52	0.68	0.65	8.731	0.99	0.301	371.83
80	4	48.02	113.31	−65.29	596.89	482.24	399.61	8.611	6.36	0.66	0.64	9.217	1.01	0.333	408.67
81	1	84.39	118.31	−33.92	615.63	503.44	416.17	9.205	5.95	0.62	0.59	9.778	1.00	0.367	454.79
81	2	99.22	118.34	−19.12	576.07	504.49	423.28	9.788	5.45	0.57	0.54	10.211	0.88	0.401	499.99
81	3	91.50	115.62	−24.13	570.64	533.48	438.99	10.367	5.30	0.55	0.53	10.608	0.89	0.431	539.79
81	4	32.60	116.37	−83.76	599.01	580.43	472.86	10.966	5.26	0.55	0.53	11.024	0.93	0.458	566.74
82	1	18.31	123.41	−105.10	611.64	584.97	489.78	11.569	5.48	0.57	0.55	11.537	0.94	0.478	609.92
82	2	72.63	131.80	−59.16	622.45	583.58	490.44	12.157	5.57	0.58	0.56	12.051	0.93	0.488	662.62
82	3	102.15	135.05	−32.90	630.02	584.35	490.42	12.726	5.58	0.58	0.56	12.524	0.92	0.490	711.47
82	4	85.14	138.36	−53.22	652.62	581.08	488.92	13.283	5.52	0.57	0.55	12.979	0.94	0.485	744.56
83	1	98.85	131.59	−32.74	656.67	615.76	506.72	13.863	4.97	0.52	0.50	13.492	0.95	0.483	804.31
83	2	89.69	135.62	−45.93	645.11	643.57	531.79	14.452	4.58	0.48	0.46	13.843	0.91	0.484	847.30
83	3	94.38	137.59	−43.21	642.64	643.93	540.57	15.025	4.50	0.47	0.45	14.210	0.91	0.494	890.95
83	4	45.24	141.18	−95.94	672.06	640.26	538.73	15.593	4.62	0.48	0.46	14.619	0.94	0.482	919.56

* ₒ difference.

TABLE 9.5
Adjusted Budget Deficit

	Financial surplus % of GDP 4 period m.a.	Inflation rate (price of domestic final expenditure) 4 period % change	Deviations of output from trend	Adjusted financial surplus
1964 (I)	−3.6	2.5	1.1	−3.7
1964 (II)	−3.8	3.9	1.1	−3.5
1964 (III)	−3.7	4.1	1.1	−3.3
1964 (IV)	−3.5	3.9	2.3	−3.8
1965 (I)	−3.0	5.6	1.8	−2.7
1965 (II)	−2.9	4.8	1.3	−2.5
1965 (III)	−2.9	5.2	1.1	−2.2
1965 (IV)	−2.7	4.6	1.5	−2.5
1966 (I)	−2.5	4.4	1.4	−2.3
1966 (II)	−2.3	4.2	1.2	−2.0
1966 (III)	−2.3	4.0	0.7	−1.7
1966 (IV)	−2.6	4.1	−0.7	−1.1
1967 (I)	−3.2	4.0	−0.6	−1.8
1967 (II)	−3.5	2.7	−0.2	−2.7
1967 (III)	−3.8	2.8	−0.4	−2.8
1967 (IV)	−4.2	2.3	0.3	−3.8
1968 (I)	−4.5	2.6	2.2	−5.2
1968 (II)	−4.5	5.3	1.3	−3.9
1968 (III)	−4.1	5.5	1.4	−3.5
1968 (IV)	−2.8	6.3	1.1	−1.8
1969 (I)	−1.5	6.5	1.1	−0.5
1969 (II)	−0.3	5.3	1.6	0.1
1969 (III)	0.6	4.9	1.1	1.2
1969 (IV)	1.1	5.3	0.3	2.2
1970 (I)	1.5	5.5	0.2	2.8
1970 (II)	1.8	6.5	0.5	3.2
1970 (III)	2.1	7.5	0.5	3.7
1970 (IV)	1.7	8.3	0.2	3.7
1971 (I)	0.7	8.5	−0.9	3.4
1971 (II)	0.4	9.4	−0.4	3.0
1971 (III)	−0.2	8.9	−0.4	2.3
1971 (IV)	−0.8	8.5	−0.3	−1.5
1972 (I)	−1.1	8.5	−2.3	2.4
1972 (II)	−2.2	6.7	0.6	−0.8
1972 (III)	−2.6	7.3	0.5	−1.1
1972 (IV)	−2.9	8.2	1.9	−2.0
1973 (I)	−3.3	9.1	4.3	−3.6
1973 (II)	−3.6	8.0	3.3	−3.5
1973 (III)	−3.8	10.2	3.7	−3.4
1973 (IV)	−4.1	11.2	3.0	−3.1

	Financial surplus % of GDP 4 period m.a.	Inflation rate (price of domestic final expenditure 4 period % change	Deviations of output from trend	Adjusted financial surplus
1974 (I)	−5.1	13.7	−0.7	−1.3
1974 (II)	−5.0	19.1	1.5	−1.1
1974 (III)	−5.6	20.7	1.9	−1.5
1974 (IV)	−6.6	21.8	−0.1	−1.1
1975 (I)	−7.0	24.2	−1.0	−0.3
1975 (II)	−7.9	26.3	−3.3	0.6
1975 (III)	−8.5	26.8	−4.6	0.9
1975 (IV)	−8.5	26.0	−4.7	0.8
1976 (I)	−8.3	19.2	−4.1	−1.1
1976 (II)	−8.3	16.4	−4.3	−1.6
1976 (III)	−8.3	13.7	−4.9	−2.0
1976 (IV)	−7.7	12.1	−3.7	−2.5
1977 (I)	−7.0	14.0	−3.8	−1.3
1977 (II)	−6.1	13.0	−5.2	0.3
1977 (III)	−5.0	13.0	−4.8	1.1
1977 (IV)	−4.6	10.4	−5.1	1.0
1978 (I)	−4.4	8.5^E	−4.5	0.4^E

but an allowance was made for changes in the inflation rate (by reference to the requirement to meet an increased money stock) and the oil balance trade deficit (it was argued that the balance of payments consequences were not caused by developments in the domestic economy). We have followed a broadly similar approach and adjusted the fiscal surplus as a proportion of GDP for inflation and output movements using the rules of thumb that a 1 per cent change in the inflation rate requires an offset of 0.25 per cent and a 1 per cent movement in output relative to trend requires an 0.6 per cent movement. The data are presented in Table 9.5 and graphed in Figure 9.2.

It is interesting to compare this with the behaviour of the growth of real money supply. This is done in Figure 9.3. The broad cyclical movement is very similar. In other words, the fiscal surplus, adjusted for movements in inflation and output, moves inversely with a measure of monetary stance. On this measure fiscal policy was being tightened during 1965 and 1966 when there was a sharp slowdown in real monetary growth. From early 1967 to early 1968 there is a period of sharp expansion on both measures, bringing with it the devaluation of sterling. Fiscal policy is then progressively tightened until late 1970; monetary policy follows the same pattern till late 1969, but then the strength of the external flows led to a monetary expansion against the background of the tight fiscal position. The expansion of the real money stock gathers pace until mid-1973 and is joined by fiscal policy from mid-1970. From mid-1973 until late 1975 there is another period of deflation which was reversed for a year and then reversed again; both measures show the same pattern.

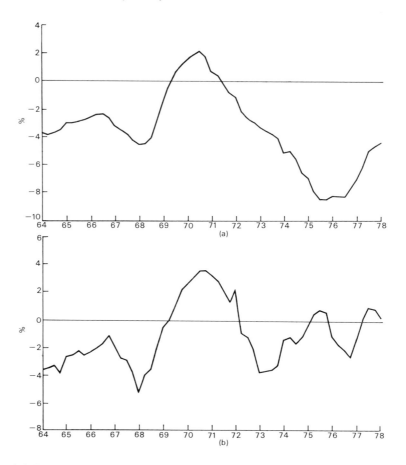

Fig. 9.2. Public sector financial surplus and adjustments for output and inflation: (a) Public sector financial surplus as a percentage of GDP; (b) Public sector financial surplus, adjusted for output and inflation, as a percentage of GDP.

It is not difficult to see why there is such a close correspondence; the periods when output is below trend and when our adjustment permits an increase in the fiscal deficit are precisely the circumstances when we expect DCE to be below the fiscal deficit as net lending will be negative. This close correspondence between the 'adjusted' fiscal deficit and the growth of the real money stock leads to the suggestion that we can think of the behaviour of the real monetary aggregates as an efficient measure of policy stance as it contains the impact of the 'adjusted' fiscal stance and also captures the influences of external flows.

The second group of simulations shows the way in which the economy adapts to a policy stance that is expansionary relative to the underlying growth of output and existing inflation rate. An expansionary policy would be here defined

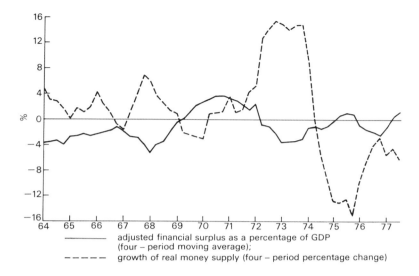

Fig. 9.3. Adjusted financial surplus and real money supply: ———— adjusted financial surplus as a percentage of GDP (four-period moving average);— — — — growth of real money supply (four-period percentage change).

as one in which the fiscal deficit was higher than justified by the current position of output relative to trend and the existing inflation rate. This would also tend to coincide with DCE less non-deposit liabilities as a proportion of the money supply being higher than the underlying growth of output plus the current inflation rate. Under these conditions we would expect the rate of currency depreciation to increase, generating a higher inflation rate and a higher private sector surplus. This continues until the fiscal deficit and DCE can be justified by the new inflation rate and higher private sector surplus.

Outstanding questions

The major outstanding issue is what happens if the stance of fiscal and monetary policy diverge in the short run, for example by the operation of 'the corset' or by a major capital inflow stemming from advantageous covered yields. 'The corset' enables monetary growth to be kept below the rate implied by fiscal policy by administrative regulation. In the model as it stands we would not directly capture any resulting squeeze upon expenditure as it is determined mainly by the fiscal variables and the inflation rate. Recently we have paid regard to the money multipliers presented in Table 9.1, adjusting private fixed investment and stock-building by the required amounts. We would like to incorporate deviations of net lending from its demand-determined level as adjustments in these functions, but so far this has not been formally done.

The second possibility is the use of large capital inflows to finance a borrowing requirement which is high relative to the monetary target. Under a floating exchange rate system, this would imply a current account deficit, a 'competitive' exchange rate and high domestic expenditure relative to output. We do not see this as a long-term possibility as it is inherently unstable; it works only as long as everyone believes it will work. If some overseas buyers lose confidence, the money supply increases; the exchange rate falls and the remaining holders of sterling experience a capital loss.

APPENDIX

VARIABLES CONTAINED IN THE TABLES

Code

ADJ	Expenditure estimate of GDP *minus* output estimate at 1970 prices
AEM	Average earnings in manufacturing, 1970=100
BAL	Current balance of payments (£m), seasonally adjusted
BALI	Invisible trade balance (£m), seasonally adjusted
BALV	Visible trade balance (£m), seasonally adjusted
BRG	Public sector borrowing requirement (£m), seasonally adjusted
BRG/	Public sector borrowing requirement as a percentage of GDP at current prices
C	Total consumers' expenditure at 1970 prices (£m), seasonally adjusted
CD	Durable consumption at 1970 prices (£m), seasonally adjusted
CND	Non-durable consumption at 1970 prices (£m), seasonally adjusted
DCE	Domestic credit expansion, seasonally adjusted
EDBA	Public sector debt interest payments (£m), seasonally adjusted
EER	Effective exchange rate for the UK, 1970=100
EGGA	Current grants from the public sector (£m), seasonally adjusted
ENIH	National Health and Insurance contributions (£m), seasonally adjusted
ESAB	Subsidies (£m), seasonally adjusted
FC	Net acquisition of financial assets by the company sector (£m), seasonally adjusted
FC/	Company sector NAFA as a percentage of GDP at current prices
FCA	Factor cost adjustment at 1970 prices (£m), seasonally adjusted
FG	Net acquisition of financial assets by the public sector (£m), seasonally adjusted
FG/	Public sector NAFA as a percentage of GDP at current prices
FJ	Net acquisition of financial assets by the personal sector (£m), seasonally adjusted
FJ/	Personal sector NAFA as a percentage of GDP at current prices
FO	Net acquisition of financial assets by the overseas sector (£m), seasonally adjusted
G	Public authorities' current expenditure on goods and services at 1970 prices (£m), seasonally adjusted
G$	Public authorities' current expenditure on goods and services (£m), seasonally adjusted
GDP	Gross domestic product (output based) at 1970 prices (£m), seasonally adjusted

GDP£	Gross domestic product (£m), seasonally adjusted
IF	Fixed investment at 1970 prices (£m), seasonally adjusted
II	Stock building at 1970 prices
INP	Private non-dwellings fixed investment at 1970 prices (£m), seasonally adjusted
KII	Stock level at 1970 prices
KM3£	Money stock sterling (£m), seasonally adjusted
LAJ/	Liquid assets of the personal sector as a proportion of disposable income
LE	Employees in employment in Great Britain (thousands)
LU	Wholly unemployed, excluding school-leavers in Great Britain (thousands), seasonally adjusted
M	Imports of goods and services at 1970 prices (£m), seasonally adjusted
M3$	UK sterling money supply (£m), seasonally adjusted
NLG/	Net lending as a percentage of GDP at current prices
PC	Consumer price index, 1970=1, seasonally adjusted
PG	Price index for government current expenditure on goods and services, 1970=1, seasonally adjusted
PGDP	Price index for the gross domestic product, 1970=1, seasonally adjusted
PIF	Price index for fixed investment, 1970=1, seasonally adjusted
PIMO	Index of wholesale prices of manufacturing output, 1970=100
PM	Price index for imports, 1970=1, seasonally adjusted
PMAN	Price index of imports of manufactured goods 1970=100
PRDM	Productivity in manufacturing industry, 1970=100
PX	Price index for exports, 1970=1, seasonally adjusted
PXGM	Price index of exports of manufactured goods, 1970=100
RL	Long-term rate of interest (2½% consols)
RLB	Minimum lending rate multiplied by 10
RS	Short-term rate of interest (91-day Treasury bills)
SJ$/	Personal sector savings ratio (%)
TEA	Taxes on expenditure (£m), seasonally adjusted
TJYP	Payments of UK personal income tax (£m), seasonally adjusted
TREF	Implicit tax rate on final expenditure index, 1970=1, seasonally adjusted
TYA	Receipts of income taxes (£m), seasonally adjusted
ULCM	Unit labour cost in manufacturing industry, 1970=100
X	Exports of goods and services at 1970 prices (£m), seasonally adjusted
YCT	Corporate gross trading profits net of stock appreciation (£m), seasonally adjusted
YD	Personal disposable income (£m), seasonally adjusted
YD/	Personal disposable income at 1970 prices (£m), seasonally adjusted
YGRA	Public sector receipts of rent, interest and dividends (£m), seasonally adjusted
YGTP	Public sector trading profits (£m), seasonally adjusted
YJG	Current grants to the personal sector from the public sector (£m), seasonally adjusted
YJO	Other personal income (£m), seasonally adjusted
YWS	Wages and salaries in the gross domestic product, seasonally adjusted (%)

FISCAL AND MONETARY POLICY IN AN OPEN ECONOMY*

M. Fetherston and W. Godley

This paper presents a model which, conditional on world trade, world prices and foreign interest rates as *exogenous* and on domestic tax rates, public expenditure authorizations, foreign trade policies, domestic interest rates and 'incomes policy' as *policy instruments*, will generate a path through time for real output, domestic prices and the movement of foreign exchange reserves as *policy targets*. One of our main purposes is to show rigorously that, on our assumptions, no presumption whatever can be established that a 'large' public sector financial deficit is 'difficult to finance' except to the extent that it has a counterpart in a loss of foreign exchange reserves; in our model, that is to say, 'crowding-out' cannot occur.

But we have reached these conclusions knowing very well that we have made some important simplifications. Our hope is that the consequence will at least be to clarify the questions at issue. Have we made wrong or inappropriate assumptions? Have we simplified crucial questions out of existence?

To put our position more aggressively, we find any macroeconomic model fundamentally defective that does not represent *all* of the following: the process of income and output determination, domestic prices, fiscal policy, interest rates, equilibrium relationships for stocks of assets, foreign trade, foreign prices and foreign interest rates, *and also adjustment processes for the whole system*.

So far as we know, all rigorous statements[1] so far published are guilty of omission in at least one of these respects; it is for instance common to see models in which full employment output is *assumed* to be constantly maintained, in which there is no representation of fiscal policy at all, and in which the 'money supply' (in one manifestation or other) is assumed to be an exogenous policy instrument without any specification of what a government would actually *do* (short of hiring a helicopter) to change it. Another approach that is quite commonly adopted, either explicitly or implicitly, is to discuss portfolio adjustment without relating this to income determination.

The deployment of our model is distinctly tedious, but unless we set out the ideas formally a verbal argument will inevitably become confused. 'Words strain, crack and sometimes break; under the burden, under the tension, slip, slide, perish, decay with imprecision, will not stay in place, will not stay still.'[2]

THE MODEL

Our expository device is first to postulate a 'baseline economy' endowed with arbitrary (though convenient) characteristics. We then consider rigorously what

*The authors are extremely grateful to Michael Anyadike Danes for extensive assistance in the preparation of this paper.

differences are made to the baseline economy if fiscal, interest rate or exchange rate policies are changed in precisely defined ways, or if the inflation rate changes because of higher import prices or because the increase in money wages changes exogenously. This procedure is similar to that used in two previous papers (Godley and May, 1977; Fetherston and Godley, 1978). The former paper was devoted to the relative impact of devaluation and import restrictions as instruments of trade policy; the latter paper introduced the asset market considerations (which are also the subject of attention in the present paper) in order to provide a specific critique of the monetary theory of the balance of payments. Here the main focus of attention is on the financing implications of budget deficits.[3]

The model presented below differs from that described in Fetherston and Godley (1978) mainly in that it introduces specific mechanisms to incorporate the effects of interest rate changes on asset demands, but much of the description of the model follows very similar lines. For convenience, all variables are defined as follows.

Definitions of variables

y	=	GDP
y_d	=	private disposable income
p	=	total domestic private expenditure
g	=	government expenditure on goods and services
x	=	exports
m	=	imports
πp	=	price of private expenditure
πg	=	price of government expenditure
πx	=	price of exports
πm	=	price of imports
πwm	=	world prices of materials
πwx	=	world prices of manufactures
t_d	=	direct tax yield
t_i	=	net indirect tax yield (assumed all to be border tariffs or export subsidies)
r	=	domestic interest rate
r_F	=	foreign interest rate
sfa	=	stocks of financial assets held by private sector
sbg	=	stocks of bonds
sbf	=	stocks of foreign assets
sc	=	stocks of cash
bof	=	balance of official settlements
$sfbg$	=	overseas holdings of public sector liabilities
ulc	=	unit labour costs
aw	=	average earnings

e = employment
cc = current normal unit costs

General: Upper and lower-case symbols represent the same variables in respectively the baseline and lower-case economies. Bars over symbols mean that the variable is denominated in constant prices; otherwise all variables are measured at current prices.

At the level of *accounting identities* our baseline economy has the following characteristics. The income–expenditure identity at current prices is given by

$$Y \equiv P + G + X - M. \tag{10.1}$$

where Y is GDP, P is total private expenditure, G is public expenditure on goods and services, and X, M are respectively exports and imports of goods and services all in current prices. The private sector, including the banks, holds as financial assets (SFA) government bonds (SBG), foreign assets (SBF) and cash (SC), measured at the end of each period:

$$SFA \equiv SBG + SBF + SC. \tag{10.2}$$

The flow of funds identities are given by

$$(G - T) + (X - M) \equiv (Y - T - P) \equiv \Delta SFA \tag{10.3}$$

where T is the tax yield, which is assumed to flow from direct taxation and also from border taxes less subsidies.

The balance of official settlements (BOF) is given by the current balance of payments less the increase in holdings of foreign assets (ΔSBF) plus any increase in overseas holdings of public sector liabilities ($\Delta SFBG$)

$$BOF \equiv X - M - \Delta SBF + \Delta SFBG. \tag{10.4}$$

Unit labour costs (ULC) are given by

$$ULC \equiv AW \cdot \frac{E}{Y} \tag{10.5}$$

where AW is average earnings and E is employment.

For simplicity it is assumed that there are no indirect taxes or subsidies and no interest payments. (A table of numerical results which do allow for interest payments is shown in Appendix 2 however. Note that, without interest payments, and assuming zero net transfers, the current balance of payments is identical with the balance on goods and services.) In the domestic financial system the banking sector is consolidated with the rest of the private sector, and together they hold three outside financial assets—money and domestic bonds issued by the government, and assets held abroad (referred to as foreign bonds). Thus in conventional terms 'money' consists of notes and coin and the reserves of the banking system, but not bank deposits. Note also that in what follows we abstract completely from the effects of changes in capital values of bonds associated with changes in interest rates. This can be accommodated by assuming that the bonds pay a variable coupon, or that they are in effect interest-bearing capital-certain deposits at the central bank. These bonds are assumed to be held by foreigners as well as by the domestic private sector.

We next assume, arbitrarily though conveniently, that the baseline economy has the following *ex post* characteristics. Real growth is steady through time at a rate that falls progressively below that of productive potential[4]; inflation is zero; the exchange rate is constant; the current balance and the balance of official settlements are both zero; domestic and foreign interest rates are constant; and all financial asset holdings rise at the same rate as (money and real) GDP. It is an implication of these assumptions that domestic holdings of foreign bonds, and foreign holdings of domestic bonds, increase in absolute terms by the same amount in each period, in order that the current and overall balances of payments be equal.

THE 'LOWER-CASE' ECONOMY

We now administer shocks to the baseline economy by changing selected policy instruments and also exogenous variables like world prices singly and in combination, and then solve, conditional on the 'lower-case' model given below, for differences compared with what would otherwise have happened.

Identities in the lower-case economy

All lower-case (l.c.) symbols refer to changes compared with the baseline economy. For flows of income and expenditure, stocks of assets and the level of average earnings, these changes are expressed as absolute differences, while costs and prices are expressed as ratios of baseline values.

The income–expenditure identity at current market prices is

$$y \equiv p + g + x - m \tag{10.6}$$

and at constant market prices,

$$\bar{y} \equiv \bar{p} + \bar{g} + \bar{x} - \bar{m} . \tag{10.7}$$

The components of expenditure in equations (10.6) and (10.7) are related by price ratios (denoted by the prefix π) such that

$$p \equiv \bar{p}.\pi p + P(\pi p - 1) \tag{10.8}$$

$$g \equiv \bar{g}.\pi g + G(\pi g - 1) \tag{10.9}$$

$$x \equiv \bar{x}.\pi x + X(\pi x - 1) \tag{10.10}$$

$$m \equiv \bar{m}.\pi m + M(\pi m - 1). \tag{10.11}$$

Private post-tax income (yd) is

$$yd \equiv y - t_d - t_i \tag{10.12}$$

where the subscripts d and i indicate respectively direct and net indirect taxation (assumed all to be border tariffs or export subsidies).

Functional relationships and policy instruments

The pivotal functional relationships assumed to hold in the l.c. economy concern stocks of financial assets held by the private sector. At the end of each year these are *always in an equilibrium relationship with the average level of disposable private income in that year.* We are deliberately making an extremely strict asset equilibrium condition in order to demonstrate that, even then, no 'crowding-out' problem can arise on our assumptions. If fiscal policy cannot generate independent problems for monetary policy under this condition it will not do so, *a fortiori*, under weaker conditions.

More precisely, it is assumed that at the end of each year *total* holdings of domestic bonds (baseline plus lower case with everything denominated in money terms) are given by

$$SBG + sbg = \lambda_1 (1-\alpha)\left(YD + \left(\frac{r}{R}\right)^{\beta_1}\left(\frac{r_F}{R_F}\right)^{\gamma_1} yd\right) \quad (10.13)$$

where r is the domestic interest rate, r_F the foreign rate, and R and R_F are their baseline equivalents. (These are defined such that $100(r-1)$ is the percentage rate of interest; i.e., a 3 per cent interest rate implies a value for r of 1.03.) Since $yd = 0$ and $r = R$, $r_F = R_F$ characterize the baseline situation where $sbg = 0$, by definition, this specification implies

$$SBG = \lambda_1 (1-\alpha)YD \quad (10.14)$$

$$sbg = \lambda_1 (1-\alpha)\left[\left(\frac{r}{R}\right)^{\beta_1}\left(\frac{r_F}{R_F}\right)^{\gamma_1}\right]. \quad (10.15)$$

Similarly, for foreign bonds and cash we write

$$SBF = \lambda_2 (1-\alpha)YD \quad (10.16)$$

$$sbf = \lambda_2 (1-\alpha)\left[\left(\frac{r}{R}\right)^{\beta_2}\left(\frac{r_F}{R_F}\right)^{\gamma_2}\right] \quad (10.17)$$

$$SC = \lambda_3 (1-\alpha)YD \quad (10.18)$$

$$sc = \lambda_3 (1-\alpha)\left[\left(\frac{r}{R}\right)^{\beta_3}\left(\frac{r_F}{R_F}\right)^{\gamma_3}\right]. \quad (10.19)$$

The portfolio allocation coefficients λ_1, λ_2, λ_3 are taken to sum to unity, so that in the baseline economy

$$SFA \equiv SBG + SBF + SC = (1-\alpha)YD \quad (10.20)$$

and $(1-\alpha)$ is thus the ratio of total financial wealth to disposable income in the baseline economy. For the l.c. economy we have

$$sfa = (1 - \alpha)\left[\lambda_1 \left(\frac{r}{R}\right)^{\beta_1}\left(\frac{r_F}{R_F}\right)^{\gamma_1} + \lambda_2 \left(\frac{r}{R}\right)^{\beta_2}\left(\frac{r_F}{R_F}\right)^{\gamma_2}\right.$$
$$\left. + \lambda_3 \left(\frac{r}{R}\right)^{\beta_3}\left(\frac{r_F}{R_F}\right)^{\gamma_3}\right] \tag{10.21}$$

which, at baseline interest rates (i.e. $r = R$, $r_F = R_F$), reduces to

$$sfa = (1-\alpha)yd \tag{10.22}$$

with $sbg = \lambda_1 (1-\alpha)yd$, etc.

Private expenditure in money terms must be inferred from the identity

$$p \equiv yd - \Delta sfa. \tag{10.23}$$

Note that at unchanged interest rates this implies

$$p = \alpha yd + (1-\alpha)yd_{-1} \tag{10.23a}$$

which is the 'New Cambridge' equation in which all of private disposable income is spent with a fairly short lag. The 'New Cambridge' empirical results (Cripps, Fetherston and Godley, 1974; 1976) are thus *consistent* with a world of rapid adjustment to equilibrium financial asset holdings, although the empirical results do not imply that the actual behaviour of asset-holding takes the precise form specified in this model.

Note also that this specification incorporates a deflationary impact of inflation on private expenditure operating via a wealth effect: a rise in the price level accompanied by higher nominal income requires an increase in nominal values of asset holdings in order to restore portfolio equilibrium, and the process of adjustment entails a rise in the ratio of net acquisition of financial assets to disposable income.

The interest rate elasticities for asset holdings are assumed to have the following signs:

$$\beta_1, \gamma_2 \geqslant 0$$
$$\beta_2, \beta_3, \gamma_1, \gamma_3 \leqslant 0.$$

For foreigners' asset holdings, a similar approach using world trade (WT) and interest rates yields the expressions

$$SFBG = \theta \cdot WT \tag{10.24}$$

$$sfbg = \theta \cdot WT \left[\left(\frac{r}{R}\right)^{\beta_4} \cdot \left(\frac{r_F}{R_F}\right)^{\gamma_4} - 1\right] \tag{10.25}$$

where $\theta, \beta_4 > 0$, $\gamma_4 < 0$.

The policy instruments assumed to be available are seven in number, and are briefly described as follows:

1. discretionary changes in the rate of direct tax (τ_d);
2. discretionary changes in real public expenditure ($\bar{g}$);
3. tariffs on all imports of goods and services (τ_m);
4. subsidies on all exports of goods and services (σ_x);
5. changing interest rates: this, under our assumptions, is done simply by announcing that interest-bearing deposits now yield more or less;
6. 'incomes policy', which shifts the outcome of the wage bargain down below where it otherwise would have been (see equation (10.26) below);
7. devaluation, which is simulated by setting $\tau_m = \sigma_x$, implies that net property income flows from abroad and capital values of internationally held assets do not change their sterling value at 'devaluation'.

Real interest rates are defined as nominal rates adjusted for expected inflation, but it will be assumed throughout that expected inflation rates are zero, and hence that real and nominal rates are equal. Domestic monetary policy is assumed to involve supplying cash and bonds in whatever amounts are necessary to maintain private (and overseas) portfolio equilibrium at specified rates of interest, so that asset holdings are always demand-determined for given interest rates. Intervention in the foreign exchange market takes the form of supporting the baseline exchange rate.

The remainder of the l.c. economy comprises conventional assumptions about trade propensities and elasticities to determine trade flows, together with rather less conventional assumptions about money wage and price determination (Godley and Nordhaus, 1972; Coutts, Godley and Nordhaus, 1978; Coutts, Tarling and Wilkinson, 1976).

Average money earnings, excluding changes in overtime (aw), are given by

$$aw = AW \left[\frac{(1-\tau)}{(1-\tau-\tau_d)_{-1}} \, \pi p_{-1} - 1 \right] + wd \cdot \frac{\pi p_{-1}}{(1-\tau-\tau_d)_{-1}} \qquad (10.26)$$

If we ignore the second term on the right-hand side (i.e. if $wd = 0$), this equation says that, if prices are altered in one period ($\pi p \neq 0$), then the money wage bargain in the succeeding period will add to money disposable income the amount that will restore, at the time the bargain is made, the *real* disposable wage to where it otherwise would have been. The variable wd permits exogenous shifts in the target real post-tax wage at settlement—a positive one to represent a wage 'explosion', a negative one perhaps to allow for the effects of incomes policy.

'Normal' unit costs (ulc) are given by the index number

$$ulc = \frac{aw}{AW} + 1 \qquad (10.27)$$

Where 'normal' here and elsewhere means that the variables are corrected for reversible cyclical effects.

Any addition to normal wages compared with the baseline economy thus adds an equal proportionate amount to unit labour costs.

The expressions for import and export prices[5] are:

$$\pi m = 1 + v(\pi p - 1) - v\tau_m + (1-v)(\pi wm - 1) \qquad (10.28)$$
$$= v(\pi p - \tau_m) + (1-v)\pi wm \qquad (10.28a)$$
$$\pi x = 1 + u(\pi p - 1) - u\sigma_x + (1-u)(\pi wx - 1) \qquad (10.29)$$
$$= u(\pi p - \sigma_x) + (1-u)\pi wx \qquad (10.29a)$$

where πwm and πwx are indices that represent exogenous shifts in world prices of raw materials (including oil) and of manufactures respectively, and $0 < v < 1$, $0 < u < 1$.

Import and export prices (compared with the baseline economy, which provides both foreign prices and world terms of trade) are each determined by domestic prices, by exogenous changes in world prices and by import taxes and export subsidies (Llewellyn, 1974). A rise in domestic or world prices thus causes a (less than proportional) rise in import prices and a tariff causes a (less than proportional) fall in (ex-tax) import prices. There is an equivalence, indicated by the parameter v, such that a rise in domestic prices of 10 per cent causes import prices to rise by the same amount as a tariff of 10 per cent causes them to fall. The same is true of exports, *mutatis mutandis*.

Current (normal) unit costs of production (as a ratio of those in the baseline) are given by the index number

$$cc = \omega.\pi m(1+\tau_m) + (1-\omega)ulc \qquad (10.30)$$

where ω represents the share of imports in costs, i.e. $\omega = (M+m)/(Y+y+M+m)$. Domestic prices are given by the index number

$$\pi p = \xi cc + (1-\xi)cc_{-1} \qquad (10.31)$$

where ξ represents the historic cost lag (determined by the average production period), so that domestic prices are determined by lagged normal unit costs. It is assumed by implication that the 'normal' profit margin on historic costs is invariant to demand pressure and is the same as in the baseline economy. For simplicity it is further assumed that the price of public expenditure is equal to the price of private expenditure, i.e., $\pi g = \pi p$.

Import and export volumes are determined conventionally as lagged responses to changes in relative prices and also, in the case of imports, by output:

$$\bar{m} = \mu\bar{y} - \eta M \{\Sigma a_i [\pi m (1 + \tau_m) / \pi p]_{-i} - 1\} \qquad (10.32)$$
$$\bar{x} = -\epsilon X (\Sigma a_i \pi x_{-i} - 1) \qquad (10.33)$$

where η, ϵ are the price elasticities of demand for imports and exports and the a_i are lag coefficients (assumed the same for exports and imports) which sum to unity.

The yield of net indirect taxation is given by

$$t_i = \tau_m (M + m) - \sigma_x (X + x) \tag{10.34}$$

and of direct taxation by

$$t_d = \tau(y - t_i) + \tau_d (Y + y - t_i). \tag{10.35}$$

The flow of funds identity may then be written as

$$(yd - p) + (t_i + t_d - g) + (m - x) \equiv 0. \tag{10.36}$$

The balance of official settlements is given by

$$bof = x - m - \Delta sbf + \Delta sfbg. \tag{10.37}$$

SOME SOLUTIONS

In this section we illustrate the properties of the system described in the preceding paragraphs by shocking the baseline economy in various different ways.

One of the main points we are trying to show is that under our assumptions funding and portfolio adjustment is a non-problem. This we do by building into the model a complete adjustment process; so *every* solution we obtain will fulfil the condition that at the end of each year the stock of financial assets and its composition will be in the desired relationship (given the level of interest rates) to the level of disposable income attained on average during the year.

The reader who has had the patience to follow us thus far may at this point be coming to the conclusion that we are demonstrating something monumentally obvious, given our assumptions. If we *assume* constant asset income equilibrium, obviously our model cannot throw up asset income *dis*equilibrium. To this the reply is that in our view the results are indeed an elaborate demonstration of the obvious; for, to put it quite generally, the government will only need (given its internal and external objectives) to create financial assets by deficit spending to the exact extent to which the private sector wishes to acquire them, i.e. to the extent to which its income exceeds its expenditure. In our view the whole controversy about crowding-out is radically misguided because it discusses portfolio equilibrium outside the context of the adjustment of the whole economy, through a multiplier process, towards dynamic equilibrium.

To return to our model, recall now that the growth rate of the baseline economy is assumed to be kept below the rate of growth of productive potential by the need to meet balance of payments constraints. In the simulations described below we first assume that the government reacts to the rising level of unemployment by applying a fiscal stimulus in year 1 of sufficient magnitude to restore employment to the 'full employment' (year 0) level in year 5 (although in the absence of further stimuli unemployment would begin to rise again thereafter). For the purpose of generating numbers it is assumed that the growth rate of the baseline economy is 3 per cent per annum, as compared with

with a full employment rate of 4 per cent. Other numerical values for the baseline economy, and the parameters of the l.c. economy, are generally chosen to correspond to a reasonable approximation with those in our large econometric model (Fetherston and Coutts, 1978), and are given in the Appendix. An exception concerns the parameters in the stylized portfolio balance equations, since our large model contains at present no equivalent relationships apart from the lags between private income and expenditure which implicitly specify the value of α.

Table 10.1 shows the results of a simulation generated just by applying and maintaining the initial stimulus to public expenditure so as to raise GDP in year 5 by just under 5 per cent (£5,504 million). Monetary policy consists of financing the increased public sector debt so as to maintain constant interest rates, and balance of payments outflows are financed by intervention at the given exchange rate. In each case the analytic solution is given in a column to the left of the numerical solution.

The first point to note about these results is that the 'long-run' effects are clearly unsustainable: for here we have the quintessential 'New Cambridge' result where the change in the *ex post* public sector deficit is, in the long run, fully reflected in a change in the current account (and in this case also in official financing). The effect of this large fiscal expansion is thus to generate a large recurring payments deficit. The short-run impact on real output and the balance of payments is smaller, while private asset holdings are adjusted upwards with the rise in disposable income. Once that rise ceases, net acquisition of financial assets (relative to the baseline situation) becomes zero.

The distribution of the private sector's asset holdings between cash, bonds and foreign assets is given solely by the parameters λ_1, λ_2 and λ_3 since interest rates are kept constant. The increased public sector deficit is thus financed partly by increased holdings of cash, partly by increased domestic holdings of bonds, and the remainder by reduction in foreign exchange reserves—which is in turn equal to the current balance plus that part of increased private asset holdings that goes overseas. In the long run, flow changes in private asset holdings are zero and the increase in the public sector deficit (in flow terms) is financed entirely by reduction in foreign exchange reserves. Private holdings of financial wealth have increased, but by just the amount and at precisely the rate that is commensurate with the rise in income, and in just such proportions as preserve the existing structure and level of interest rates.

In Table 10.1 it is assumed that monetary policy is operated so as to maintain the baseline domestic interest rate. In the simulation shown in Table 10.2 the initial step adjustment in public expenditure designed to achieve an output target in year 5 is now accompanied by a maintained rise in the domestic interest rate (here assumed to move from 3 to 5 per cent; i.e., $R = 1.03, r = 1.05$). This is done mainly to illustrate the properties of the portfolio balance mechanism, as there is no inherent reason why the authorities should wish to permit interest

TABLE 10.1

Effects of an Increase in Real Public Expenditure, $\bar{g}$†

	1st year			Long run
Real output ($\bar{y}$)	$\dfrac{\bar{g}}{1+\alpha(1-\tau)+\mu}$	3,765	$\dfrac{\bar{g}}{\tau+\mu}$	5,522
Real private expenditure ($\bar{p}$)	$\dfrac{\alpha(1-\tau)\bar{g}}{1-\alpha(1-\tau)+\mu}$	1,581	$\dfrac{(1-\tau)\bar{g}}{\tau+\mu}$	3,865
Private net acquisition of financial assets (Δsfa)	$\dfrac{(1-\alpha)(1-\tau)\bar{g}}{1-\alpha(1-\tau)+\mu}$	1,054	0	0
Private stocks of bonds (sbg)	$\dfrac{\lambda_1(1-\alpha)(1-\tau)\bar{g}}{1-\alpha(1-\tau)+\mu}$	527	$\dfrac{\lambda_1(1-\alpha)(1-\tau)\bar{g}}{\tau+\mu}$	773
Public sector deficit ($g-t_d-t_i$)	$\dfrac{[(1-\alpha)(1-\tau)+\mu]\bar{g}}{1-\alpha(1-\tau)+\mu}$	2,184	$\dfrac{\mu\bar{g}}{\tau+\mu}$	1,657
Current balance of payments ($x-m$)	$\dfrac{-\mu\bar{g}}{1-\alpha(1-\tau)+\mu}$	−1,129	$\dfrac{-\mu\bar{g}}{\tau+\mu}$	−1,657
Balance of official settlements (bof)	$\dfrac{-[\mu+\lambda_2(1-\alpha)(1-\tau)]\bar{g}}{1-\alpha(1-\tau)+\mu}$	−1,235	$\dfrac{-\mu\bar{g}}{\tau+\mu}$	−1,657
		Ratios		
Price level (πp)		1.0		1.0
Terms of trade ($\pi x/\pi m$)		1.0		1.0

†Numerical values are given for $\bar{g} = 3,313$.

rates to rise in this fashion, unless in an attempt to offset the adverse balance of payments impact of expansionary fiscal policy by attracting a capital inflow. Such an attempt can be seen to have rather limited impact in the simulation, for two reasons: first, the effect on asset holdings is virtually once-and-for-all, as portfolios are adjusted in the first period following the interest rate change; and second, the arbitrary, though in our view plausible, numbers chosen for β_1, β_2, β_3, β_4 generate rather small responses even initially, while on the capital account substitution effects are partly offset by an income effect on the demand for foreign bonds. Larger coefficients would certainly improve the first period response, by amplifying the switch from foreign to domestic bonds by both the private sector and foreigners, but they could not help with the long-run problem,

TABLE 10.2

Effects of Increased Public Expenditure Accompanied by a Rise in Interest Rates

		1st year		Long run
		£m		£m
Real output ($\bar{y}$)	$\dfrac{\bar{g}}{1+\mu-(1-(1-\alpha)\phi)(1-\tau)}$	3649	$\dfrac{\bar{g}}{\tau+\mu}$	5535
Real private expenditure ($\bar{p}$)	$(1-(1-\alpha)\phi)(1-\tau)\bar{y}$	1423	$(1+\mu)\bar{y}-\bar{g}$	3875
Private net acquisition of financial assets (Δsfa)	$(1-\alpha)\phi(1-\tau)\bar{y}$	1131		0
Private holdings of bonds (sbg)	$\lambda_1\left(\dfrac{r}{R}\right)^{\beta_1}(1-\alpha)(1-\tau)\bar{y}$	1042	$\lambda_1(1-\alpha)\bar{y}(1-\tau)\left(\dfrac{r}{R}\right)^{\beta_1}$	791
Public sector deficit ($g-t_i-t_d$)	$\bar{g}-\tau\bar{y}$	2226	$\bar{g}-\tau\bar{y}$	1661
Current balance of payments ($x-m$)	$-\mu\bar{y}$	-1095	$-\mu\bar{y}$	-1661
Balance of official settlements (bof)	see note (a)	-1194	$-\mu\bar{y}$	-1661
			Ratios	
Price level (πp)		1.0		1.0
Terms of trade ($\pi x/\pi m$)		1.0		1.0

Notes:

$$\bar{g} = 3321$$

$$\phi = \left(\lambda_1\left(\frac{r}{R}\right)^{\beta_1} + \lambda_2\left(\frac{r}{R}\right)^{\beta_2} + \lambda_3\left(\frac{r}{R}\right)^{\beta_3}\right)$$

(a) First year effect on $bof = -\mu\bar{y}-\lambda_2\left(\dfrac{r}{R}\right)^{\beta_4}(1-\alpha)(1-\tau)\bar{y} + \theta(WT-WT_{-1})\left(\dfrac{r}{R}\right)^{\beta_4} - 1$

namely that in a model where interest rates influence *stock* asset demands, only continuing changes in interest rates can offset a permanent *flow* imbalance on the current account.

Note that there is a small increase in the required degree of fiscal expansion as compared with Table 10.1, owing to the small deflationary impact of the interest rate change still operating by year 5.

Neither of the simulations in Tables 10.1 and 10.2 can be regarded as feasible in policy terms because of the adverse impact of fiscal expansion on the balance of payments. Table 10.3 thus shows results of a simulation where another instrument, 'devaluation' (i.e. a combination of export subsidies and import tariffs), is brought into play alongside fiscal policy. The targets now in force are the 'full employment' level of output in year 5, and a zero current balance, also in year 5. Here we show only numerical results, as explicit analytic solutions are not easily obtainable.

The required degree of fiscal expansion is roughly halved, owing to the expansionary impact of devaluation on real demand (despite the fact that under these assumptions the devaluation is fully eroded in the long run by a higher domestic price level). The current balance deteriorates initially with the J-curve effect before reaching balance in year 5: subsequently, however, slow deterioration recurs as the real impact of devaluation is diminished. As in Table 10.1, the fiscal deficit is financed by supplying appropriate quantities of financial assets to preserve portfolio equilibrium at baseline interest rates.

Table 10.4 shows the results of a simulation with a significant inflationary impulse. It is assumed that there is an exogenous wage 'explosion', with workers attempting in year 1 to achieve a gain of 10 per cent in their real post-tax wage at settlement, and seeking thereafter to preserve this gain through compensation for subsequent price changes. The tariff/subsidy scheme acting as a proxy for devaluation is operated to preserve trade competitiveness, with fiscal policy in the shape of public expenditure adjusted in each period to maintain baseline GDP (and thus, given the immediately preceding assumptions, to maintain a zero current balance also).

The figures in the table clearly illustrate the positive impact of inflation on the private sector's demand for financial assets, and on the consequent need to run a fiscal deficit in order to meet this demand and at the same time to sustain the baseline level of aggregate demand (given that the current account is being kept in balance). Note, however, that our assumption of zero inflation expectations, already somewhat undermined by the step devaluation of Table 10.3, becomes very hard to justify in this context when wage pressure combined with devaluation establishes a continuous inflationary process at a rate of around 7 per cent per annum. It might therefore be expected that nominal interest rates would have to rise in order to preserve the baseline real interest rate. The effects of this would then need to be taken into account in simulations that include the effects of interest *payments* on the distribution of disposable incomes between sectors, such as that shown in Appendix 2.

Finally, Table 10.5 shows the impact of a 10 per cent increase in world raw materials prices (see n.5), assuming no offsetting changes in the values of policy instruments. In the long run, domestic prices and wages respond in full, but there is a permanent loss on the terms of trade as export prices are partially held in check by competing world prices. Throughout there are substantial losses of real output and on the balance of payments which render the long-run

TABLE 10.3

Effects of Increased Public Expenditure Accompanied by 'Devaluation'

	Year 1	Year 5
	£m.	£m.
Real output ($\bar{y}$)	1,929	5,504
(% of baseline)	(1.95)	(4.95)
Real private expenditure ($\bar{p}$)	256	3,397
(% of baseline)	(0.37)	(4.41)
Private net acquisition of financial assets (Δsfa)	559	194
(% of baseline GDP)	(0.57)	(0.17)
Private holdings of bonds (sbg)	280	1,260
(% of baseline GDP)	(0.28)	(1.13)
Public sector deficit ($g-t_i-t_d$)	1,312	194
(% of baseline GDP)	(1.33)	(0.17)
Current balance of payments ($x-m$)	−753	0
(% of baseline GDP)	(−0.76)	(0.00)
Balance of official settlements (bof)	−809	−20
(% of baseline GDP)	(−0.82)	(−0.02)
	Ratios	
Price level (πp)	1.009	1.034
Terms of trade ($\pi x/\pi m$)	0.975	0.988

Notes: $\bar{g} = 1682$
$\tau_m = \sigma_x = 0.05796$

TABLE 10.4

Effects of Wage-inflation Impulse Accompanied by Offsetting 'Devaluation'

	Year 1	Year 5
	£m.	£m.
Real output ($\bar{y}$)	0	0
Real private expenditure ($\bar{p}$)	−1,621	−2,017
(% of baseline)	(−2.37)	(−2.62)
Private net acquisition of financial assets (Δsfa)	1,776	3,201
(% of baseline GDP)	(1.80)	(2.88)
Private holdings of bonds (sbg)	888	6,305
(% of baseline GDP)	(0.90)	(5.67)
Public sector deficit ($g-t_d-t_i$)	1,776	3,201
(% of baseline GDP)	(1.80)	(2.88)
Current balance of payments ($x-m$)	0	0
(% of baseline GDP)		
Balance of official settlements (bof)	−178	−320
(% of baseline GDP)	(−0.18)	(−0.29)
	Ratios	
Price level (πp)	1.064	1.405
Terms of trade ($kx/\pi m$)	1.0	1.0

TABLE 10.5

Effects of a 10% Increase in World Raw Materials Prices (πwm)†

	Year 1		Year 5
	£m.		£m.
Real output ($\bar{y}$)	−1,463		−4.473
(% of baseline)	(−1.48)		(−4.02)
Real private expenditure ($\bar{p}$)	−1,996		−4,386
(% of baseline)	(−2.92)		(−5.70)
Private net acquisition of financial assets (Δsfa)	−681		49
(% of baseline GDP)	(−0.70)		(0.04)
Private stocks of bonds (sbg)	−340		−25
(% of baseline GDP)	(−0.34)		(−0.02)
Public sector deficit ($g-t_i-t_d$)	1,177		2,043
(% of baseline GDP)	(1.19)		(1.84)
Current balance of payments ($x-m$)	−1,858		−1,994
(% of baseline GDP)	(−1.88)		(−1.79)
Balance of official settlements (bof)	−1,790		−1,999
(% of baseline GDP)	(−1.81)		(−1.80)
	Ratios		Long run
Price level (πp)	1.015	1.058	1.1
Terms of trade ($\pi x/\pi m$)	0.924	0.944	0.964

† $\pi wm = 1.1$

outcome purely academic, as the intervening payments deficits would impose heavy financing burdens which might in practice have to be averted by off-setting policy measures.

CONCLUSION

We end by reiterating the specific nature of our arguments that financing a large budget deficit need not be a problem. As should be apparent from the simulations, we are in no way arguing that fiscal policy never runs into difficulties for, on the contrary, we have many times (in other contexts) propounded the view that fiscal mismanagement has contributed significantly to Britain's poor economic performance in recent decades. In particular, inappropriate fiscal expansion may well cause severe balance of payments difficulties when associated with a high propensity to import or with adverse shifts in speculative sentiment. We have made no attempt to model such speculative behaviour, as to do so seems an impossible task; however, we finish with the observation that fiscal policy may in fact encounter difficulties when high private sector demand for public sector liabilities requires a large budget deficit to sustain a given level of output, and yet speculators are accustomed to reacting adversely to publication of large PSBR figures.

APPENDIX 1

PARAMETER VALUES

Parameter	Value
μ	0.3
τ	0.3
α	0.6
λ_1	0.5
λ_2	0.1
λ_3	0.4
β_1	1.0
β_2	−0.2
β_3	−0.3
β_4	2.0
γ_1	−0.04
γ_2	1.0
γ_3	−0.05
γ_4	−0.04
h	0.03
ν	0.1
u	0.6
ξ	0.7
η	0.5
a_1	0.2
a_2	0.3
a_3	0.3
a_4	0.2
ϵ	2.5
θ	0.0093

THE BASELINE ECONOMY IN YEAR 1

	(£m.)
P	68,367
G	30,451
X	29,645
M	29,645
Y	98,818
T	29,645
SBG	13,835
SBF	2,767
SC	11,068
SFA	27,670
ΔSFA	806

ΔSBF	81
$\Delta SFBG$	81
BOF	0
WT	296,454
E (thousands)	23,042
AW (£ thousand)	3.139
ULC (£ thousand)	0.732
R	1.03
R_F	1.03

APPENDIX 2

Table 10.A repeats the numerical results of Table 10.1 in the main text but allowing for the effects of interest payments on the distribution of disposable income between sectors. Interest is assumed to be paid annually in arrears. The necessary additions to the model of the l.c. economy in the text are equations determining net interest receipts/payments by each sector—private, public and overseas—as functions of asset stocks and interest rates, and to redefine private pre-tax income, the public sector deficit and the current balance of payments to allow for intersectoral flows of interest payments.

TABLE 10.A

Effects of an Increase in Real Public Expenditure, $\bar{g}$

	1st year	Long run
	£m.	£m.
$\bar{y}$	3,744	5,524
$\bar{p}$	1,573	3,886
Δsfa	1,048	0
sbg	524	777
$g-t_i-t_d+ig$	2,171	1,652
$x-m-io$	−1,123	−1,652
bof	−1,228	−1,652
	Ratios	
πp	1.0	1.0
$\pi x/\pi m$	1.0	1.0

Notes

$\bar{g} = 3,295$

Net interest payments to foreigners, io, now enter the current balance as a debit item, and public sector interest payments, ig, augment the public sector deficit.

NOTES

CHAPTER 1 FISCAL AND MONETARY POLICY—THE ISSUES

[1] With imperfect capital mobility and an exchange rate that is not expected to change (even though it does!), the domestic interest rate could stand above (or below) world rates, and interest parity would be observed. However, permanent equilibria of this type following a bond-financed fiscal expansion are in general ruled out, since the exchange rate is required either to appreciate to eliminate an incipient overall surplus (as in the perfect mobility case and with identical results) or to depreciate to eliminate an incipient deficit (in which event the result is unstable, requiring limitless depreciation and ever-increasing output).

[2] A more extended treatment is given in Brown *et al.* (1980); see also Artis and Currie (1981).

[3] Illustrating the complaint against the counterfactual nature of simulations of this type, see Ball, Burns and Warburton (1978, pp. 14–15), where dissatisfaction with this kind of long-run property motivates the employment of a revised export pricing function which appears to alleviate (though not completely to remove) this implication of assuming a fixed lag structure.

[4] See Denham and Lomax (1978).

[5] The Fetherston and Godley account, and their interest rate simulations, are eloquent on this score.

[6] Thus, the Fetherston and Godley simulation reported in Table 1.1 is not closely comparable with the others reported there. It does, however, have the property that the exchange rate is so changed as to clear the current account, which—as suggested above—is a stylized equivalent of the long-run exchange rate requirement in the other models.

[7] Strictly speaking, the term 'crowding-out' is something of a misnomer here, since the table does not show, as would be required for conventional measures of crowding-out, the difference between the simulated effects of a given fiscal shock conditional upon *alternative* patterns of financing. Rather, one particular financing path, specific to the model in question, is assumed for each simulation.

[8] The constant interest rate–no devaluation multiplier is, as Fetherston and Godley point out (p. 173 below) nothing but $(m + t)^{-1}$, where m is the marginal propensity to import and t the marginal tax rate. Ignoring the added volume of net exports needed to counter the terms of trade deterioration implicit in the devaluation, and assuming that the marginal propensity to import *is* invariant with respect to the expenditure composition of GDP, and with respect to the exchange rate, the requirement to hold the current account constant must require that the incipient import leakage attributable to this fiscal policy be offset by an equivalent increase in net exports after taking account of the associated further income-induced imports. Simplifying in this way, if $\Delta M = m(m + t)^{-1} \Delta G$ represents the incipient worsening in the current account, an increase in net exports associated with devaluation of ΔX is required such that $\Delta X - m(m + t)^{-1} \Delta X = m(m + t)^{-1} \Delta G$. Since m and t are of the same order of magnitude, this means that $\Delta X = \Delta G$.

CHAPTER 2 MONETARY AND FISCAL POLICY AND THE CROWDING-OUT ISSUE

[1] There are a number of reasons why crowding-out need not occur even at full employment. (For a recent discussion opposing the view of Barro, 1974, see Tobin, 1978.) These issues are largely neglected in what follows.

[2] These longer-run effects are rarely theorized explicitly, which makes it hard in what follows to derive analytical results for the long run from this perspective.

[3] This applies only to the extent that high-powered money comprises only a subset of government liabilities and, is, therefore, influenced only by open-market operations. In

practice in the UK, reserve assets may be created to a degree by the private sector. However, this is not of major significance, so the statement in the text retains approximate validity.

[4] The use of the term 'bond-financed fiscal deficits' is somewhat ambiguous. In the following, we take it to mean a fiscal deficit unaccompanied by a change in monetary policy. If constant monetary policy is defined with respect to a broad monetary aggregate, it follows that bonds must be issued not only to finance the fiscal deficit, but also to offset any increase in the broadly defined supply of money consequent upon the induced rise in interest rates. If bonds were issued only to finance the deficit, bond-financed fiscal deficits would necessarily be accompanied by a change in monetary policy as we define it.

[5] The formal condition is that

$$\frac{\dot{h}}{\dot{b}} = \left(\frac{\eta_w^h}{\eta_w^b}\right)\left(\frac{h}{b}\right)$$

where h is the stock of money, b the stock of bonds, and η_w^h, η_w^b denote the wealth elasticities in the money and bond demand functions respectively.

[6] An alternative specification, which is often used is to include the difference between long-run desired and actual levels of wealth. This may be shown to be equivalent to the specification proposed in the text.

[7] To upset the ultra-rational argument, it suffices that just one individual bond-holder is not ultra-rational. This raises the more general issue of the dependence of ultra-rational behaviour on the actions of others, and, therefore, the possibility of multiple forms of ultra-rational behaviour (see Shiller, 1978).

[8] In an open economy, wealth effects also result from current account surpluses or deficits: see Section 3.

[9] Note, however, the theoretical reservations of Tobin in his comments on this paper. See also the comments of Brunner and Meltzer on Modigliani and Ando (1976).

[10] This channel is inoperative in our case, since we assume that interest payments on government debt are offset by changes in other transfers.

[11] For a useful analysis, see Meyer (1974). Meyer neglects wealth effects in the money demand function, and therefore arrives at somewhat different conclusions.

[12] This is, of course, diminished to the extent that Tobin's argument, discussed at the end of Section 1, is valid.

[13] It is of interest to note that the condition under which fiscal policy is less effective in the short run is the condition under which bond-financed deficits are effective in the long run, at least for the fixed-price case; see below.

[14] Benavie (1976) uses a two-sector model to argue that the effects of fiscal policy (in the form of a stimulus to consumer demand) may be ambiguous whereas monetary policy has the usual expansionary effect. This arises because an increase in consumer prices lowers real wealth (defined relative to consumer prices) and has an ambiguous effect on the demand for equities. In extreme cases, the fall in investment demand may offset the rise in consumer demand. The significance of this result seems doubtful, particularly in view of the arguments in the following paragraph.

[15] This is based on the reasonable assumption that the relevant interest rate in the expenditure and money demand functions are real and nominal measures respectively.

[16] If uncertainty concerning future price levels is also increased, this may act as a deterrent to higher investment (see Flemming *et al.* (1976)).

[17] For theoretically possible parameter values, the savings ratio may fall, in which case the effect of inflationary expectations is necessarily expansionary. However, this case does not seem to be of relevance to recent experience in the UK and elsewhere. It may be noted that the attempt to run down asset holdings is necessarily unsuccessful in a closed economy with a balanced government budget: asset prices and the level of aggregate demand adjust in such a way as to make the private sector willing to hold existing asset stocks.

[18] Money is not neutral in the long run in such models (except in the absence of wealth effects in both the expenditure and money demand function) because of the fall in the real value of nominally denominated wealth caused by the rise in prices. It should perhaps be reiterated that the effect of the latter is ambiguous. The fall in real wealth will tend to raise

the private sector savings ratio unless desired wealth holdings fall more than proportionately to the rise in inflation. But the fall in the real supply of bonds could lower the real rate of interest and hence stimulate investment. Whether this second effect could outweigh the first would seem to be a fruitful area of investigation. In the UK, the evidence suggests that the decline in real interest rates has been a factor offsetting declining profitability (Flemming *et al.*, 1976). Whether the decline in real financial net wealth is a factor in the decline in real interest rates is less clear.

[19] The importance of this effect is diminished to the extent that Tobin's argument, discussed at the end of Section 1, is applicable. Open-market operations at the short end of the maturity spectrum may have very limited effects.

[20] This argument underlies the explanation provided by Bacon and Eltis (1976) for the relative industrial decline of the UK in the post-war period.

[21] The effects of changing debt interest are neglected here (see the introduction).

[22] This conclusion is modified somewhat if inflationary or growing stock-flow equilibria are considered (for references, see Currie, 1978). In this case, long-run equilibrium is charac-terized by asset flows to maintain and augment real asset holdings in line with the growth of the economy. Monetary policy has some role to play in determining the long-run equilibrium asset stocks and hence asset flows. In this case, monetary policy has some influence along with fiscal policy in the determination of long-run levels of real income. The relative efficacy of the two policies in the long run is then a complex function of the parameters of private sector asset demand and expenditure functions, government fiscal and financing parameters and the long-run rate of growth. The analysis of this case is relatively under-developed in the literature, and offers extensive scope for further research.

[23] A further contrast is that effects on labour supply will be absent provided that the marginal tax rate is unchanged.

[24] If, on ultra-rational grounds, it is argued that government debt does not count (or counts only partially) in net private sector wealth except to the extent that it is backed by government holdings of overseas assets, then it could be argued that the likelihood of in-stability arising from the sterilization of the balance of payments is less than that arising from bond financing of the budget deficit; for budget deficit financing will then have zero (or weaker) wealth effects in the goods market, while considerations of portfolio balance in the money market may lead to some rise in the rate of interest, with contractionary effects on demand. Increases in wealth arising from a balance of payments surplus are more likely to generate a rise in demand sufficient to offset this money market effect. However, this argument rests on an assumed high degree of ultra-rationality on the part of the private sector, particularly for the present case of zero capital mobility, where all increases in wealth are in the form of government bonds, so that the private sector must take note of changes in foreign exchange reserves in arriving at an assessment of its net wealth holdings. A more straightforward argument rests on the differential effects on confidence of budget deficits and balance of payments surpluses.

[25] Some components of government spending may have a higher import propensity that the average for the economy (e.g. military expenditure overseas). In this case, super-crowding-out will result.

[26] If imports depend on national income, relative competitiveness will, in fact, return to its initial level in order to ensure external trade equilibrium, so that the full adjustment occurs through wealth changes. For this to happen, income must fall below its initial (and long-run) level along the adjustment path. If the import content of government expendi-tures is less than the average, however, balanced-budget fiscal policy must lead to some loss of competitiveness in order to restore external equilibrium, so that prices will rise in the long run. A fall in output because of capital-shallowing increases, while capital-deepening lowers, prices in the long run.

[27] The analysis of this paragraph rests heavily on the neoclassical analysis of the long run—see n.2 above.

[28] This is not the case if balanced budget fiscal policy generates an initial trade surplus (as discussed above); for then sterilization will increase the ratio of non-monetary to mone-tary wealth, as wealth rises via the balance-of-payments, raising interest rates; while non-sterilization will lower it.

[29] Sales of bonds to the overseas sector, perhaps resulting from attempted sterilization, may be used to offset this reserve loss.

[30] This assumes that government bonds issued as the counterpart to a fiscal deficit count as private sector net wealth. If they count only in part, then the external deficit will be correspondingly smaller than the government deficit in long-run equilibrium.

[31] This assumes an absence of risk aversion, for otherwise financial assets denominated in different currencies cannot be perfect substitutes.

[32] For a useful discussion, see Dornbusch and Krugman (1976). However, they omit several of the points in the following.

[33] Regressive expectations concerning exchange rates might be justified on the argument of the following paragraph.

[34] It can be shown that, if imports depend primarily on private sector expenditures because government expenditures have a low or zero import content, the long-run level of income is unaffected. However, the balanced budget fiscal policy leads to an appreciation of the exchange rate in the long run.

[35] As before, the inclusion of interest payments modifies these results. A fiscal stimulus increases overseas indebtedness of the private sector, requiring a larger trade surplus in the long run to meet the higher interest payments. Thus allowance for this effect means that fiscal policy is less effective. The converse applies to monetary policy. However, as before, the direction of this modification may be reversed if allowance is made for growth and inflation; see above.

[36] The process is likely to be curtailed by a failure of confidence in the international creditworthiness of the government. If the government meets the added interest payments by higher taxes on the private sector, cumulative instability ensues.

CHAPTER 3 WEALTH EFFECTS AND EXPENDITURE FUNCTIONS: A SURVEY OF THE EVIDENCE

[1] Barro (1974) has shown that this objection does not apply if individuals' utility derives from their descendants' welfare as well as their own. He produces some evidence from bequests that this is so but it does not appear to settle the issue conclusively.

[2] In an earlier paper to these seminars, (see Chapter 2) Currie has also cast doubt on the ultra-rationality proposition and has separately drawn attention to the importance of what the government does with its revenues. I would suggest that on these grounds the two issues may be more closely linked than he allows.

CHAPTER 4 THE MEASUREMENT OF FISCAL POLICY

[1] Various definitions of the balance are possible, e.g. the net acquisition of financial assets or the public sector borrowing requirement and its counterparts. For our view, see below.

[2] In defining these, one must decide whether endogenous changes caused, say, by fiscal drag are to be included with discretionary changes.

[3] The comparison should be by reference to target income, if it differs from the constant employment income.

CHAPTER 5 THE MEASUREMENT OF MONETARY POLICY

[1] In practice there will always be sizeable residuals between the recent past and model forecasts. These reminders of uncertainty and possible mis-specification will increase the other pressures on model-builders, not only to adjust constant terms in their equations (massaging the residuals), but also to override and adjust coefficients on the basis of informal judgement. Although the practice of forecasting is less deterministic than often thought, I stick to the analytical argument above.

[2] It will also be the case that the effect of any policy change will depend on the initial conditions in the model if the model contains non-linearities.

[3] But note that there has been a change in the Fed's operating procedures — in October 1979 — since this was written (Eds.).

[4] This sounds a more accommodating type of policy than it actually is. If nominal in-

comes are rising fast, federal funds rate will have to rise to hold M1 to its intended path. The increase in interest rates and/or fall in real money balances will in turn serve to constrain nominal incomes, but probably not seriously so for several months. It is this lag that allows the Fed. to treat nominal income as predetermined for the next few months.

CHAPTER 7 THE RELATIONSHIPS BETWEEN MONETARY AND FISCAL POLICY

[1] In the 1978 Budget the Chancellor announced a target range for sterling M3 of 8–12 per cent for the year to mid-April 1979. On 9 November 1978 this target was rolled forward when the Chancellor announced a target range of 8–12 per cent for £M3 growth for the year to mid-October 1979. The new Conservative Chancellor, in his Budget speech of June 1979, promised to roll his M3 target forward the following autumn. [Eds].

CHAPTER 8 MONETARY AND FISCAL POLICY IN THE NATIONAL INSTITUTE MODEL

[1] See Bank of England (1973).

[2] Although, given the present institutional setting, it would seem very difficult to regulate the reserve base very precisely. Since the Treasury bill issue is the residual source of public sector finance, the base is affected by such unpredictable events as foreign exchange fluctuations.

[3] Although predictions of the external capital flows component of *OSLP* are not in fact generated by the present NIESR model.

[4] See Price (1973; and 1978a, pp. 167–71).

[5] *ECPRI* is included because it is identified in the national accounts instead of the pensions paid from private funds (which are taxable).

[6] The model also includes a different consumption function from that given in the model listing (NIESR, 1977). The equation for (non-durable) consumption is:

$$\Delta_4 \, QCND = 0.428 \, \Delta_4 \, QRDY - 0.148 \Delta_1 \, \Delta_4 \, QRDY - 0.144 (QCND/QRDY)_{t-4}$$
$$+ \, 0.011 \Delta_4 \, D68 - 0.186 \, \Delta_4 \, CPI - 0.174 \, \Delta_1 \Delta_4 \, CPI + 0.028 \, QE_{t-2} - 0.343$$

where the variables are in logs, Q signifies constant (1970) prices, Δ_4 signifies the change on the corresponding quarter a year earlier and Δ_1 is the quarter-to-quarter change. RDY is personal disposable income, CPI is the consumer price index, W is personal wealth and $D68$ is a dummy variable for the first quarter of 1968.

CHAPTER 10 FISCAL AND MONETARY POLICY IN AN OPEN ECONOMY

[1] This sweeping statement applies only to those models that are simple enough for analytic solutions to be found; it does not apply to the numerous large econometric models of national economies, the analytic properties of which are generally obscure.

[2] From 'Burnt Norton' by T.S. Eliot.

[3] Since this paper was written Fetherston and Godley (1978) has been published in K. Brunner and A.H. Meltzer (eds), *Public Policies in Open Economies,* Carnegie-Rochester Conference Series on Public Policy, vol. 9, together with extensive comments, most particularly from Alan Blinder (1978) in the same volume. To have taken full account of these comments would have required us completely to rewrite the present paper. We have instead made some comments and amendments (with due acknowledgement) to Blinder and certain other contributors to that conference volume.

[4] Blinder (1978) criticized us for failing to model the supply side of the economy. Without conceding his point in general, a sufficient reason for us to ignore supply constraints, to the extent that we are concerned with UK problems, is that the strongly adverse trends in foreign trade imply a progressive recession if, as assumed, the current balance is held at zero by fiscal and monetary policy and real exchange rates do not change.

[5] In Fetherston and Godley (1978) we erred in omitting the last term from equations (10.28)–(10.29), leading Blinder (1978) to infer, quite reasonably, that in our model domestic prices are entirely unaffected by world prices—even that of oil. In this paper changes in world prices are modelled explicitly and a simulation of the consequences of such a change is shown in Table 10.5.

BIBLIOGRAPHY

Ando, A. and Modigliani, F. (1963), 'The "Life Cycle" Hypothesis of Saving: Aggregate Implications and Tests', *American Economic Review*, 53, 55–84.

Ando, A. and Modigliani, F., (1965), 'Velocity and the Investment Multiplier', *American Economic Review*, 55, 639–728.

Ando, A. and Modigliani, F. (1975), 'Some Reflections on Describing Structures of Financial Sectors', in *The Brookings Model: Perspective and Recent Developments*, ed. G. Fromm and L. Klein, (Amsterdam, North Holland).

Arena, J. J. (1963), 'The Wealth Effect and Consumption: A Statistical Inquiry', *Yale Economic Essays*, 3, 251–304.

Artis, M.J. and Currie, D.A. (1981), 'Monetary and exchange rate targets', in *Monetarism: Traditions, Debates and Policy*, ed. A.S. Courakis and R.L. Harrington (London: Macmillan).

Ashenfelter, O. and Heckman, J. (1974), 'The Estimation of Income and Substitution Effects in a Model of Family Labour Supply', *Econometrica*, 42, 73–85.

Bacon, R. and Eltis, W. (1976), *Britain's Economic Problem: Too Few Producers* (London: Macmillan).

Bailey, M. J. (1971), *National Income and the Price Level*, 2nd edn. (New York: McGraw-Hill).

Ball, R. J. (1978), *Committee on Policy Optimisation*, Cmnd 7148 (London: HMSO).

Ball, R. J. and Drake, P. S. (1964), 'The Relationship Between Aggregate Consumption and Wealth', *International Economic Review*, 5, 63–81.

Ball, R. J., Boatwright, B. D., Burns, T., Lobban, P. W. M. and Miller, G. W. (1975), 'The London Business School Quarterly Econometric Model of the UK Economy' in *Modelling the Economy*, ed. G. A. Renton (London: Heinemann).

Ball, R. J., Burns, T. and Warburton, P. J. (1978), 'The London Business School Model of the UK: An Exercise in International Monetarism', mimeo, London Business School Econometric Forecasting Unit, Discussion Paper no. 49.

Bank of England (1973), 'Competition and Credit Control: Modified Arrangements for the Discount Market', *Bank of England Quarterly Bulletin*, no. 13, 306–7.

Bank of England (1977), 'The Personal Sector 1966–1975', *Bank of England Quarterly Bulletin*, 17, 27–33.

Bank of England (1978), 'Reflections on the Conduct of Monetary Policy', Governor's speech reported in *Bank of England Quarterly Bulletin*, 18, 64–5.

Barge, J. and Wise, P. J. (1977), 'Competition and Credit Control–Six Years On', *Journal of the Institute of Bankers*, 98, 67–9.

Barro, R. J. (1974), 'Are Government Bonds Net Wealth?' *Journal of Political Economy*, 82, 1095–1117.

Barro, R. J. (1976), 'Rational Expectations and the Role of Monetary Policy', *Journal of Monetary Economics*, 2, 1–32.

Barzel, Y. and McDonald, R. J. (1973), 'Assets, Subsistence and the Supply Curve of Labour', *American Economic Review*, 63, 621–33.

Bean, C. R. (1978), 'The Determination of Consumers' Expenditure in the United Kingdom' (Treasury Working Paper no. 5).

Becker, G. S. (1965), 'A Theory of the Allocation of Time', *Economic Journal*, 75, 493–517.

Beenstock, M. and Bell, S. (1979), 'A Quarterly Econometric Model of the Capital Account of the UK Balance of Payments', *Manchester School*, 37, 33–62.

Benavie, A. (1976), 'Monetary and Fiscal Policy in a Two-Sector Keynesian Model', *Journal of Money, Credit and Banking*, 8, 63–84.

Blinder, A. S. (1978), 'What's New and What's "Keynesian" in the "New Cambridge" Keynesianism?', in *Public Policies in Open Economies*, ed. K. Brunner and A. H. Meltzer (Carnegie–Rochester Conference Series, vol. 9), pp. 67–86 (Amsterdam: North-Holland).

Brainard, W. and Tobin, J. (1968), 'Pitfalls in Financial Model Building', *American Economic Review*, Papers and Proceedings, 58, 99–122.

Branson, W. H. and Klevorick, A. K. (1969), 'Money Illusion and Aggregate Consumption Function', *American Economic Review*, 59, 832–49.

Brown, R. N., Enoch, C. A., and Mortimer-Lee, P. D. (1980), 'The interrelationships between costs and prices in the United Kingdom', Bank of England mimeo.

Brumberg, R. (1953), 'Utility Analysis and Aggregate Consumption', unpublished PhD thesis, Johns Hopkins University, Baltimore.

Brunner, K. and Meltzer, A. H. (1972), 'Money, Debt and Economic Activity', *Journal of Political Economy*, 80, 951–77.

Brunner, K. and Meltzer, A. H. (1976), 'An Aggregate Theory for a Closed Economy', in *Monetarism*, ed. J. L. Stein (Amsterdam: North-Holland).

Buchanan, J. M. (1958), *Public Principles of Public Debt: A Defence and Restatement* (Homewood, Ill.: Irwin).

Buiter, W. H. (1977), 'Crowding Out and the Effectiveness of Fiscal Policy', *Journal of Public Economics*, 7, 309–828.

Burns, T., Lobban, P. J. and Warburton, P. J. (1977), 'Forecasting and the Real Exchange Rate', *Economic Outlook 1977–81*, vol. 2, no. 1 (Farnborough: Gower Press).

Cambridge Economic Policy Group (1975–8), *Economic Policy Review*, various issues.

Central Statistical Office (1978), 'Personal Sector Balance Sheets', *Economic Trends* (January).

Christ, C. (1951), 'A Test of an Econometric Model for the United States 1921–47' in *Conference on Business Cycles* (New York: National Bureau of Economic Research).

Christ, C. F. (1978), 'Some Dynamic theory of Macro-Economic Policy Effects on Income and Prices Under the Government Budget Restraint', *Journal of Monetary Economics*, 4, 45–70.

Coghlan, R. T. (1978), 'A Transactions Demand for Money', *Bank of England Quarterly Bulletin*, 18, 48–60.

Coutts, K. J., Godley, W. A. H. and Nordhaus, W. D. (1978), *Industrial Pricing in the United Kingdom* (Cambridge: University Press).

Coutts, K. J., Tarling, R. J. and Wilkinson, S. F. (1976), 'Wage Bargaining and the Inflation Process', Chapter 2 of *Economic Policy Review*, no. 2, 20–7 (Cambridge: Department of Applied Economics).

Cripps, T. F., Fetherston, M. J. and Godley, W. A. H. (1974), 'Public Expenditure and the Management of the Economy', in *Public Expenditure, Inflation and the Balance of Payments* (Ninth Report from the Expenditure Committee, Session 1974, HC328) (London: HMSO).

Cripps, T. F., Fetherston, M. J. and Godley, W. A. H. (1976), 'What is Left of New Cambridge?' chapter 6 of *Economic Policy Review*, no. 2, 46–9 (Cambridge: Department of Applied Economics).

Cripps, T. F., Fetherston, M. J. and Godley, W. A. H. (1978), 'Simulations with the Cambridge Economic Policy Group Model', chapter 1 in *Demand Management*, ed. M. V. Posner (London: Heinemann Educational).

Currie, D. A. (1977), 'On the Stability of Modified Keynesian Stabilisation Techniques', *Queen Mary College Discussion Paper in Economics*.

Currie, D. A. (1978), 'Macroeconomic Policy and the Government Financing Requirement: A Survey of Recent Development', in *Contemporary Economic Analysis*, ed. M. J. Artis and A. R. Nobay (London: Croom-Helm).

Davidson, J. E. H., Hendry, D. F., Srba, F. and Yeo, S. (1978), 'Econometric Modelling of the Aggregate Time-Series Relationship between Consumers' Expenditure and Income in the United Kingdom', *Economic Journal*, 88, 661–92.

Deaton, A. S. (1972), 'Wealth Effects on Consumption in a Modified Life Cycle Model', *Review of Economic Studies*, 39, 443–53.

Deaton, A. S. (1977), 'Involuntary Saving through Unanticipated Inflation', *American Economic Review*, 67, 899–910.

Defris, L. V. (1977), 'Australian Consumer Expectations, Evaluations, Uncertainty and the Savings Ratio', *Australian Economic Review*, 37, 36–42.

Denham, M. and Lomax, R. (1978), 'The Model of External Capital Flows', part two of *A Financial Sector for the Treasury Model* (Government Economic Service Working Paper no. 17, Treasury Working Paper no. 8) (London: HM Treasury).

Dornbusch, R. (1976), 'Exchange Rate Expectation and Monetary Policy', *Journal of International Economics*, 6, 231–44.

Dornbusch, R. and Krugman, P. (1976), 'Flexible Exchange Rates in the Short Run', *Brookings Papers on Economic Activity*, no. 3, 537–84.

Eisner, R. (1969), 'Fiscal and Monetary Policy Reconsidered', *American Economic Review*, 59, 897–905.

Evans, M. K. (1967), 'The Importance of Wealth in the Consumption Function', *Journal of Political Economy*, 75, 335–51.

Feldstein, M. S. (1976), 'Social Security and Savings: The Extended Life Cycle Theory', *American Economic Review Papers and Proceedings*, 66, 77–86.

Feldstein, M.S. and Flemming, J. S. (1971), 'Tax Policy, Corporate Saving and Investment Behaviour in Britain', *Review of Economic Studies*, 38, 415–34.

Fetherston, M. J. (1976), 'Estimation of Simultaneous Relationships: A UK Private Expenditure Function', *mimeo*, Cambridge Department of Applied Economics.

Fetherston, M. J. (1977), *Technical Manual on the CEPG Model*, 2nd edn. mimeo (Cambridge: Department of Applied Economics).

Fetherston, M. J. and Coutts, K. J. (1978), *Technical Manual on the CEPG Model*, 3rd edn. (Cambridge: Department of Applied Economics).

Fetherston, M. J. and Godley, W. A. H. (1978), ' "New Cambridge" Macroeconomics and Global Monetarism', in *Public Policies in Open Economies*, ed. K. Brunner and A. H. Meltzer (Carnegie-Rochester Conference Series, vol. 9), pp. 33–66 (Amsterdam: North-Holland).

Fisher, M. R. (1956), 'Explorations in Savings Behaviour', *Bulletin of Oxford University Institute of Economics and Statistics*, 18, 201–77.

Fischer, S. (1977), 'Long-Term Contracts, Rational Expectations and the Optimal Money Supply Rule', *Journal of Political Economy*, 85, 191–205.

Flemming, J. S., Price, L. D. D. and Byers, S. A. (1976), 'The Cost of Capital, Finance and Investment', *Bank of England Quarterly Bulletin*, 16, 193–205.

Flemming, M. (1962), 'Domestic Financial Policies Under Fixed and Under Floating Exchange Rates', *IMF Staff Papers*, 9, 369–80.

Forsythe, J. (1975), 'A New Analysis of the Savings Ratio', *Morgan Grenfell Economic Review*, 1–6.

Fox, K. A. (1956), 'Econometric Models of the United States', *Journal of Political Economy*, 64, 128–42.

Friedman, B. (1977), 'The Inefficiency of Short-Run Monetary Targets for Monetary Policy', *Brookings Papers on Economic Activity*, no. 2, 293–346.

Friedman, M. and Meiselman, D. (1965), 'Reply', *American Economic Review*, 55, 753–85.

Godley, W. A. H. (1977), 'Inflation in the United Kingdom', in *Worldwide Inflation*, ed. L. B. Krause and W. S. Salant, (Washington DC: Brookings Institution).

Godley, W. A. H. and May, R. M. (1977), 'The Macroeconomic Implications of Devaluation and Import Restriction', Chapter 2 of *Economic Policy Review* no. 3, 32–42 (Cambridge: Department of Applied Economics).

Godley, W. A. H. and Nordhaus, W. D. (1972), 'Pricing in the Trade Cycle', *Economic Journal*, 82, 853–82.

Goldfeld, S. M. (1973), 'The Demand for Money Revisited', *Brookings Papers on Economic Activity*, 3, 577–638.

Goldsmith, R. W. (1956), *A Study of Saving in the United States-1955* (Princeton: University Press).

Greenhalgh, C. (1977), 'Labour Supply Functions for Married Women in Great Britain', *Economica*, 44, 249–65.

Greenwell, W. and Co. (1978), *see* W. Greenwell & Company.

Grice, J. W. (1977), 'Wealth Effects, Multipliers and Inflation', paper presented to the Money Study Group, mimeo (September).

Griliches, Z., Maddala, G. S., Lucas, R. and Wallace, N. (1962), 'Notes on Estimated Aggregate Quarterly Consumption Functions', *Econometrica*, 30, 491–500.

Haberler, G. (1941), *Prosperity and Depression*, 3rd edn. (Geneva: League of Nations).

Hall, R. E. (1977), 'Investment, Interest Rates, and the Effect of Stabilization Policies', *Brookings Papers on Economic Activity*, no. 1, 61–103.

Hamburger, W. (1955), 'The Relation of Consumption to Wealth and the Wage Rate', *Econometrica*, 23, 1–7.

Hartley, N. and Bean, C. (1978), 'The Standardised Budget Balance', *Government Economic Service Working Paper*, no. 1, 1–32.

Henry, S. G. B., Sawyer, M. C. and Smith, P. (1976), 'Models of Inflation in the UK: An Evaluation', *National Institute Economic Review*, no. 77, 60–71.

Hendry, D. F. (1974), 'Stochastic Specification in an Aggregate Demand Model of the United Kingdom', *Econometrica*, 42, 559–78.

Hendry, D. F. and Mizon, Grayham E. (1978), 'Serial Correlation as a Convenient Simplification, not a Nuisance: A Comment on a Study of the Demand for Money by the Bank of England', *Economic Journal*, 88, 549–63.

HM Treasury (1978), *H.M. Treasury Macroeconomic Model, Technical Manual* (London: HM Treasury).

Hewitt, M. E. (1977), 'Financial Forecasts in the United Kingdom', *Bank of England Quarterly Bulletin*, 17, 188–96.

Hilton, K. and Crossfield, D. H. (1970), 'Short-run Consumption Functions for the UK, 1955–66', in the *Econometrica* study of the United Kingdom, ed. K. Hilton and D. F. Heathfield, (London: Macmillan).

Juster, F. T. and Wachtel, P. (1972), 'Inflation and the Consumer', *Brookings Papers on Economic Activity*, 1, 72–122.

Katz, E. (1977), 'The Efficacy of Fiscal and Monetary Policies Under Floating Exchange Rates: The Implications of Capital Mobility Reconsidered', *Queen Mary College Discussion Paper*.

Kenen, P. B. (1977), 'New Views of Exchange Rates and Old Views of Policy', mimeo.

Keynes, J. M. (1936), *The General Theory of Employment, Interest and Money*, Chapter 6 (London: Macmillan).

Khan, M. (1974), 'The Stability of the Demand-for-Money Function in the US 1909–1965', *Journal of Political Economy*, 82, 1205–19.

Klein, L. R. (1950), *Economic Fluctuations in the United States, 1920–1941*, (Cowles Commission Monograph no. 2), pp. 80–85 (New York: John Wiley).

Klein, L. R. (1954), 'Statistical Estimation of Economic Relationships from Survey Data' in *Contributions to Survey Methods in Economics*, ed. L. R. Klein (New York: Columbia University Press).

Klein, L. R. and Goldberger, A. S. (1955), *An Econometric Model of the United States 1929–1959* (Amsterdam: North-Holland).

Laidler, D. W. (1978), 'An Essay on the Transmission Mechanism', *Journal of Monetary Economics*, 14, 151–91.

Laury, J. S. E., Lewis, G. R. and Ormerod, P. A. (1978), 'Properties of Macroeconomic Models of the UK Economy: A Comparative Study', *National Institute Economic Review*, no. 83, 52–72.

Llewellyn, G. E. J. (1974), 'The Determinants of United Kingdom Import Prices', *Economic Journal*, 84, 18–31.

Lucas, R. E. (1976), ed. Karl Brunner and Alan Meltzer 'Econometric Policy Evaluations: a Critique', in *The Phillips Curve and Labor Markets* (Carnegie-Rochester Conference Series vol. 1), (Amsterdam: North-Holland).

Maddala, G. S. (1966), 'Some Notes on Aggregate Savings Function', Stanford University Research Center in Economic Growth, memorandum no. 42.

May, J. (1970), 'Period Analysis and Continuous Analysis in Patinkin's Macroeconomic Model', *Journal of Economic Theory*, 2, 1–9.

Mayer, T. (1972), *Permanent Income, Wealth and Consumption* (Berkeley: University of California Press).

Meyer, L. (1974), 'Wealth Effects and the Effectiveness of Monetary and Fiscal Policies', *Journal of Money, Credit and Banking*, 6, 481–502.

Midland Bank (1977), 'The paradox of personal saving', *Midland Bank Review*, Winter, 12–18.

Mishkin, F. S. (1976), 'Illiquidity, Consumer Durable Expenditure and Monetary Policy', *American Economic Review*, 66, 642–54.

Mishkin, F. S. (1977), 'What Depressed the Consumer: The Household Balance Sheet and the 1973–75 Recession', *Brookings Papers on Economic Activity*, no. 1 123–74.

Modigliani, F. (1971), 'Monetary Policy and Consumption' in *Consumer Spending and Monetary Policy: the Linkages*, ed. Federal Reserve Bank Boston (Monetary Conference Series, no. 5, Boston, June), pp. 9–84.

Modigliani, F. and Ando, A. (1976), 'Impacts of Fiscal Actions on Aggregate Income and the Monetarist Controversy: Theory and Evidence', in *Monetarism*, ed. J. L. Stein (Amerstam: North-Holland).

Morishima, M. and Saito, M. (1964), 'A Dynamic Analysis of the American Economy 1902–1952', *International Economic Review*, 5, 125–64.

Mundell, R. A. (1968), *International Economics* (New York: Macmillan).

Munnell, A. H. (1974), *The Effect of Social Security on Personal Saving* (Cambridge Mass.: Ballinger).

National Institute of Economic and Social Research, (1977), 'A Listing of National Institute Model 3', *National Institute Discussion Papers*, no. 7.

Neild, R. R. (1963), *Pricing and Employment in the Trade Cycle* (Cambridge: University Press).

Niehans, J. (1975), 'Some Doubts about the Efficacy of Monetary Policy Under Flexible Exchange Rates, *Journal of International Economics*, 5, 275–81.

Nordhaus, W. D. and Godley, W. (1972), 'Pricing in the Trade Cycle', *Economic Journal*, 82, 853–82.

Patinkin, D. (1965), *Money, Interest and Prices*, 2nd edn. (New York: Harper and Row).

Patinkin, D. (1967), *On the Nature of Monetary Mechanism* (Stockholm).

Patinkin, D. (1969), 'Money and Wealth: A Review Article', *Journal of Economic Literature*, 7, 1140–57.

Perry, G. L. (1976), 'Stabilization Policy and Inflation', in *Setting National Priorities—the Next Ten Years*, eds. Henry Owen and Charles L. Schultze (Washington: Brookings Institution).

Pesek, B. and Saving, T. (1967), *Money, Wealth and Economic Theory* (New York: Macmillan).

Pigou, A. C. (1943), 'The Classical Stationary State', *Economic Journal*, 53, 343–51.

Poole, W., (1970), 'Optimal Choice of Monetary Policy Instruments in a Simple Stochastic Macro Model', *Quarterly Journal of Economics*, 82, 197–216.

Price, R. W. R. (1973), 'Some Aspects of the Progressive Income Tax Structure', *National Institute Economic Review*, 65, 52–63.

Price, R. W. R. (1978a), 'Modelling Fiscal Policy: The Personal Income Tax System', *National Institute Discussion Papers*, no. 22.

Price, R. W. R. (1978b), 'Budgetary Policy', chapter 4 in *British Economic Policy 1960–1974*, ed. F. T. Blackaby (Cambridge: University Press).

Rees, R. D. and Layard, P. R. G. (1972), *The Determinants of UK Imports* (Government Service Occasional Paper no. 3).

Revell, J. R. S. (1967), *The Wealth of the Nation* (Cambridge: University Press).

Rowthorn, R. E. (1977), 'Conflict, Money and Inflation', *Cambridge Journal of Economics*, 1, 215–39.

Russell, T. and Wakeman, L. M. (1978), ' "New Cambridge"–Economics Without Markets', in *Public Policies in Open Economies*, ed. K. Brunner and A. H. Meltzer (Carnegie-Rochester Conference Series, vol. 9), pp. 95–102 (Amsterdam: North-Holland).

Sargent, T. J. (1976), 'A Classical Macro-Econometric Model for the United States', *Journal of Political Economy*, 84, 207–37.

Sargent, T. J. and Wallace, N. (1975), ' "Rational" Expectations, the Optimal Monetary Instrument, and the Optimal Money Supply Rule', *Journal of Political Economy*, 83, 241–54.

Sargent, T. J. and Wallace, N. (1976), 'Rational Expectations and the theory of economic policy', *Journal of Monetary Economics*, 2, 169–84.

Savage, D. (1978), 'The Monetary Sector of the NIESR Model', *National Institute Discussion Papers*, no. 21.

Shiller, R. J. (1978), 'Rational Expectations and the Dynamic Structure of Macroeconomic Models', *Journal of Monetary Economics*, 4, pp. 1–44.

Sjaastad, L. A. (1976), 'Why Stable Inflations Fail', in *Inflation in the World Economy*, ed. J. M. Parkin and G. Zis (Manchester: University Press).

Spencer, P. and Mowl, C. (1978), 'The Model of the Domestic Monetary System', part one of *A Financial Sector for the Treasury Model* (Government Economic Service Working Paper no. 17, Treasury Working Paper no. 8) (London: HM Treasury).

Spiro, A. (1962), 'Wealth and the Consumption Function', *Journal of Political Economy*, 70, 339–54.

Stein, J. L. (ed.) (1976), *Monetarism, Studies in Monetary Economics*, vol. 1 (Amsterdam: North-Holland).

Stone, R. (1964), 'Private Saving in Britain, Past, Present and Future', *Manchester School*, 32, 79–112.

Thore, S. (1961), *Household Saving and the Price Level* (Stockholm: National Institute of Economic Research).

Tobin, J. (1958), 'Liquidity Preference as Behaviour Towards Risk', *Review of Economic Studies*, 25, 65–86.

Tobin, J. (1971), 'Essays on the Principles of Debt Management', in Essays in Economics, Vol. I: *Macroecnomics* (Amsterdam: North-Holland).

Tobin, J. (1975), 'Keynesian Models of Recession and Depression', *American Economic Review, Papers and Proceedings*, 88, 195–202.

Tobin, J. (1978), 'Government Deficits, Capital Accumulation and Inflation', in *Contemporary Economic Analysis*, ed. W. Peters and D. Currie (London: Croom-Helm).

Tobin, J. and Buiter, W. H. (1976), 'Long Run Effects of Fiscal and Monetary Policy on Aggregate Demand', in *Monetarism*, ed. J. L. Stein (Amsterdam: North-Holland).

Townend, J. C. (1976), 'The Personal Savings Ratio', *Bank of England Quarterly Bulletin*, 16, 53–73.

Tucker, D. (1968), 'Credit Rationing, Interest Rate Lags, and Monetary Policy Speed', *Quarterly Journal of Economics*, 82, 54–84.

Turnovsky, S. J. and Kingston, G. H. (1977), 'Monetary and Fiscal Policies Under Flexible Exchange Rates and Perfect Myopic Foresight in an Inflationary World', *Scandinavian Journal of Economics*, 79, 424–41.

W. Greenwell & Company (1978), 'Measures of Fiscal Stance', *Monetary Bulletin*, 3–6.

Wall, K. D., Preston, A. J., Bray, J. W. and Peston, H. M. (1975), 'Estimates of a Simple Control Model of the UK Economy' in *Modelling the Economy*, ed. G. A. Renton (London: Heinemann).

Ward, T. S. and Neild, R. R. (1978), *The Measurement and Reform of Budgetary Policy* (London: He

Ward, T. S. and Neild, R. R. (1978), *The Measurement and Reform of Budgetary Policy* (London: Heinemann, for the Institute of Fiscal Studies).

Wass, Sir Douglas (1978), 'The Changing Problems of Economic Management', *Economic Trends*, 293, 97–104.

Zellner, A. (1957), 'The Short-Run Consumption Function', *Econometrica*, 25, 552–67.

AUTHOR INDEX

GENERAL INDEX